THE CHELTENHAM GOLD CUP

Anne, Duchess of
Westminster's
legendary Arkle,
winner of the Gold
Cup in 1964, 1965,
1966.

John Welcome

THE CHELTENHAM GOLD CUP

THE STORY OF
A GREAT
STEEPLECHASE

PELHAM BOOKS: LONDON

Published in Great Britain by
Pelham Books Ltd
44 Bedford Square
London WC1B 3DU
1984

© 1984 by John Welcome
First published in Great Britain by Messrs Constable 1957
First published by Pelham Books 1973
This edition first published 1984

British Library Cataloguing in Publication Data

Welcome, John
  The Cheltenham Gold Cup.—3rd ed.
  1. Steeplechasing—History   2. Cheltenham Gold Cup.—History
  I. Title
  798.4′5′094241   SF359

ISBN 0-7207-1499-0

Filmset, printed and bound in Great Britain by
Butler & Tanner Limited, Frome and London

ACKNOWLEDGEMENTS

The author and publishers are grateful to the following for their
help in supplying illustrations: Major J.M. Crawford, Mr E.W.
Davis, Miss V. Dreaper, Lord Fermoy, The Countess of Fingall,
Mrs J. Roberts and Sir John and Lady Thomson. For permission
to reproduce copyright illustrations thanks are due to: BBC
Hulton Picture Library pages 49, 53, 54, 73; Peter Biegel front
cover and page 159; Gerry Cranham page 181 and back cover;
Geoffrey Hammonds page 105 (bottom); Clive Hiles page 152;
Bobby Hopkins page 138; Illustrated London News Picture
Library pages 2, 5, 6, 7, 8, 10, 12, 14, 16, 18, 19, 22, 23, 25, 27,
28, 32, 34, 36, 39, 41, 42, 43, 46, 57, 58, 60, 61, 67, 68, 70, 77;
Keystone Press Agency page 147; Press Association pages 93, 94,
114, 149, 214; George Selwyn pages 187, 189, 192, 193, 200, 202,
204, 207, 212; Sport and General pages 65, 81, 105, (top), 107,
109, 117, 121, 126, 131, 133, 134, 142, 144, 150, 154, 157, 160,
164, 167, 174, 182, 196, 199, 210; Sporting Pictures (UK) page
180; Times Newspapers pages 86, 96, 98, 101, 190, 213. In a few
instances it has not been possible to ascertain the copyright owner
and it is hoped that any omissions will be excused.

Contents

Author's Note

In preparing this, the third edition of *The Cheltenham Gold Cup*, I should like to repeat my thanks to all who have helped me in this and the previous editions, answered my queries and given me their advice. Amongst so many it would be invidious to single out a few and I can only hope that all those who so generously gave of their time will accept this as an expression of gratitude.

For permission to reproduce copyright material I am grateful to the following: Mary Comyn Carr author of *The Dikler and His Circle* published by J.A. Allen & Co Ltd; Ivor Herbert author of *Winter's Tale* published by Pelham Books Ltd; Pat Taaffe author of *My Life and Arkle's* published by Stanley Paul Ltd; Phil Bull author of *Chasers and Hurdlers* published by Portway Press.

1

Background

THE RACE KNOWN as the Cheltenham Gold Cup, a weight-for-age steeplechase for a gold cup value two hundred sovereigns with added money, distance three miles and a quarter, was first run on Wednesday, March 12th, 1924.

In the year 1924, weight-for-age races under National Hunt Rules were a novelty. With the exception of the National Hunt Steeplechase, also run at Cheltenham, which was then open only to maidens at starting ridden by gentlemen riders, and the Champion Chase at Liverpool, all the principal races were handicaps. There was no true championship to determine which was the best long-distance staying steeplechaser over park courses and at level weights, for the Grand National was of course a handicap.

On the flat, things were very different. The classics were run at level weights, and many, if not most, of the important races were weight-for-age.

It was felt by many that the preponderance of handicaps was not in the best interests of steeplechasing and that the institution of a race, broadly similar to the Ascot Gold Cup, which would provide an opportunity for the best long-distance chasers to compete against each other annually on level terms would be for the benefit of steeplechasing generally. The Cheltenham executive under the chairmanship of Mr F.H. Cathcart put this feeling to the test when they founded the race. The conditions were simple. The race was for five years old and upwards; weights: 11 st 5 lb and 12 st.

From the first the race filled. It has grown steadily in prestige and importance over the years until it is now the recognised championship of steeplechasing, and the horse who wins it is entitled as of right to be called the champion chaser of the year.

At first regarded by trainers and owners in the light of another National trial, a prize to be picked up on the way to Aintree, it is now an objective quite on its own, and since 1946 it has not been won by a horse other than one who has been especially trained for it. Only one horse in the history has succeeded in winning both the great events in one year. This was the mighty Golden Miller, and this alone underlines the fact that the Gold Cup is not and probably never was a mere side issue to the Grand National but is a true championship requiring a preparation quite of its own.

In the year 1924 the new race was worth only £685 to the winner; it was not even the chief event of the National Hunt Meeting, which was still the National Hunt Steeplechase,

1 Hon. A. Hastings; 2 Meyrick Good; 3 M.D. Blair; 4 Capt. R.E. Sassoon; 5 Bob Gore; 6 Lord Stalbridge; 7 Billy Payne; 8 Eric Foster; 9 Ted Leader; 10 Capt. A.F.W. Gossage; 11 'Billy Barton' Ober; 12 H.A. Brown; 13 T. Coulthwaite; 14 G. Poole; 15 G. Martin.
Some of the leading national hunt figures of the 1920s from a contemporary cartoon.

then worth £1,285. Nevertheless, the Gold Cup got off to a good start, for the conditions of the race made it certain even then that it would attract top-class horses, and this it did. Before going on to deal with the 1924 race in detail it is advisable, however, to spare a glance at the general background against which the sport was then carried on.

The Grand National, with its unrivalled prestige and enormous prize money, far in excess of that to be won in any other race, dominated the steeplechasing season. Being run late in the year, at the end of March or the beginning of April, some time after the start of the flat, this made the whole programme top-heavy. It was the ambition of every owner, trainer and rider to win the Grand National. The good horses had their training programmes mapped out with it and little else in view. There was, in fact, little other point in running or training a good steeplechaser but to have a cut at the National. With the exception of the National Hunt Steeplechase already mentioned and the other Aintree races such as the Grand Sefton and the Champion Chase, it might almost be said that no other race had any prestige value at all. In 1924 only two races in the whole season other than the National and those mentioned above offered prize money to the winner of over £1,000. In all, only eighteen races were worth more than £500 to the winner, and of these no less than nine were run either at Liverpool or the National Hunt Meeting at Cheltenham. No race except the National was worth over £2,000. The most valuable other race was the Lancashire Steeplechase, worth £1,780.

The result of this was that the leading horses were seen out, obviously unready, once or twice early in the season. They were then put away until they came out for their winding-up races for the National. In the great race itself they clashed with others who by no stretch of the imagination could be called good horses but whose owners were hoping for some near miracle, as was to happen in 1928 when Tipperary Tim came home alone out of the mud and the murk at 100-1. Thus the Grand National fields became swollen to grotesque sizes (sixty-six faced the starter in 1929, Gregalach's year), the risk of interference became increased, and the chance of any given horse getting round proportionately diminished. Nevertheless, because of its unparalleled prestige and prize money, all eyes were turned to it. It was the be-all and end-all of the National Hunt season. But fields in other races sank and public interest fell away.

There were other reasons, too, for the slackening of public interest. Steeplechasing in 1924 was something of a closed shop. Most of those taking part were active enthusiasts, young men out for sport or older men with a young man's outlook. The rigour of the game was strictly applied. If I did you one week, you did me the week after and we had a drink together to the next time. The sport was, in fact, run by the participants for the participants. This was more or less inevitable, for the rewards to be gained at steeplechasing at that time were very small and trivial indeed compared with those to be won on the flat.

The average jumping programme was then framed to give four races value £100 and one of £200. Of the £100, the fortunate winning owner received £85. From this he had to give his jockey five guineas for a winning ride, and most trainers in addition took 10 per cent of the stake. Thus the owner was left with £71 5s. Even this small sum he could not count on putting into his pocket, for the jockey had still to receive a present for his win. The latter was not an essential payment, but it was - and is - the custom, and if the rider was a successful one and the owner wished to secure his services again, it was as well not to overlook it. Finally, to complete the account, there were the rider's travelling expenses and those of the trainer if he charged for them, the owner's personal travelling expenses, the cost of getting the horse to the meeting and a present to the stable-hands. If it was a cold day and the owner's friends were anxious to warm themselves at his expense, his win, in so far as the prize was concerned, probably cost him money.

The £100 stake has been mentioned as the average for a race. At one or two meetings the stakes were higher. There were also some where they were lower. One country meeting in 1924 offered six races, two with stakes of £50, one (the feature race) of £55 and, to wind-up with, a steeplechase of £30, value to the winner £25, £5 to the second.

Obviously, with prizes such as these, owners and trainers, unless they were very rich men – and there were then few rich men in National Hunt racing – were practically forced to bet, not so much to make money, but to enable them to carry on at all. This betting had little in common with the inspired wagering and colossal coups of the flat; it was tough, hard-working betting for existence.

Many of the prominent flat-racing bookmakers refused to brave the winter weather and go steeplechasing. As a result, the ring was small and weak and there was some difficulty in placing a substantial amount of money. 'Evens each of two. Three to one others,' was a usual market for the followers of steeplechasing. The methods employed to secure a good price for the horse upon whom, in the idiom of the day, the trainer wished to wager his wife and family, were many and devious. Steeplechasing was still very much the poor relation of flat racing. As is the way with many poor relations, its behaviour was just this side of disreputable – and very entertaining. Some of the stories of the stratagems then employed – one of which concerns a later pillar of Irish racing ensconced as a signaller in a smoke-stack – would read as racily and almost as improbably as the *Arabian Nights* if one were allowed to print them. But, amusing and – sometimes – profitable as they were to the participants, these diversions accentuated the 'private army' atmosphere of steeplechasing at the time. The public did not benefit from them. The public wanted spectacle, lots of runners and something to bet on; they were, in addition, being enticed by the counter-attractions of football, greyhound racing and that new-fangled invention, the wireless, and they stayed away.

The press, too, was disapproving. Bob Sievier's *The Winning Post*, which in pre-war days had been the scourge of crooked racing and inefficient stewards, was a fading voice and was soon to fold. But there was another to take its place. This was the voice of a young man of good family who had enthusiasm, expert and practical knowledge of racing, for he had ridden races himself, a crusading spirit and a facile pen. 'He preferred,' his brother wrote of him, 'spotting a non-trier down the course to backing a winner on the stand.' And when he did spot a non-trier he said so in no uncertain fashion whoever owned him and whoever rode him, for he was no respecter of persons. He was a brilliant racing journalist, he became the racing correspondent of one of the most influential papers in the land, and others enlisted themselves under his banner. His name was Geoffrey Gilbey.

The criticisms in the press were sometimes aimed at the actual participants and sometimes at the stewards, for at this time control of the sport was lax at some meetings and in one or two instances more than lax. There were then no stewards' secretaries, and some local stewards appeared to be chosen for any reason but their knowledge of racing or their probity.

The journalist already referred to told a tale of the times, stating that he heard this conversation himself:

'Did you see that?' said the young steward to the old steward. 'Yes, I saw it,' said the old steward to the young steward. 'What are you going to do?' said the young steward to the old steward. 'Do?' said the old steward to the young steward. 'Do? Back it next time out, of course.'

It is perhaps no wonder that Sydney Galtrey, the then Hotspur of the *Daily Telegraph*, writing in 1934 of the previous decade of steeplechasing, said: 'Only the brave and the faithful – some have cynically described them as the needy and the greedy – were followers of the winter sport.'

So much for the general background against which steeplechasing was conducted in the year 1924. It is now necessary to move from the general to the particular and to say something of the men and horses who were then prominent, and some of whom were to clash in the first race for the Cup.

Of the trainers, Tom Coulthwaite of Hednesford 'Old Tom' as he styled himself, had the greatest reputation and the largest string. By that time he had already trained two Grand National winners, Eremon and Jenkinstown, and was to add another to his name with Grakle in 1931. His reputation stood high, and deservedly so, but he had a most unusual background for a National Hunt trainer for he was said never to have sat on a horse in his life. Originally he had made his name training footballers and athletes. Becoming interested in racing, he had decided to apply to horses the principles he learnt with humans, and this he did with immediate and resounding success.

Tom Coulthwaite from a contemporary caricature.

TOM COULTHWAITE ANOTHER OF THE WIZARDS — WHEN HE ISN'T TRAINING ROSES HE'S TRAINING NATIONAL WINNERS — BUT UP TO THE TIME OF GOING TO PRESS I DON'T KNOW IF IT'S TO BE "FRAU KARL" OR "FLY MASK" THIS YEAR!

The Hon. Aubrey
Hastings – a leading
trainer of the day.

Two other trainers must be mentioned, the likeable and friendly
Fred Withington and the Hon. Aubrey Hastings. Both these men
had been distinguished amateur riders. Fred Withington, who had
started riding races in the year 1891 – with a bad fall, incidentally,
from a horse inaptly named Spring Captain – had won the Champion Chase at Liverpool in 1896. After his marriage in 1908 he
started to train, first near Banbury then moving to Danebury, where
he trained under both rules for a long and distinguished list of
patrons, sending out, amongst other winners, Rubio, to win the
Grand National in 1908 at 66-1. Later in life Mr Withington cut
down his string and moved to Bicester where he trained a few
selected horses for his friends, and where he was established in 1924
when the first Gold Cup was run.

The Hon. Aubrey Hastings had won the Grand National in 1906
on Ascetic's Silver, trained by himself, and had wasted down to
10 st 9 lb to do it. In the same year he almost completed a magnificent double, for on Port
Light II he was only just beaten in the National Hunt Steeplechase. In addition to Ascetic's
Silver, Hastings sent out the winners of two War Nationals, Ally Sloper in 1915 and
Ballymacad in 1917, and was to win yet another in the year of which we are speaking, 1924,
with Master Robert.

In this year Aubrey Hastings had no less than forty-two horses in training at Wroughton
including Forewarned, who was to start favourite at 3-1 for the first Gold Cup. Jack and
Ivor Anthony, two members of a very famous racing family, were the stable professionals.
Jack, the younger of the two, won the Grand National as an amateur three times, on
Glenside in 1911, Ally Sloper in 1915 and Troytown in 1920. As a professional he was
second in consecutive years, 1925 and 1926, on Old Tay Bridge, and third in 1927 on
Bright's Boy. This is a record at Aintree which will probably never be equalled. A rider of
tremendous strength, probably he and he alone could have held the massive and hard-
pulling Troytown in the gale-force winds that tore across Aintree in 1920. Ivor's successes
cannot be compared with that of his more brilliant brother, but he was placed three times
in the National, the years being 1912, 1917 and 1918. When Mr Hastings dropped dead
playing polo in 1929, Ivor, who had retired from riding, ran the Wroughton stable for Mrs
Hastings with such success that he not only maintained, but also enhanced its great
reputation.

Jack was due to ride Forewarned in the first Gold Cup for Mr Hastings. Mr Withington
also had a runner, a potentially brilliant young horse called Red Splash, but with his small
string he had no professional attached to the stable and he was in some doubt whether he
could get a rider who would do his young horse justice. He had a wide field from which to
choose, for the standard of riding – both amateur and professional – was exceptionally high
in the early 'twenties.

The acknowledged leader amongst the professionals and, appropriately, the leading jockey
in the list published on January 1st, 1924, was F. B. Rees. Rees, known to his friends as
'Dick' Rees was, like the Anthonys, a Welshman. In fact, they came from adjoining counties,
the Anthonys from Camarthenshire, Rees from Pembroke. Like Jack Anthony, Rees had
ridden as an amateur for a year or two after the First World War, in which he had served

with some distinction in the R.F.C. In 1921, his first year as a professional, he won the Grand National on Shaun Spadah. A beautiful horseman, he was, in addition, a quick thinker and a brilliant tactician throughout a race. Indeed, the skill with which he rode his races and his ability to win them on horses apparently hopelessly beaten two fences out brings him as near to being a genius as makes no matter. Many steeplechase jockeys, excellent though they may be in other aspects of their art, fail to get the best out of their mounts in a finish. Rees was superb in a finish and could hold his own with any of the leading flat-race jockeys. He is generally acknowledged to have been the best steeplechase rider to have been seen in the British Isles during the twenty years between the two wars. Some have gone so far as to call him incomparable. Perhaps he was. This much is certain: he was a supreme master of his art, and if he was not the greatest steeplechase jockey of all time he is amongst the very few who have genuine claims to that honour.

Jack Anthony.

Like many another genius he was wayward. The calls of the flesh were perhaps too readily answered. In his later years in the saddle weight troubles beset him. But, to the end, the old genius remained undimmed. On one occasion towards the close of his career, when his figure had become noticeably corpulent, he rode and won a hurdle race on a horse which probably no one else could have got into the first three. In the weighroom afterwards a young jockey congratulated him. 'Ah, my boy,' he answered, stripping off his jacket, 'if I could do ten stone again I'd show you who would still head the ——list!' And it was not an idle boast.

Like Anthony, Dick Rees had a less brilliant brother. L. B. ('Bill') Rees was, nevertheless, no mean performer in his own right and he had won the National on Music Hall in 1922.

If the Anthonys and the Rees brothers were the leaders among the professionals, there were giants, too, in those days amongst the amateurs. Captain Tuppy Bennett was the leading amateur in 1923. He won the National on Sergeant Murphy that year, and had 62

F.B. ('Dick') Rees (*left*) with his brother L.B. ('Bill') Rees.

winners out of 267 rides. As Rees only bettered this by having 64 winners out of 245 rides, it will be seen that, on figures, there was nothing much between them. In fact Bennett, who was a veterinary surgeon, could more than hold his own with the leading professionals. Unfortunately his career had a sudden and tragic ending. Early in January 1924 a horse called Ardeen fell with him at Wolverhampton, fracturing his skull, and he died a few days later.

One famous name was missing from the list of leading jockeys published at the beginning of 1924. The redoubtable Mr H.A. Brown had broken an ankle at Tunstall Park very early in the season and had not ridden since. Of all those then riding, amateurs and professionals, Mr Brown probably ranked second only to Dick Rees. In 1919 he had defeated Rees for the championship and had headed the list of leading jockeys – no mean feat indeed for an amateur. In fact Harry Brown and Jack Anthony, who topped the list in 1914 with a total of sixty winners, are the only two amateurs ever to have accomplished it.

The racecourse was a duller place through the absence of Mr Brown. He was, amongst other things, the steeple-chasing mentor of the then Prince of Wales. He was given to speaking his mind, and he was born to incident as the sparks fly upwards. His brother has told how, when walking the Aintree course with the Prince of Wales before the 1923 Grand National, he put the future Monarch off backing Serjeant Murphy with the brash announcement, 'Good God, no. He's as old as I am. He isn't a horse at all!'

When Sergeant Murphy strolled home to win at his ease at 100–6 Harry though it prudent to remove himself from H.R.H.'s side, and take refuge in the nearest champagne bar. His most spectacular exploit was in 1921, when his own horse, The Bore, fell with him at the second last fence in the Grand National. At the time of their fall Brown and The Bore were upsides with Dick Rees on Shaun Spadah; everything else was beaten out of sight. Brown's collar-bone was broken by his fall, but he had laid a substantial bet that he would finish 'in the money'. A bystander slung him up and when handing him the reins gave them to him, by mistake, both on one side of The Bore's neck. In this condition and in this position Brown rode The Bore over the last fence to occupy second place and to land his bet.

His feats on Lord Londesborough's Dudley have passed into legend. On one occasion he laid a bet that he and Dudley would win twelve successive steeplechases. In fact, they won fourteen in unbroken sequence. But, when getting near his goal, he found himself opposed in a race only by a horse owned by his brother Frank, also a successful amateur rider. Frank refused to take his horse out and so denied Harry the walkover he wanted. Dudley won all right but it is recorded that some very unbrotherly remarks flew across the unsaddling enclosure after the race.

Harry Brown won neither the National nor the Gold Cup. We have seen how unlucky he was in the National of 1923, and it will shortly be shown how near he went to winning the first Gold Cup.

2

Beginnings

CONJUROR II HAD BEEN third in the National of 1923. Captain Bennett, who rode Sergeant Murphy, made no secret of the fact that, in his opinion, had Conjuror II been ridden by a stronger and more experienced jockey the result might have been different. Mr Dewhurst, the owner's son, at that time an Oxford undergraduate, had ridden Conjuror II. He had had to waste hard to do the weight and, considering his inexperience, he had done extremely well to finish third. But the horse had shown what he could do and it was felt that someone of greater strength and experience was needed to do him full justice. So Harry Brown had been asked to ride him in all his races, including the Gold Cup and the Grand National. The horse was trained by Tom Coulthwaite.

It was, however, by no means certain that Harry Brown would be able to ride him. Owing to his injury he did not take any rides during the month of January, and when Conjuror II first appeared in public young Mr Dewhurst was on him again. On February 12th Mr Brown, still limping from his injured ankle, had his first ride in public since his accident, and on the following day he won a race on his old friend Dudley at Windsor. He then commenced to run up a series of victories all over the place and it was announced that he would definitely ride Conjuror II in the Grand National and his other engagements. It is worth noting that the Gold Cup was then very definitely included amongst the 'other engagements'.

Conjuror II trained by Tom Coulthwaite and second in the 1924 Gold Cup.

It was not being a very good season. The weather was vile; runners were few; there were one or two incidents. Major Doyle, a leading amateur, received an ultimatum from the stewards requiring him to turn professional or confine himself to riding in amateur races; there was trouble over foul riding at Plumpton. Press comment was generally acid, one racing reporter being moved to fill in his column with a review of a racing novel by H. S. 'Atty' Persse, the trainer and former amateur rider, the review ending with the following quotation from the book: 'He stepped back, startled, pleasantly shocked. His cheek had brushed the warm lips of a woman!'

However, the National Hunt Meeting opened in brilliant weather. The National Hunt Steeplechase was run on the first day and won by Patsey V. The first race for the Gold Cup was due to be run the following day, on Wednesday, March 12th.

The weather held; it was a soft, springlike day. The going was reported to be excellent. The Prince of Wales, last year's bad tip long forgotten and forgiven, had arrived to see Harry Brown ride Conjuror II. The omens were auspicious for a splendid start to the new race.

The day before, almost every sporting writer had given as the likely winner of the Gold Cup an entire horse called Alcazar, trained by George Poole for whom Dick Rees had a retainer. Alcazar was expected to start a very-short-priced favourite, and he was tipped as a certainty. There was every justification for this, for he had a fine record over park courses; he was not in the National and it was thought that the National horses such as Conjuror II, Gerald L and Old Tay Bridge might not be fully wound up. There were other good horses in the field: Mr Bankier's Forewarned, trained by Aubrey Hastings and ridden by Jack Anthony, had started favourite in the National the year before, Mr Dixon's Old Tay Bridge, who was to start favourite and to finish second in that race in two years time, and Sir Keith Fraser's Ardeen, the 'patent safety' from which Tuppy Bennett had been killed. There was also Major Wyndham's chestnut gelding, Red Splash, the youngest horse in the race. No one, except perhaps Mr Withington his trainer, took Red Splash very seriously amongst these good horses, although he had previously, when ridden by F. Rees, won over three miles at Hawthorn Hill, beating Old Tay Bridge by four lengths in the process.

No great race is complete without a touch of drama, and drama was not wanting here. Over dinner on Tuesday night Mr Withington confided to a friend that he did not think he would start Red Splash. He said that the horse was young (he was in fact a May foal, so that in actual years he was not yet five), that in a handicap Alcazar would be set to give him lumps of weight while here the difference was only 9 lb, and that he didn't think he could find a suitable jockey. He wanted Dick Rees, who had ridden Red Splash before, but Rees was claimed for Alcazar. Finally, Mr Withington pointed out that his horse's training had been held up by an accident and that he had had to give him a hurried preparation. Mr Withington had a particular interest in Red Splash, for he had trained both the sire and the dam and had owned the horse himself before selling him to his present owner, who was in the Household Cavalry. Major Wyndham was no stranger to the saddle, for he had won the Grand Military in 1912 and 1913, on his horse Another Delight. Subsequently he became the doyen of the National Hunt Committee, dying in 1970 at the age of eighty-two.

At that 1924 meeting, the next morning, when Mr Withington arrived at the course, he was told that Alcazar would not be started. He lost no time in engaging Dick Rees to ride and in declaring his horse a runner.

Prestbury Park, the Cheltenham racecourse, lies in a fold of the Cotswold Hills above the town of Cheltenham. It is overlooked and dominated by Cleeve Hill on whose heights the first races at Cheltenham took place over a century ago. On a fine day such as this was, Prestbury Park is a particularly lovely place. The very air is impregnated with the history of steeplechasing. Adam Lindsay Gordon rode in one of the early Grand Annual Steeplechases; George Stevens, who rode the winners of five Grand Nationals was killed when his cob bolted down Cleeve Hill; and in the little village of Prestbury was started the training career of Dr 'Fogo' Rowlands. In 1844 Rowlands had given up his medical practice to ride steeplechases with great success. He was one of the characters of the time. When he started training, no lesser celebrities than the Prince of Wales, the 'Red' Duke of Hamilton and Sir John Astley sent their horses to him at Prestbury. It was to Sir John Astley, when both of them were backing the latter's horse, Scamp, in the Croydon Hurdle, that Rowlands sent probably the most confident telegram in the history of steeplechasing: 'Finished his work rare and well. I fear nothing. Fogo.'

William Archer, father of the great Fred Archer, lived at Prestbury, and Fred was born and reared there. William was himself a fine steeplechase jockey and won the Grand National in 1858 on Little Charley. His elder son, also named William, was killed riding in a steeplechase at Cheltenham in 1878. Fred, as a small boy, rode his first race near Prestbury on a pony. He did not win, and came home crying!

'Black Tom Oliver' was another Prestbury worthy. He rode the winners of three Grand

Old Tay Bridge, a runner in the first Gold Cup.

Nationals and taught Adam Lindsay Gordon and George Stevens what they knew about riding races. Towards the end of his life from Wroughton, another name famous in steeplechasing history, Oliver wrote a friend a letter of advice to give to Stevens before Stevens rode The Colonel in the National of 1870. This letter is, unfortunately, too long to quote in full, but a few lines will do to show that Oliver could be as expressive with his pen as he was in speech:

> The master means it, the jockey rides honest and they have got a good horse. If Stevens lays away from his horses and not to be interfered with it will be like a lot of terriers leading a stag-hound a gallop. . . . . Tell him it is a long way home from the last half-mile. I have no doubt he will say I am a d——d old fool, but recollect Old Tom Oliver's *words*: be cautious and not to go too soon, the post is the place to win at.
> Yours truly,
> OLD TOM OLIVER.

There was a Gold Cup run for at Cheltenham before 1924 – over a hundred years before in fact. Flat racing took place on the windy heights of Cleeve Hill in the eighteen-twenties. The principal prize at these meetings was the Cheltenham Gold Cup, a three-mile, weight-for-age flat race for three-year-olds and upwards. Later, when steeplechasing started, racing moved from the hilltop to the vale below, and the steeplechases were run over natural courses around or about Prestbury. It was one of these courses near Knoverton which Gordon described in *How We Beat The Favourite*. Over fifty years ago two enthusiasts retraced the Knoverton course and found and had photographed some of the fences in it, including the stone wall where, as every reader of galloping rhymes will remember:

> Mantrap and Mermaid refused the stone wall;
> And Giles and the grayling came down at the paling
> And I was left sailing in front of them all.

It was not until 1902 that the present course at Prestbury came into being. In 1907 Messrs. Pratt took over the management and have continued in control ever since.

The course over which the Gold Cup was run then and for many years afterwards started behind the stands beyond the enclosures. The first fence was the same first fence as that of the National Hunt Steeplechase. The horses then crossed the racecourse and jumped the second fence, which was parallel to the rails. The third fence was a plain one, and after it was the water. Then came an open ditch, two plain fences on rising ground, a turn and another open ditch. The ground commenced to fall here and there were two more plain fences. Then there was the turn for home and the hill towards the stands where there was a plain fence. The horses turned left at the stands and went round again, the water and the open ditches being jumped twice. The open ditch round the turn at the top of the hill for home was the fourth last fence and an important one.

To act on the Cheltenham course a horse must be able to gallop both up and down hill, and it is a severe test of both his courage and his conformation. It was sometimes said that it was not, as Sandown is, a true stayers' course, for a horse who does not really get three miles could often steal a race if he was cleverly ridden. When the pace was not too strong a jockey could sometimes slip his field at the last open ditch and be into a six-length lead before anyone knew what was happening. The course was a test of brains as well as horsemanship and jockeyship. Not generally rated a front-runner's course, it was yet one where it was almost essential to lie up and not to lose one's place. It was difficult to ride a waiting race and disastrous to lie out of one's ground. It was a course which was a first-class test of both horse and jockey. It was a course over which Dick Rees was superb.

In the absence of Alcazar, Forewarned was made favourite at 3–1 for the 1924 Gold Cup. The National horses were virtually neglected in the betting.

From the outset it was apparent that it was going to be a strongly run race and that none of the fancied horses was going to have much to do with it. Rees took Red Splash to the front, and they stayed there until they had covered two and a half miles. Here Red Splash appeared to be tiring and began to drop back. It looked to those on the stands as if the young horse had had enough. However, he received a reminder from Rees which woke him up again and he commenced to run on. Between the last two fences he was still in charge, going strongly in front. But he was being challenged by Gerald L, and Harry Brown on Conjuror II was in hot pursuit of them both. These three horses had drawn clear of the field. At the last, Conjuror II had closed on the others. The three of them rose to it abreast and came storming up the hill. Red Splash had been a fraction in front all the way and, responding to Rees' urging, he just held on to his lead. Conjuror II mastered Gerald L but he could not quite catch the young horse. The judge's decision was a head and a neck. Red Splash had

Red Splash, Conjuror II and Gerald L taking the last jump together in the first Gold Cup. Major Wyndham's Red Splash went on to win.

made practically all the running, being headed only once. It was a magnificent performance and it was hailed as such. The leading professional was on the winner and the best amateur in the country on the second – what a send-off for the new race!

Both the placed horses had good records. Gerald L had won the National Hunt Handicap Steeplechase in 1920 and had started third favourite for the National in that year. He had won over four miles at Hurst Park in 1923 and was the ante-post favourite for the National until he was taken out through injury. Conjuror II had won the National Hunt Steeplechase in 1922 and, as we have seen, was placed third in the National of 1923. In the 1924 Grand National, partly as a result of his showing in the Gold Cup, partly because of stable confidence and partly because Harry Brown was to ride him, he was to start the second hottest favourite in the history of the race. Money poured on to him from Hednesford, from the punters, from everywhere, and his final price was 5-2. Conjuror II was an unlucky horse, as, indeed, his rider was unlucky round Aintree, and they fell at Becher's first time round. But we shall meet Conjuror II again in these pages.

After the race Red Splash was immediately recognised to be a potential champion. The word 'potential' is used advisedly since The Gold Cup was not yet, nor was it for some years to come, to be recognised as the race for the championship. He was also seen to be an uncommonly good-looking horse. In fact, the only criticism one writer could find to make of his appearance was that he was 'too much like a racehorse' ever to win a Grand National. He was only five years old, there was plenty of time for him. If he kept sound, he might go anywhere and do anything – if he kept sound, that was the trouble.

Throughout the summer months of steeplechasing and the early part of the season proper rumours of Red Splash's unsoundness persisted. It was said, amongst other things, that his wind had gone. He did not reappear until January 19th, 1925, when he ran in a small race at Leicester. He had filled out in the intervening months and was now clearly seen to be a magnificent type of steeplechaser, full of scope and quality. In looks as well as performance he was fitted to be a champion. One writer put him down as the best-looking steeplechaser seen in training. In this race he ran well, but, obviously unready yet for serious racing, he faded before the finish. His trainer announced that his objective this year would be neither the Gold Cup nor the National but the Champion Chase at Liverpool. Rumour seemed to be scotched. But, unfortunately, it was all too true. Red Splash did not run in the Champion Chase, and never contested another Gold Cup.

Alcazar was again in the Gold Cup in 1925 and seemed likely to start at an even shorter price than that forecast for him the year before. Alcazar was now being hailed as the best three-mile chaser in the country over park courses. The Saturday before the Gold Cup was due to be run he gave Silvo, the reigning favourite for the National, 3 lb and a short head beating over three miles. In addition, Alcazar appeared to have much less to beat. It was true that Conjuror II was again in the field, but Conjuror II, at thirteen, had lost much of his former brilliance. He had taken to making mistakes and had all but fallen at the water in Alcazar's race at Leicester. He had changed stables, too, since last year and was now trained by Aubrey Hastings at Wroughton, and, finally, he had lost the assistance of Harry Brown could give him. He was to be ridden once more by his owner's son, Mr C. Dewhurst.

The field in 1925 was small, though what it lacked in numbers it more than made up for in quality. Patsey V, last year's winner of the National Hunt Steeplechase, and Ballinode,

'The Sligo Mare', were the only other runners. Ballinode was trained at the Curragh in Ireland by Frank Morgan, whence she was brought to England on periodic raids. The raids were almost invariably successful, for Morgan, a most skilful trainer who had introduced the famous Dudley to racing, had always succeeded in bringing her to the post in exact tune with her objective. He had secured as her jockey in England Ted Leader, son of the trainer Tom Leader and one of the most promising of the younger steeplechase riders, who learnt her ways and rode her beautifully. She needed riding, for she was a fast, flippant jumper and inclined to take chances. Twice before during the season Morgan had brought her to England and had won with her. In November she beat a good field, which included Silvo, to win the Grand Sefton.

Morgan intended to ride her himself in this race, but was taken ill the day before. It was a chance ride for Leader, and he did so well that he rode her in the remainder of her races. On February 3rd she survived a bad blunder at the water to win the Nottinghamshire Handicap Chase at 6–1 carrying 11 st 7 lb, the third top weight. Now she had arrived to run

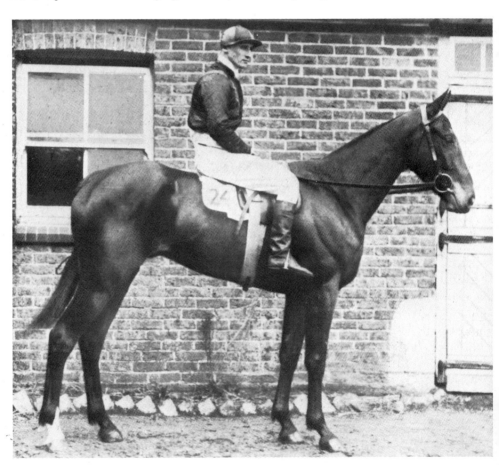

Mr W. McAlpine's Alcazar (F.B. Rees up).

in the Gold Cup. Twice before her trainer had been able to produce her just right to win a big race in England. The omens were there for all who wished to see, but bookmakers, tipsters and the public, as is their wont, preferred the more recent form. Alcazar's victory over Silvo was good enough for them. He started a raging favourite at 13–8 on.

Dick Rees took Alcazar to the front from the start, apparently trying to repeat the tactics which had served him so well the year before. Conjuror II went with him, and Leader on Ballinode was content to let them go. Rees really turned on the pace at the water the second time round. Here Conjuror II blundered badly and was out of it. Patsey V was outjumped and outclassed and could not go the pace. But, do what he would, Rees could not shake off Ballinode. Three fences from home Leader let Ballinode go up to him. It was immediately apparent that Alcazar was in trouble. Rees was hard at him to keep alongside the mare. She outjumped him at the second last and then drew away at her ease. She won in a canter by five lengths. She was the first of the three mares to have won the Cup, and by an extraordinary coincidence she had run a dead heat in a two-horse race at Sligo a year or so before with Koko, who won the Cup the following year.

There was tragedy as well as triumph here. Conjuror II broke down shortly after his blunder at the water. Mr Dewhurst dismounted and walked him home. The horse's tendon was badly gone; he was thirteen years old; it looked like the end of him. However he was fired, given time and a summer's grass, and was back on the racecourse the following year to run again but without success. After this he was hunted; he stayed sound and went through every season until his eventual retirement at the age of nineteen. This is all the more remarkable because in his early days, before ever he had seen a racecourse, when he was hunted, he almost always came home lame. Indeed on one occasion Mr Dewhurst, senior, so exasperated by this, said to a friend, 'I'll give you this damned horse if you'll have him.' The friend's answer was immediate: 'Not on your life. What would I or anyone else do with that broken-down beggar!'

Conjuror was a most unlucky horse – third in the National, second, beaten by a head in the first Gold Cup, and an unlucky faller in that year's National; the only big win he registered was in his victory in the National Hunt Steeplechase in 1922, though in his younger days he had won the Lady Dudley Cup, the blue riband of point-to-pointing.

Ballinode lost her form in the following steeplechase season, and she was not started in the 1926 Gold Cup. After two years the race had definitely established itself. By the standards of the day it was now, from the financial point of view, well worth winning, being worth £880 to the winner this year and the year before.* It was not yet one of the principal events in the calendar, but it was beginning to be noticed that its conditions were so framed that it attracted the best three-mile steeplechasers in training. It was, too, being realised that it was a difficult race to win; and already considerable prestige was attached to the winner. It had not of course, as yet, even begun to threaten the supremacy of the Grand National. Owners and trainers of National horses looked upon it as another, if severe, Grand National trial.

There were two distinguished National horses in the 1926 field – Old Tay Bridge and Gerald L. Both were, in 1926, twelve years of age, but age in a steeplechase horse did not perhaps count against him so much in those days as it does now, when races are run at a faster pace, and each was expected to give a good account of himself. Old Tay Bridge and

*Oddly enough, its value did not exceed this figure until 1939, when it passed £1,000 for the first time.

Gerald L were second and third favourites respectively. A mishap prevented Jack Anthony, his usual jockey, from riding Old Tay Bridge, or he might have started at a shorter price, for he was not by any means everybody's ride. As it was, Mr W. Filmer Sankey's Ruddyglow, with his owner in the saddle, started favourite. None of these horses was, however, to win the race. That honour fell to Mr Frank Barbour's Koko, who started at 10–1. Mr Barbour, who was an enthusiastic and most successful supporter of steeplechasing, trained his own horses at Trimblestown, Co. Meath, where he had built a steeplechase course of his own and reproductions of many famous fences over which he schooled his horses. He had a great eye for a horse in the rough – a gift which had served him well during his term in Ireland, where he had bought Koko and, more recently, another young horse, a tearaway youngster called Easter Hero. Mr Barbour had, in addition, a most astute sense of the best time at which to part with his horses at a profit. This sense was to serve him well with both of these horses, Koko and Easter Hero.

Koko, a magnificent-looking bay gelding, was eight years old at the time of this race. He liked to go in front and he was inclined to take the most terrible chances with his fences. In his previous two races he had fallen at the first fence at Nottingham, and had put his backers' hearts into their mouths by the chances he had taken when beating Bright's Boy at Sandown. But when he happened to meet them right he fairly flew.

Everything went as it should have done for him in the Gold Cup. He was allowed to make his own pace in front and gave a breath-taking exhibition of quick, accurate fencing. No one

Koko beating Old Tay Bridge in the 1926 Gold Cup.

could get near him to hustle or unbalance him, though both Mr Filmer Sankey on Ruddyglow and Hogan on Old Tay Bridge made the effort. Both were beaten off with almost contemptuous ease. Old Gerald L at the end of it all looked more dangerous than any of them, but he could not match the speed of Koko's jumping. In trying to do so, he came down four fences out. Koko won by four lengths from Old Tay Bridge. Ruddyglow was a further five lengths away, third. But these distances flatter the placed horses. Neither had any chance of troubling the winner.

The heroes of the 1927 Gold Cup were the Hon. Hugh Grosvenor and his horse Thrown In. Prior to this Mr Grosvenor had only ridden in eight steeplechases, although one of these had been the National of the year before. Thrown In, who had been bought for Mr Grosvenor by his father, Lord Stalbridge, had had a varied career. He had run on the flat as a two-year-old, and proved useless. Ted Gwilt, the trainer, had him as a three-year-old and, finding him just as bad a year later, sold him cheaply to Mr Morgan Blair. Mr Blair hunted him for two years and then passed him on again. Finally Lord Stalbridge, then joint Master of the Fernie, bought him for his son.

Mr Grosvenor's decision to run his horse and ride himself was regarded as a sporting one, but no one gave him much chance against the cracks. Silvo, for whom £10,000 had been paid before the 1926 National and still, at eleven, regarded as one of the best chasers over any course in the country, was a confident favourite at 13–8. Lady Helen McCalmont's Amberwave shared second favouritism with a promising but difficult five-year-old called

Grakle, who was to be ridden by a young Irishman, Jack Moloney. Thrown In, like Koko the year before, was at 10–1.

The fences had been stiffened this year for the first time since the war. They were now, in the opinion of many, the stiffest outside Aintree. Certainly horses could not take the liberties with them which had formerly been permitted. Amberwave found this out to his cost when he tried conclusions with the first open ditch and came down.

Coming to the second last, Thrown In was in front. Here Grakle and Silvo challenged him. Silvo's effort was short-lived and he was soon done with. Grakle, driven by Moloney, and Thrown In, running freely for his amateur rider, matched strides and rose at the last fence together. Grakle, as he was wont to do, tried to run up this fence. Moloney's great strength kept him all but straight. He did

The Hon. Hugh Grosvenor aboard his father's yacht *The Tally Ho*. Mr Grosvenor rode Thrown In to victory in the 1927 race.

succeed in veering away very slightly, but this did not cost him the race.

Mr Grosvenor had let Thrown In run his own race throughout. Now, with admirable coolness, he kept his horse going. Thrown In had plenty in reserve. He drew away to win by two lengths. Silvo, now seen to be past his best, was a further length and a half away, third. Gallant old Gerald L, ridden by Bill Rees, was fourth.

Thrown In's next appearance was at Aintree, where he attracted some popular fancy and was the Prince of Wales's tip. Unfortunately, he had the bad luck to be knocked over at the first fence. Mr Grosvenor, it is sad to relate, was never to ride in public again. Shortly after the 1927 National he went to Australia to take up an appointment, and was killed there in an aeroplane crash a year or so later.

Koko was back in the field for 1928 and he was strongly fancied to win. It was generally thought that he was a better horse than when he won in 1926, for his jumping had improved and he did not now take such chances at his fences. He started at 5–4 on. A five-year-old horse called Patron Saint ridden by Dick Rees was second favourite at 7–2. Sprig, the National winner of the year before, was next in demand at 5–1.

It was by no means certain that the race would be run at all, for there had been heavy snow followed by a severe frost. Luckily Prestbury Park had not caught the worst of the snowstorm and a bright sun came out early on the day of the race and melted the frost. The going was, however, desperately heavy, and the race was run at a slow pace.

Backers of the favourite were still on good terms with themselves when Koko, going easily and jumping beautifully, jumped to the front a mile out. But Patron Saint, ridden and driven with all Rees's genius, got the inside at the last turn. Patron Saint jumped the last under pressure but still in the lead. Koko, lying second, was on the bit and being ridden as if he had the race in his pocket. Landing over the last, Powell asked Koko for his effort, and to the amazement of the watchers the favourite stopped dead in two strides. He was passed on the run in by Vive and finished a bad third. Patron Saint won by four lengths.

After the race Koko was found to have broken a small blood vessel, and whether or not he would have beaten the winner provided enthusiasts with a subject for argument for weeks to come.

But there was something else to talk about too. Mr Barbour had now moved his training quarters to Bishop's Cannings in Wiltshire. There he trained a brilliant young horse, Easter Hero, who had a couple of seasons ago been falling over every steeplechase course in Ireland. His impetuosity curbed, he had proved himself virtually unbeatable over two and a half miles. Tremendously fast, a brilliant and breath-taking fencer when he stood up, he was thought, however, to be a short-distance chaser. But at Kempton on March 4th, carrying top weight of 12 st 7 lb, he had beaten a high-class field over three and a half miles. Easter Hero had suddenly produced another mile from nowhere, as it were, and his chances for the Gold Cup and the National, in both of which he was entered, had all at once to be taken seriously.

3

Easter Hero

EASTER HERO WAS not started for the Gold Cup, his astute trainer probably deciding not to subject him to a test of such severity so soon before the National. It was decided to run him instead for the National Hunt Handicap Steeplechase the next day. However, he did not start for that race, either.

Easter Hero was, as events were to show, a great horse, and things do not happen in an ordinary way either to great horses, or to great men. On the eve of the National Hunt Handicap Steeplechase Easter Hero was sold. The greatest secrecy was preserved as to both the purchaser and the price. Rumour put the price at £10,000 and one commentator sourly observed that at least he could reveal that the purchaser was not the King of Afghanistan. Because of the sale Easter Hero was not started at Cheltenham, but is was made clear that he would definitely run in the National. A little later the purchaser was disclosed as Captain A. Lowenstein, the Belgian financier, and the price as £7,000, with a contingency of £3,000 if the horse won the National. Since he had purchased the horse for a little over £500, and Easter Hero had won him good races when in his ownership, this was a nice profit for Mr Barbour. There was, however, some speculation as to why Mr Barbour, who was a wealthy man, sold Easter Hero at all. It is said that he had refused a large sum for Jerpoint some years before and Jerpoint had been killed shortly afterwards, and that, as a result of this, he had determined never to refuse a good offer in future.

Easter Hero was not yet done with sensation that year. Although his jumping had greatly improved, he had never seen Aintree before, and he was still impetuous to a degree. Fine horse though he was, many people looked forward with a lively anticipation to his first appearance at Aintree. They expected fireworks, and they were not disappointed.

Easter Hero went off in front, going great guns and flipping over the fences as if this were a park course and the race a two-mile steeplechase. At Becher's the first time round he was many lengths ahead of his field.

Aintree, however, has a way of exacting penalties from horses who treat its fences with contempt. At the Canal Turn Easter Hero took off yards too soon, hit the top of it, straddled it – and stayed there. The Canal Turn at that time had a ditch on the take-off side. Struggling to free himself, Easter Hero fell back into the ditch. He got to his feet, but could not get out. His presence there baulked all but nine of the horses following him. As there were forty-two runners that year, the mêlée may well be imagined. Eventually the tubed Tipperary Tim won

Easter Hero who was sold by Frank Barbour for £10,000 in 1928 and Captain Alfred Loewenstein the Belgian financier and one-time owner of Easter Hero.

what was probably the most fantastic National ever run. Koko also had a spectacular fall; for he went into the ditch at Becher's first time round and stuck there. He was hauled out with ropes only an instant before the five horses then standing came round for the second time.

Before the year was out, Easter Hero had changed hands again. Captain Lowenstein was lost in an aeroplane over the North Sea, and his executors sold the horse to the American multi-millionaire John Hay Whitney. The sale was private, and the price was not disclosed. His new owner sent him to Jack Anthony, who had now given up riding and taken to training, to be trained for the coming steeplechase season.

It has been necessary to dwell in some detail on the earlier exploits of Easter Hero because he was the first of the really great horses to run for and win the Gold Cup. The others, and they may as well be set down now, are Golden Miller, Prince Regent, Cottage Rake and, of course, the towering and majestic Arkle.

But, in a way, Easter Hero was more than just a great horse. He was a symbol of a change for the better in steeplechasing. In colour a brilliant chestnut, in appearance handsome to a degree, he was the first horse since the First World War to possess the presence or personality or whatever is the correct word to describe the particular set of qualities which makes a horse a public draw. Perhaps in his case it was a combination of three things – he was good-looking, he was spectacular and he won. The public knew, when they bet on him, that they were on a trier and that they would probably get their money back plus a dividend. If they did not, then they had compensation in watching in action one of the most splendid horses and spectacular jumpers in the history of steeplechasing. Easter Hero, in the late 'twenties, put steeplechasing on the map as a popular public sport.

Then, too, Easter Hero was the means of introducing Mr J. H. Whitney to top-class English steeplechasing. This was one of the greatest services anyone could have rendered to the sport, for Mr Whitney was an owner of the finest type. A multi-millionaire, he was a discriminating and selective buyer of high-class horses with the object of winning the leading races; his horses, when they ran, ran to win. Down the years successes commensurate with his efforts and his deserts, on the whole, eluded him; he had never won the Grand National, and Easter Hero was the only one of his horses which won him the Gold Cup. But, as in other walks of life, luck in racing does not always go to the most deserving. In fact Easter Hero, the first of his good horses, was also the best, but then Easter Hero was a great horse and Mr Whitney would have been lucky indeed had he got another like him.

Round about the time when Easter Hero began his run of victories in Mr Whitney's colours, the Hon. Dorothy Paget, Mr Whitney's cousin, was becoming interested in racing. In 1930 she had financed Sir Henry Birkin's team of $4\frac{1}{2}$-litre Bentleys round the road circuits of Europe. But her interest in motor-racing was not lasting, and her thoughts were turning to horses. At her command, also, was an immense fortune. Coming down to breakfast on her twenty-first birthday she had found waiting for her an envelope that contained a cheque made out for £1,000,000. This was by way of an advance of the money coming to her on her majority from her American grandfather's estate. Her agents, both in Ireland and in England, were instructed to search for horses likely to be successful under both rules. She acquired many good horses, some bad ones and one or two which were to reach greatness. It is not, perhaps, entirely fanciful to suppose that Miss Paget's desire to enter into steeplechasing may have been encouraged by the spectacular successes of her cousin's horse, Easter Hero.

A little later than Miss Paget another enormously wealthy person was actively to interest himself in the sport. The 'royal blue and primrose quartered' colours of Mr J. V. Rank had been registered in 1920, but he does not come into this story nor does he figure largely in steeplechasing until his horse Southern Hero was to run in the Gold Cup of 1935. He, too,

Mr J. H. Whitney with his wife. Mr Whitney, who died in 1982, was a great supporter of the turf and the owner of Easter Hero.

was to secure a great horse, by some regarded as, perhaps, the greatest of them all, though he never had a chance to prove his true worth – Prince Regent. A little later the banker, the late Lord Bicester, was to enter the arena. Some very good horses ran in his colours and he won good races, including the Gold Cup in 1951 with Silver Fame, but again luck in proportion to the scale of his ownership and his efforts did not come his way.

These were indeed owners of some magnitude. They could command great resources both of wealth and power; they could afford to buy the best horses and to keep them in training year after year. They were not buying to sell at a profit, nor did they depend on betting to keep them in the game. But, because of these things, neither were they likely to countenance laxity of control nor oddities of form. It is perhaps not a coincidence that about this time steeplechasing began to put its house in order. Stewards' secretaries – the euphemistic name given to stipendiaries in these islands – were appointed in 1936. The secretaries were chosen with care and wisdom and have helped immeasurably in the smooth running and ever-increasing wellbeing of the sport.

Control was tightening up, wealthy and responsible owners were coming in, the number of high-class horses in training was increasing, and the crowds were thronging through the turnstiles to see them. Truly steeplechasing could be said to be rapidly pulling out of the doldrums of the early 'twenties.

The race of 1929 was the first of Easter Hero's two Gold Cup victories. The field of ten runners this year was the largest since the inception of the race. It was an exceptionally high-class field and included Koko, Grakle and Bright's Boy. Patron Saint, last year's winner and considered the best young horse in training, had been entered, but he went wrong and was struck out. Grakle had run in the Gold Cup before – in 1927, when he was second to Thrown In. At that time he had been owned by Mr T. K. Laidlaw and had been in training with Coulthwaite for a short time. Grakle was then young and inexperienced, his jumping was unreliable and there was more than a suspicion that he was ungenerous. Coulthwaite had, however, realised the horse's possibilities. When Mr Laidlaw went abroad in 1927 and sent Grakle to the July sales at Newmarket, the trainer advised Mr Cecil Taylor, a Liverpool cotton-broker, to buy him. Mr Taylor had had to go to 4,000 guineas to get the horse, and now, two years later, time and Tom Coulthwaite had turned him into a high-class steeplechaser. In all, Grakle was to run in four Gold Cups and to start an odds-on favourite in one of them, but in this race he could never do better than finish second. He did, however, win the Grand National in 1931. Bright's Boy had a good record over park courses and had been third in the National in successive years, on the second occasion carrying top weight of 12 st 7 lb. Koko had won in 1926 and started an odds-on favourite in 1928. Altogether Easter Hero had something to beat in his first Gold Cup.

He had been given a very careful preparation, aimed, as was then universal, at the Grand National. The Gold Cup was to be his first and only race over fences before Aintree. Each time that he had been out previously had been over hurdles, and each time he had won.

Once more the race very nearly did not take place at all, being postponed from March 5th to the 12th owing to frost and snow. Rees was to ride Easter Hero, and he was at what now appears to have been the very liberal odds of 7–4 against. Grakle and Koko were second and third favourites, Grakle's price being no more than 11–4. From the prices someone must have expected Grakle to have made a fight of it.

Easter Hero, with the greatest of ease, galloped the lot of them into the ground. He was no less than thirty lengths in the lead coming past the stands for the first time. Here Rees gave him an easy and Bright's Boy and Grakle closed on him. Rees was, however, only toying with them. Bright's Boy fell at the first fence after turning for home; Grakle was in hopeless difficulties trying to match speed and stride with the favourite. Easter Hero went away as he liked and won by twenty lengths.

It is just possible that Easter Hero's old stablemate Koko might have made a race of it. He, too, was a handsome, spectacular horse, and a front runner. He was not allowed, however, to go to the front and, restrained with the field, he made mistake after mistake, dragging his hind legs through the fences, and fell at the first water. This is where we say farewell to Koko, another horse who did not get all the luck that should have come to him.

After this race Easter Hero, even with top weight of 12 st 7 lb, was made and stayed favourite for the Grand National. He started at 9–2, and it would have been fitting had he won it. He was, however, greater in defeat than the majority of winners are in victory. Ridden by Moloney, he made all the running until the second last, when he was passed by Gregalach, to whom he was giving 16 lb. Gregalach beat him by six lengths. After the race it was found that he had spread a plate at Valentine's the second time round. That he was able to struggle into second place under this handicap and his great weight is in itself convincing proof of his class and his courage. In addition, even with the spread plate, he confirmed the Gold Cup form, for Grakle, who was getting 12 lb from him, could only finish sixth.

A new star arose in 1930 to take on Easter Hero. This was Gib. Bred, brought up, and introduced to chasing by Lord Killeen in County Meath, Gib was sold to Mr B. D. Davis

(LEFT) Easter Hero in the 1929 race – the first of his two Gold Cup wins. (RIGHT) Grakle, the winner of the 1931 Grand National and runner in four Gold Cups. His name lives on in the 'grakle noseband' which was specially designed for use on him.

early in 1930 and proceeded to win all the seven steeplechases in which he had been started before the Gold Cup. His final performance before the race was to carry 12 st 9 lb at Lingfield and to give 6 lb and a trouncing to no less a horse than Gregalach. He was trained by Percy Woodland, who in his younger days had ridden the winners of two Grand Nationals. Mr Woodland had many successes as a trainer, but perhaps his stables at Cholderton near Tidworth were best known as being a sort of university for amateur riders. General McReery, Captain Brownhill, Brigadier Mark Roddick and Lord Killeen himself were a few of those who graduated there. Lord Killeen kept his horses with Woodland and, when Gib was sold, Woodland continued to train him. Mr Davis liked his horses to run often and to win often. He had won those seven races, but the handicapper had kept pace with him and they had been won under ever-increasing weights. Gib was a seven-year-old and this was his first year of top-class steeplechasing. It is no disparagement of anyone concerned to say that those seven races do not now seem to have been the best of preparations for a race against such a one as Easter Hero in the Gold Cup. Still, Easter Hero was in the National, which Gib was not. Easter Hero's main objective was certainly Aintree, for which he was the ante post favourite. It was possible that at Cheltenham he might not be fully wound up; he had had a desperate race in the National last year; he was a year older; he might not be as good as he had been. These points were canvassed and discussed wherever racing men met. But best of all in Gib's favour was the fact that Rees was to ride him. Apart from his natural genius, Rees had ridden Easter Hero to victory the year before, so that if anyone knew how to ride a race to beat him, Rees did. Taken all in all, Gib was generally expected at worst to make Easter Hero run for his life and at best to beat him. They were at level weights, nothing was likely to get in the way, for Grakle and Donzelon were the only other acceptors. The prospect of taking on the cracks without any advantage in the weights had frightened off everybody else. Public interest was terrific.

Easter Hero had again been given a very quiet preparation. Anthony scouted any suggestion that he had gone off and maintained that he was better than ever. Tim Cullinan, a young ex-amateur from Ireland who had ridden Billy Barton into second place in the National of the year before and who was regarded as one of the most brilliant of the younger jockeys, had been engaged to ride him. There was plenty of stable confidence behind Easter Hero, and he started at 11-8 on.

It was a wonderful day for the race. The weather was bright and sunny, the light and the going were perfect. Both the cracks were front-runners; both liked to go a good gallop; it looked as if it might be the race of the century. Certainly the public thought so; they poured in in their thousands to see it. The attendance was a record for the first day. It showed how well the chances of Gib were rated that the bookmakers would give no more than 13-8 against him.

The start of the race was sensational. Easter Hero, as has been said, never did things in an ordinary way. He dashed into the lead, went at the first fence as if it had been the last, and hit it the most terrible crack. Such was his speed that the mistake barely checked him, but he rushed the second fence, too, and this time it looked as if he might be down. He was not, however, and before the third Cullinan had him steadied and balanced. He jumped this fence perfectly and then began to draw steadily away from his field.

At the stands the favourite was ten lengths ahead of Gib. Donzelon had fallen after a mile and Grakle was hopelessly out of the hunt. Cullinan now employed tactics identical to those of Rees the previous year. He looked over his shoulder to see if anyone else was about at all, and then gave Easter Hero an easy.

Gib closed the distance to two lengths; and all down the far side of the course he chased the champion. He pecked slightly at the water and made another mistake two fences later. But he had Rees on him, and Rees was at that time probably worth a stone to any horse. Two fences out, Rees had driven Gib up to the other. The two horses appeared to rise at the fence together. Gib went through the top of it and made a terrible mistake on landing. For a moment it looked as if Rees and he would stay up. Then they were gone and the interest of the race with them. Easter Hero won his second Gold Cup as easily as his first. The official verdict was the same – twenty lengths.

There were the usual post-mortems directed to what would have happened if Gib had not fallen. Such post-mortems are, it is suggested, on the whole, valueless things. The horse which stands up is, after all, the better horse on the day, unless, perhaps, the other horse is desperately unlucky in being interfered with or knocked over. With small fields and level weights this sort of bad luck plays little part in the Gold Cup, although, as will be seen, there is a suggestion that it may have helped Golden Miller to win in 1933. But this much may be said about the Gib-Easter Hero battle: Gib had been driven up to Easter Hero and was under pressure when he fell. Moreover, fall he did, and Rees' genius was probably at its brightest when he was driving and lifting a tired horse. Cullinan, at the time of Gib's fall, had not moved on Easter Hero. The champion, in fact, gave the impression that he could go away as and when he liked, as he had done the year before. Finally, Gib was never much use again, the not unusual fate of a good horse who is slammed by a better in a top-class steeplechase.

That afternoon Anthony and Cullinan won the Champion Hurdle, which was then run on the same day as the Gold Cup, with Brown Tony, thus being the first pair to complete the double. But still

Gib ridden by F.B. Rees before his fall in the 1930 race.

better things were in store for Cullinan. He was engaged to ride Easter Hero in the National, but somewhere in the race for the Gold Cup the champion hurt himself. He went lame and could not be started at Aintree. Cullinan, without a ride at a time when most riding arrangements were completed, was offered and took the ride on Shaun Goilin. He won, without one iron, which he lost in a mêlée at the last fence, by a head and a length and a half from Melleray's Belle and Sir Lindsay. To win the three principal races of the year in one year is, so far as the writer has been able to ascertain, a record. What a crowded and wonderful three weeks it must have been for Cullinan!

There was no Gold Cup in 1931, Cheltenham's old bogey the weather making racing impossible. The National Hunt Steeplechase was reopened and run on April 16th. Although, financially, this race was the best-endowed at the meeting, it could not at this time be by any means regarded as the most important, the Gold Cup having for some years superseded it in public interest. It was a matter for comment in certain quarters that it was the National Hunt Steeplechase and not the Gold Cup which was reopened. Nowadays, of course, there would be no question which would be reopened and take precedence, and when similar situations arose in later years, it was the Gold Cup which was run on the later date.

Whether Easter Hero would have won his third Gold Cup had it been held is open to question. At the beginning of the season the race looked to be at his mercy. It was said that he had quite recovered from his injury, but as the season progressed his performances seemed to show that something had left its mark on him. Maybe it was merely the passing of the years, for he was eleven, not a great age perhaps, but one which also saw the first defeat at Cheltenham of his mighty successor, Golden Miller.

He still retained his position as a public favourite and, unfortunately for him, his position at the top of the handicap. Once more he appeared as top weight in the National, and that weight was 12 st 7 lb. This year he was

Jack Anthony at the 1930 Cheltenham meeting where he trained the winner of both the Gold Cup and the Champion Hurdle.

again ridden by Dick Rees. At Lingfield shortly before the National, with odds of 6–1 laid on him, Easter Hero was beaten by a head by Major Colin Davy's old horse Desert Chief. Desert Chief was receiving no less than 23 lb from the champion, but still this was the first time that Easter Hero had been beaten in England over a park course. It did look as if some of the old splendour had gone. Despite this beating, Easter Hero remained the public fancy for the National and he started favourite at 5–1. He was knocked over at Becher's the second time round, but he was not going like a winner when he fell. The next day he was brought out for the Champion Chase. Here, at level weights, it required all Rees' skill in a finish to drive him up to a dead-heat with the little-known French horse Coup de Chapeau. Coup de Chapeau was ridden by Gerald Wilson, then at the beginning of a great career.

After this race it was obvious that Easter Hero had lost the brilliance of his former years. Mr Whitney wisely and kindly decided to retire him, so he was spared, as not all great horses have been spared, the sadness of defeats on the scenes of his former victories.

A contemporary writer said of Easter Hero that he was a racehorse turned steeplechaser. It is true that he was built on more handsome lines than the then fashionable close-coupled, deep-girthed 'Aintree types', but this verdict is unfair to Easter Hero, who was a true steeplechaser and a very great one. The yardstick of Liverpool was then applied ruthlessly to every horse, and if he failed to win the National, greatness was denied him. Easter Hero, as we have seen, did not win the National, but Dick Rees, who rode him in his last race at Aintree, is reported to have said that he was the best horse that never won it. Jack Anthony, too, said that Easter Hero was the best horse he ever knew. This is a weighty testimony. Moreover, he was by that great sire of great chasers, My Prince, who, amongst others, got the National winners Gregalach, Reynoldstown and Royal Mail, and the later – and great – Gold Cup winner, Prince Regent. His dam, Easter Week, was, however, not in the stud-book. He won two Gold Cups, being the first horse to do so. Only Golden Miller, Cottage Rake and Arkle have won more than this number.

He was not the luckiest of horses, as his owner was not the luckiest of owners. Had he been started in 1928 he might, perhaps, have made his tally of Gold Cups up to three. His spread plate in the National of 1929 has already been mentioned; he was unable, owing to injury, to be started in the National of 1930, when he was probably in prime. He carried 12 st 5 lb and 12 st 7 lb in the Nationals in which he did start. He was greater horse than Conjuror II, but, like Conjuror II, his merits exceeded his achievements. Moreover, as has been said, he ushered in a new and better age of steeplechasing, and many of the public who flocked to see him stayed to see his successors.

The twilight of Easter Hero's career saw the end of one decade of steeplechasing and the beginning of another. The scene was changing, actors who had held the limelight for years were stepping out of it and younger men were coming forward to take their places. By 1931 Harry Brown had retired from riding, Dick Rees had ridden in his last Gold Cup when Gib took his hammering from Easter Hero, and the Anthonys had given up riding and taken with great success to training. Ted Leader, who as a comparative newcomer had won the Gold Cup on Ballinode, was now and had been for some time amongst the leading riders; Moloney and Tim Cullinan, too, had made their names and established themselves, Gerald Wilson and Danny Morgan were coming to the fore, and so, too, were 'the two Billys', Stott and Speck, great characters and brilliant riders, both of whom were destined to die too soon.

It was to be a great decade of steeplechasing, during which was to be run the Gold Cup of 1935, often spoken of as the greatest steeplechase of all time, and which was to see, too, what is generally regarded as the best National of the present century. This is the 1933 race won by Kellsboro Jack in the then record time of 9 minutes, 28 seconds. This race was run at a breathtaking pace on the top of the ground; twenty-seven horses completed the first circuit and nineteen finished. During the 'thirties the record for the National was to be broken three times; the standard of horses running and jockeys riding was exceptionally high; the sport was admirably conducted, and public interest and attendances were constant and well maintained. But perhaps the decade really owes its splendour to the fact that it was to be dominated by one who must rank amongst the immortals of steeplechasing. He was called Golden Miller.

4

The Mighty Miller

THE STORY OF the Gold Cup from 1932 to 1938 is largely the story of Golden Miller, and for that reason his history must be set down in some detail.

Early in the year 1914 Mr Julius Solomon, a Dublin businessman, was in his club talking to his friends. The talk turned, as club talk will, especially amongst businessmen, to money and thence to ways in which money might be made. It was decided amongst the circle of men that one who had money to spare could do a great deal worse than invest it in bloodstock. Thinking it over at home, Mr Solomon decided that his friends were right. Thereupon he made up his mind to acquire a brood mare. Summoning his motor-car, he drove out of the city to the farm of Mr James Nugent.

As to Dr Johnson one green field was much the same as another, so to Mr Solomon one horse – or mare – was much the same as another. He remained in his motor-car and sent his chauffeur off with Mr Nugent 'down the land' to choose the mare. History, unfortunately, does not record the chauffeur's name, but he either had luck, knowledge, or an eye for a horse. He chose a mare and the deal was completed at £100. The mare's name was Miller's Pride. Then the chauffeur returned to the motor-car and Mr Solomon drove off back to his business in Dublin.

But, having bought his mare, Mr Solomon had nowhere to keep her, so she was sent to board with Mr Laurence Geraghty at Drumree, Co. Meath (the romantic story of 'the unknown British officer' is, unfortunately, a romantic story and no more). It was thought at the time that the mare was in foal. At this distance of time it is impossible to trace the name of the sire who covered her, but it is said that he was one of the notable ones and Mr Solomon, it seems, had high hopes of his investment. Unfortunately, the hopes were not fulfilled, for the mare proved to be barren. Then the First World War broke out.

During the war there was little or no demand for bloodstock and Mr Solomon lost interest in his mare. By arrangement Mr Geraghty took her over for her keep. To his later and lasting regret Mr Geraghty did not take any steps to commit this arrangement to paper nor to register a change of ownership. But through the years he treated the mare as if she were his own, caring for her well and breeding several foals from her, mostly by sires from the Flat House Stud. One of these foals became May Crescent, of whom there were National hopes in 1930. May Crescent plays a part later on in the story of Golden Miller. When he sent the mare to stud, Mr Geraghty paid the fees for these visits. Mr Solomon continued to show no interest in the mare and went about his business in Dublin, having apparently written off his venture into the bloodstock industry as unprofitable.

The Flat House Stud closed down and Mr Geraghty looked about him for somewhere else to send the mare. He decided on a sire called Goldcourt owned by Mr Patsy Byrne of Copperally, Maynooth, Co. Meath, not far from Drumree. Goldcourt had never run, he had produced nothing of any great value and his fee was only five guineas. He could not, in fact, be described as being anything approaching a fashionable or high-class sire. But then Mr Geraghty was doing day-to-day breeding with a rather ordinary chasing mare. He was not aiming at nor did he anticipate producing the prodigy which he did.

In due course, in the year 1927, a colt foal was born. Mr Geraghty's experienced eye told him that the foal was a good one. He cared for him and did him well and sent him as a yearling to Goff's sales at Ballsbridge. Here he was sold for 100 guineas, not at all a bad price for a store yearling at the time, to Mr P. Quinn from Tipperary. Mr Geraghty appeared as the vendor and the sale was made in his name. This yearling was the future Golden Miller. The mare never had another foal, for she died the following year. There were to be

Mr J. O'Riordan's Goldcourt – the sire of Golden Miller.

no full brothers or sisters to Golden Miller. He was unique in the truest sense of the word.

Mr Geraghty's name, as well as appearing as the vendor, also appeared as the breeder of this yearling. There was no reason why it should not, for he had kept the mare, arranged the mating and paid the service fee. But there was still the fatal flaw of 'the papers'.

Some years later, when Golden Miller was running prominently in England, Mr Solomon appears to have woken up to the fact that his investment in bloodstock, whilst it might not have been profitable in terms of cash, could well pay off in prestige. He approached an agent well known in the bloodstock world with a view to having his name credited as the breeder of Golden Miller. After some little difficulty this was done. So if anyone now takes the trouble to look up volume twenty-eight of the General Stud Book he will see Mr Geraghty appearing as the breeder of Golden Miller, but he will also see himself referred to an Errata List at the end of the book. If he pursues the matter into the Errata List he will then see the name of the breeder corrected from that of Mr Geraghty to that of Mr J. Solomon. Such is the extraordinary story of the breeding and begetting of Golden Miller.

Mr Geraghty, naturally enough, was not best pleased at being deprived of the honour of having bred the steeplechaser of the century. On the other hand Mr Solomon knew his rights, and he was entitled to insist on them. Doing justice to both of the parties it would appear fair to say that if Mr Solomon was the breeder of Golden Miller in name — as he undoubtedly was and rightly is – then Mr Geraghty was the breeder in act and deed.

During the time these events were taking place a young man was growing up in England. He went to Eton and on to Cambridge, for he was the son of wealthy parents. He enjoyed himself in the way of young men of sporting tastes, hunting, riding in point-to-points and making a start at riding under Rules. He loved horses and was passionately interested in all forms of sport connected with them. Above all else he wanted to train racehorses. His father, however, was not in favour of the son's ambition to take up training as a career. After coming down from Cambridge the young man went round the world and then, at his father's behest, spent two years in an estate office. During those two years he went on hunting and riding, but his riding now took him more frequently on to the racecourse proper. He began to register wins as a G. R. and began, too, to take an occasional tilt at the ring. Finally, at the end of the two years, his desire to train racehorses having become more compelling, he took out a licence and set up as a trainer at Maddingly, outside Cambridge. He was still very young and the horses which he trained were at first all his own. But he had his successes and very soon it was noticed that his horses were well schooled, well done and well brought out. The young man's name was Basil Briscoe.

Amongst his horses at Maddingly was May Crescent, a bay gelding out of an Irish mare called Miller's Pride. Briscoe hunted this horse, ran him in point-to-points and raced him. He won good money for his owner-trainer, who only parted with him because it was thought that his heart was unsound. But Briscoe remembered May Crescent with affection, and he made a mental note to look out for others out of the dam that had bred him.

After a year at Maddingly, Briscoe moved to the family home at Longstowe, and here he was kept busy, for outside owners began to send him horses. Briscoe was a gifted young man, a true lover of horses, devoted to his chosen profession, and with that flair for racing which sometimes comes close to genius. As his successes increased, so did his string; quite suddenly the stables at Longstowe became a power in the racing world. Throughout all this

Briscoe kept his head. More important still, he kept his eye for a horse and his patience in giving a young one time to develop. These two qualities were to serve him well when another of the progeny of Miller's Pride was to come under his care. For Briscoe and Golden Miller were to meet, and together they were to make history.

In March 1930 Briscoe found waiting for him one evening a telegram from a Captain Farmer, who was in Ireland looking for horses. It was Captain Farmer from whom Briscoe had bought May Crescent. The telegram asked him if he would buy a good-looking three-year-old out of Miller's Pride. The price was £500. Briscoe, remembering both May Crescent and his dam, decided to buy the horse sight unseen and wired his acceptance.

When the horse arrived, Briscoe began to regret his purchase. He was wretched-looking, listless and generally miserable. Although he was no trouble to break, the three-year-old showed no interest in his work and no promise of developing into even a moderate racehorse. When the trainer told his head lad that he had named the three-year-old Golden Miller, the head lad's comment was: 'A good name for a bad horse.'

Golden Miller's first appearance on a racecourse was at Southwell on September 1st, 1930. His performance there seemed to bear out the head lad's opinion. He finished well back in a field of twenty-five and ran like a horse that did not want to race.

In despair, thinking that if he had thrown his money away on a bad racehorse he might at least have got a good hunter, Briscoe took him out with the Fitzwilliam. Let him tell the story in his own words: 'I doubt if I have ever experienced a worse day's hunting. ... To pick up with the hounds we had to cross over a smallish fence with a stiff rail laid through it. ... I set the Miller at this small fence. He took it by the roots, nearly flung me out of the saddle and was all but on the ground. This did not give me much confidence in my new purchase. ... The next obstacle we met was a post and rails; this he went clean through,

shattering the rails to smithereens. ... We went through the roots of every fence he jumped, and try as hard as I could to coax him to take an interest, my efforts were all in vain. Not only that, he appeared to me so slow that I even could not keep up with the hounds.'

Briscoe returned to Longstowe tired and depressed. Next morning, as a crowning blow, Golden Miller's off foreleg was found to be filled. A vet who was called in diagnosed a sprung tendon. One can only imagine what the trainer's feelings were when he heard this news.

One of the earliest and most faithful of Briscoe's patrons was a Mr Philip Carr. Mr Carr was a wealthy man, he had owned and raced horses for years and was sensible and knowledgeable about them. He

Basil Briscoe, the trainer responsible for four of Golden Miller's Gold Cup wins.

was, incidentally, the father of A. W. Carr, who captained England at cricket and also his county, Nottinghamshire, in the days of its glory when Larwood and Voce hurled down thunder and lightning from either end. Mr Carr was a frequent visitor to Longstowe. He had seen Golden Miller and he liked his looks, as well he might, for the Miller had by this time, whatever his actual worth as a performer, grown into a most impressive-looking horse, full of strength, scope and quality. Moreover, he had even then a kindly and intelligent way with him. An intelligence far above that of the average horse was one of the Miller's outstanding attributes. This, without any doubt, materially contributed to his winning the great races which he did and to his wonderful run of victories in the Gold Cup; it may well also have played a part in bringing about the disasters which befell him at Aintree and elsewhere.

Mr Carr asked Briscoe if he would sell the horse. The trainer told his patron candidly his opinion of the horse and the vet's diagnosis. Mr Carr was, like his son, a man of decided opinions. He liked to back his fancy, and he had the money to do it. He told Briscoe that he still wanted the horse. So Golden Miller changed hands again, this time for £1,000.

The tendon meanwhile had been yielding to treatment. The leg improved rapidly, and in a much shorter time than anyone had expected the horse was sound and ready to run. Ten days after the sale he ran in a handicap hurdle at Newbury and ran a splendid race. He was third, beaten three lengths and two lengths by much more experienced horses. His rider, Lyall, who was to win the Grand National on Grakle the following year, was loud in his praises. Both Mr Carr and Briscoe now realised that they had got hold of a good horse – and perhaps a very good one. All this was extremely bad luck on Briscoe, who had parted with the horse just ten days too soon. Moreover, he had persevered with the Miller when the rest of the stable were laughing at him. But at least he had the consolation of training the horse and watching him advance under his care from a supposedly useless three-year-old into a very great racehorse.

Golden Miller was not eligible for the Gold Cup of 1931, which was in any event abandoned, as has been told. He was, however, eligible and entered for the race in 1932. But in the meantime he had changed hands again.

In the winter of 1931 Mr Carr was very ill and he let it be known that his horses would be sold. This was about the time that Miss Paget was entering the market for steeplechasers. In her search she rang up Briscoe. Briscoe, who was not given to hiding the lights of his horses under bushels, told her that he had in his care the best steeplechaser in the world and the best hurdler, Insurance, in the country. Miss Paget bought them both, paying £6,000 for Golden Miller. They both continued to be trained by Briscoe.

Before the Gold Cup of 1932 Golden Miller ran in four hurdle races and four steeplechases. He won two of the hurdles and finished third in the other two. Of the steeplechases he won three (although he was disqualified from the winning of one owing to his trainer having misread the conditions) and was second in the other. This was a formidable record, and it made the horse a public favourite. It shows how important a race the Gold Cup had become and how difficult it already was to win that he did not start favourite in it, or anything like it. It was held that his youth and inexperience would more than offset the slight advantage which he would have at the weights with the older horses. As a matter of fact Golden Miller very nearly did not run at all. The ground was iron hard, which he never liked, and Briscoe did not want to risk him on it. Miss Paget was, however, adamant. She gave instructions that ground or no ground Golden Miller would run, and Briscoe had no option but to comply.

Golden Miller was the first really top-class horse Miss Paget was to own, and she was already displaying towards him and his trainer those qualities of wilfulness and unpredictability which were to make her one of the most famous and notorious figures on the racing scene during a career as an owner that spanned over a quarter of a century.

Dorothy Wyndham Paget, or 'Miss P' as she came to be known, was a true eccentric. She was also, save for her few and loyal intimates who formed what was almost a court about her, whom she treated thoughtfully and well and who rewarded her with affection and devotion, a domineering and, at times, a disagreeable woman. Her wealth brought her little satisfaction, and she appears to have remained deeply unhappy to the end of her short life.

Much of this may well have stemmed from her upbringing. Her father, the first and the last Lord Queenborough, was not himself a particularly lovable man. He longed for a son to carry on his newly-won title. Instead, from two marriages he had five daughters. It would appear that it was on Miss Paget, the second daughter of his first marriage, that he vented most of his disappointment. In addition to being a daughter, she was ungainly, ineffective and almost pathologically shy. During her minority she and her father conducted a sort of running warfare interspersed with short truces. When she came into her fortune she determined to go her own way heedless of accepted convention, good taste, fashion and deportment, and this indeed she did. Her racing attire of blue beret and shapeless, ankle-

length brown coat never changed until the day of her death. Their appearance on the racecourse emerging from a convoy of expensive motor-cars was a sort of battle flag to the bookmakers, for through-out her career she was a fear-less and compulsive plunger.

In some thirty years of racing she had over thirty trainers and spent upwards of £5,000,000 on the purchase of racehorses. What she spent on gambling is anybody's guess.

Tom Coulthwaite always said that Cheltenham was his unlucky course. There had been some chopping and changing of stable plans at

The Hon. Dorothy Paget with Golden Miller.

Hednesford this year, it being originally intended to run Sir Lindsay in the Gold Cup and to keep Grakle, last year's National winner, for another cut at Aintree. Then Coulthwaite changed his mind and decided to run Grakle in the Gold Cup. Mr J. Fawcus, one of the most promising of the young amateurs, was to ride him. Perhaps Coulthwaite, who had never won this race, saw it within his grasp at last and the laying of his Cheltenham bogey with it. At any rate Grakle started as an odds-on favourite at 11-10. Gib was back in the field again, but Gib had sadly fallen from his high estate of two years ago. He was neglected in the betting and started at 100-8. Besides Golden Miller, the other horses do not merit much mention. They were Inverse, Aruntius and Kingsford, although Kingsford started at a shorter price than Golden Miller, being 3-1 to the other's 13-2.

Inverse made the running from Aruntius and Golden Miller. Gib fell at the second fence. Golden Miller, feeling the ground, did the first two fences exceedingly badly but he kept his place. Grakle, going very easily throughout and looking and moving like a champion, was tucked in last. This order was unchanged as they came past the stands and went away down the far side of the course.

The Inspector of Courses had visited Cheltenham the weekend before the meeting and had had some hard things to say about the fences. As a result some six inches had been taken off the top of each. There was, therefore, no 'soft top' to the fences through which the horses could brush. Whether this had anything to do with the débâcle which took place at the fence before the water it is impossible to say. It is a fact, however, that there were more falls than usual at the meeting that year.* What appears to have happened is this: Aruntius hit the fence and made a bad mistake; Kingsford, just behind him, unsighted perhaps, hit it half-way up and took a smashing fall. Grakle, behind both of them, cleared the fence but swerved on landing to avoid Kingsford and his jockey. This swerve put Mr Fawcus out of the saddle and Grakle went on without his jockey. Coulthwaite's bogey was working overtime.

Golden Miller, now warmed up, was left with the race at his mercy, and he went on to win very much as he liked from Inverse and Aruntius, the only other two finishers. He was ridden by Ted Leader, whose second Gold Cup victory it was. It was also the second time that Leader had upset an odds-on favourite, for when he won on Ballinode in 1925 Alcazar had started at 13-8 on.

As Leader passed the post he saw a riderless horse go by him. He went on, caught it, and brought it back with him. The unusual sight was then seen of the winner of a big race leading a loose horse with him towards the unsaddling enclosure. The horse was Grakle, and he might well have done himself injury had he been allowed to go on. Both Mr Taylor and Coulthwaite were exceedingly grateful to Leader for this kindly and thoughtful act, and Tom Coulthwaite presented him with a cigarette case inscribed: '*Actions speak louder than words. From Tom Coulthwaite to Ted Leader. Cheltenham 1932.*'

In a way this first victory of the Miller's was a hollow one, and it was not greeted with any very great critical acclaim. It was pointed out that Grakle had not fallen and that he had been going very easily when he went out of the race, and that Golden Miller had made two bad mistakes in the first two miles and had been all but down. It was not then realised, nor was it to be for some time to come, that the Miller could do almost anything to a fence and remain on his feet. Even now it is worth repeating that, though in his later career he got up to all sorts of tricks and refused and blundered and got rid of jockeys, he never actually fell

---

*One well-known rider has told the writer that there were fifty-six and this he could vouch for as he took six of them! He expressed the opinion that it was like hitting concrete.

during the entire eight-and-a-half seasons and fifty-two races of his steeplechasing career except in the National of 1936, when he was brought down by a fallen horse at the first fence.

Briscoe was confident that he had a champion who was going to be, if he was not already, a really great horse. He did not bother about the critics, and he did nothing to disillusion them. He knew now how good his horse was and he knew that he had something to bet on. He had a wonderful Cheltenham that year, for he won the Champion Hurdle for Miss Paget with her other purchase, Insurance. His brave words on the telephone were being borne out.

During the year that followed the critics continued to give Golden Miller only grudging admiration. Looking back over the years at the astounding record of the horse even so early in his career, one finds this attitude difficult to understand. Perhaps it was because, unlike his great predecessor Easter Hero, the Miller was neither showy nor spectacular. He was not a tearaway front-runner full of dash and fireworks. The Miller was, in fact, an uncommonly lazy horse. If not from the very start of his races, then from the point when the first mile was passed he had to be niggled and kicked at to keep his place. He would never do anything more than he had to do. Even in his great jumping he was the same. There was never daylight between him and his fences. It was economical jumping carried out with the tremendous stride and speed which made him so formidable over park courses. But there was nothing dramatic about him. He was a placid horse both in his box and on the racecourse. He had not the *panache* of Easter Hero nor the breath-taking acceleration from the last fence of Cottage Rake. He knew what he had to do, and he did it with the least possible exertion to himself. Despite his laziness and the driving and kicking which he asked for and duly received, there was nothing ungenerous about him. One who has ridden him has said that although he had to be booted along, whenever one kicked there was always an answer. He was, as time was to show, a really great stayer, perhaps the greatest of them all. Two years later and again three years after that he was to win over three miles five furlongs at Sandown carrying 12 st 7 lb. That distance at Sandown is regarded as the test *par excellence* of a stayer, and the weight, of course, speaks for itself. And he had in abundance that quality without which neither horse nor man can succeed in racing or in any other walk of life – the quality of courage.

He won his races of three miles and over by outstaying his opponents. Especially at Cheltenham, from three fences out that great relentless stride would begin to tell. On and on he would stay and stride while the others wore themselves out trying to keep with him. More than of any other horse can it with truth be said of him that he galloped his opponents into the ground.

He was in the Gold Cup again in 1933, though this year he was eligible for the Grand National and was trained for it. He was given a long rest after the previous season's racing and during that time Briscoe moved from Longstowe to Beechwood, near Newmarket. The Miller's first appearance was in a two-and-a-half-mile chase at Kempton Park on December 1st. This he duly won by five lengths. His next three races were all over three miles and he won them all, being ridden in each by Billy Stott. It is perhaps worth mentioning that in the second of these three-mile chases, the Open Steeplechase at Lingfield, Gib was third, beaten three lengths and a distance.

Dorothy Paget leads in Golden Miller after winning his second Gold Cup in 1933.

Then came the Gold Cup. Stott again had the ride. In opposition was Kellsboro Jack, a very good horse though perhaps better over Liverpool than over park courses. Kellsboro Jack belonged to Mr Ambrose Clark, an American who was an enthusiastic supporter of English steeplechasing. Mr Clark had been trying for many years to win the Grand National, but bad luck seemed always to pursue him. In an effort to defeat his jinx he decided that Kellsboro Jack would no longer run in his name, and he sold the horse to his wife for the sum of £1. He ran in Mrs Clark's name and colours in this year's Gold Cup and Grand National.

Delaneige, ridden by Moloney, and Thomond II, then a comparative novice but later to give Golden Miller the fright of his life, were also in the field. The other runners were Holmes, Inverse and Brown Talisman.

The press, while conceding that Golden Miller had every right to start a hot favourite, were not, on the whole, enthusiastic about his chances of being the second horse to win the race twice in succession. This was so, even though the field this year could not by any stretch of the imagination be called a brilliant one. The Miller's fencing, it was said, left something to be desired. Perhaps, at this stage of his career, it did, but no one had as yet fully realised (except, of course, the horse's trainer and those who would listen to him) that such was Golden Miller's intelligence that he seemed to know how to rectify his mistakes almost before he made them, and such was his strength that it swept him on through recovery and into his stride without losing either time or distance.

It was a showery day and the going was heavy. The fences had been reconstructed since the year before, so a repetition of the mix-up when Grakle had been put out of the race was unlikely. The public remained faithful to Golden Miller, who was rapidly becoming the most popular chaser of the century. He started at 7–4 on, and, in the event, that was a long price.

Delaneige made the pace and Thomond II jumped the last open ditch in front. That is all, really, that can be said about the race. At the third last Golden Miller took command. He jumped past Thomond II and drew away, galloping strongly and at his ease to win as he liked by ten lengths. For the record and for all that it mattered, Thomond II was second and Delaneige, a further three lengths away, third. It is almost an insult to the Miller to say that he won this race without being extended. He won it as if he had been cantering at home.

It was pointed out against the Miller's performance that he had taken off too soon at the second last and had knocked a piece out of it, and that he had jumped to the right and sprawled at the last. Neither mistake, if mistakes they were, cost him an inch of ground. Captain Lyle, the racing correspondent of *The Times*, and one of the most graceful writers on the sport of his day, who before the race had expressed the opinion that Golden Miller was not as good as generally rated, made a most handsome recantation. His words are worth quoting: 'Galloping with ease, resolution and obvious enjoyment he went on by himself and in his glory to win without being challenged. It was done in the style of a great horse – *at last he must be admitted to be that.*'*

Miss Paget and Briscoe completed the double for the second time with Insurance. The final touches were then put on Golden Miller's preparation for the National, and he went to Aintree with the high hopes of his stable behind him. He was, however, still only six, and it was an exceptionally good National field that year.

There was a change of jockeys before the National. Stott had ridden the Miller in all his races this season, but it is believed to have been thought that Stott had not sufficient experience of Aintree nor had he the length of leg of Leader, who was substituted for him. Leader, it will be remembered, had ridden the Miller in most of his races the previous year.

Golden Miller did not win that National. He made a mistake at Becher's the second time round and, hitting the next fence hard, parted with his jockey. This National would have been a good one to win. As has already been mentioned, it is generally regarded as being the best National of modern times. The time of 9 minutes, 28 seconds was then a record. The winner was Kellsboro Jack, who came over the last fence level with Pelorous Jack ridden by Golden Miller's cast-off jockey, Billy Stott. Pelorous Jack fell, and Kellsboro Jack went on

*The italics are the author's.

In 1933 Dorothy Paget also won the Champion Hurdle and she is seen here with her winner, Insurance.

to win as he liked. His owner's luck had been well and truly changed by his wife's pound note.

Golden Miller was back in the field for the 1934 Gold Cup, and so was Kellsboro Jack. This year Kellsboro Jack was not in the Grand National. As there had been a story to tell about him before the 1933 Grand National, so there was one to tell after it. When he had won the National, Mr Clark declared that the horse had done enough at Aintree and that he would run there no more. In fact, he wanted to retire him and take him home to America with him. He was prevailed upon, however, to leave him in training with Ivor Anthony for the coming season at least. One stipulation he made in giving his consent, and that was that though the horse was to be kept fit and would take his chance in any of the races which his trainer picked for him, he was not to be subjected to an arduous or specific preparation for any given race. And, of course, he was not again to run at Liverpool. So, although at first sight, in view of his missing the National this year, it looked as though Kellsboro Jack must have been specially kept for and trained for the Gold Cup, this was not, in fact, the case.

Golden Miller's preparation in 1934 was aimed at the National. Although it was now being said that, great horse though he was, Golden Miller would not jump at Aintree, or if he did, that he would not stay the four-and-a-half miles, Briscoe maintained his belief that the horse would win the National and set the seal of such a victory on his career and his greatness.

This year Gerry Wilson was engaged to ride him. Wilson had ridden him in his first steeplechase, a race at Newbury in 1931. He has put it on record that when he came back to him the Miller was running across his fences and that he had to hit him on the side of the face to keep him straight. It will be remembered that it had been noticed that he had jumped to the right at the last fence of his last Gold Cup.

The first race the new partnership had was at Lingfield on November 25th. This they won, Thomond II being behind them. Thomond II had revenge a month later over two-and-a-half miles at Kempton Park. This was a fine performance on the part of Thomond II, for he was only getting 7 lb – a small amount of weight for the Miller to give away, for he was usually conceding stones. A few weeks later the Miller was again beaten, this time by Southern Hero, a very good horse of Mr Rank's who was receiving no less than 2 st. The Miller did not have another race before the Gold Cup.

The field in 1934 was a good one. It included Mrs Mundy's Avenger, a most promis-

Sir Peter Grant Lawson broke a collar-bone when Inverse fell in the 1934 race. As can be seen from the position of the legs of the horse above him, Sir Peter was fortunate not to receive more serious injuries. (RIGHT) Golden Miller clear of the last fence in the 1934 Gold Cup.

ing five-year-old later to be killed at Aintree; Kellsboro Jack; Royal Ransom, a good horse of Mr Whitney's; and a French horse, El Haljar, who came over with a certain amount of ballyhoo behind him and started second favourite. Two old friends, Delaneige and Inverse, completed the field but this was to be Inverse's last race. He touched Avenger at the fence below the stands, fell, broke a leg and was destroyed. There had been rain on hard ground and the going was slippery, which was not just as Golden Miller liked it. He could act on any going, but he preferred the soft. He started favourite, but at better odds than the year before, being 6–5 against.

The race boils down to the simple statement that everyone had a cut at Golden Miller and that everyone failed. El Haljar took him on three from home and promptly fell. Then Kellsboro Jack, ridden by Danny Morgan, had a go three out and actually headed him for a few strides. It was only for a few strides. Then he dropped back, beaten. Avenger joined issue at the last, but the great, remorseless stride of the champion up the hill saw him off too. Golden Miller once more galloped past the Gold Cup winning-post alone, at ease, and with his ears pricked. This was his third successive Gold Cup. He had beaten Easter Hero's record. Despite the quality of the horses opposed to him, he had had an easy race. Now, in 1934, all that remained for him to do was to win the Grand National and to establish another record.

At this time the Miller was only seven years old. If he kept sound, and if he could show that he could jump Liverpool and win the National, it looked as if he might set up such a series of records at Cheltenham and Aintree as might never begin to be challenged. Briscoe was confident that the Miller could do it.

Golden Miller won that Grand National by six lengths and five lengths from Delaneige and Thomond II. The time was a record, and the fact that he is the only horse to win both the Gold Cup and the National in one year is a record to this day.

By his greatness, Golden Miller stood out far above even the good horses which were then racing. So clear was his superiority that his victories in his big races had been easily

gained. The Fates were, however, conspiring to produce a situation in 1935 in which Golden Miller would have to run for his very life. The instruments which the Fates decided to use in bringing about this situation were the Miller's old rival Thomond II and his owner, Mr J. H. Whitney.

In view of the race which Thomond II was to give the Miller the following year, a little more must be said about him and his history. He was bred by the Duc de Stacpoole in County Meath not far from the Miller's birthplace. His dam was not in the stud-book. The Duc de Stacpoole bought her from a butcher in Trim when she was eighteen years old and in foal to Drinmore. This foal was Thomond II. The dam had only one eye, having lost the other in strange circumstances. She was out at grass during 'the troubles' in a field studded with rocks. A lorry-load of Black and Tans passing by loosed a volley into the blue – this being a playful way they had. One of the shots hit a rock in the field and a sliver of stone penetrated the mare's eye. Fortunately she did not die and lived on to produce Thomond II.

The Duc de Stacpoole hunted Thomond II as a three-year-old and put him in training the following year because, to use his own words, 'Out hunting, you could turn Thomond II but not stop him.' He won six races off the reel and was then sold because there was some doubt whether he would carry 12 st or over when he got to the top of the handicap. This doubt was well founded, for Thomond II had not much physique and no middle-piece, but when put to the test he disproved it. He carried 12 st 7 lb more than once to victory over good horses in England, though he had little but his courage to help him to carry it.

Briscoe looked forward to winning both the Gold Cup and the National for a second time with Golden Miller in 1935. The horse was trained to win the National and his whole progress was mapped out with that race in view. The Gold Cup was that year regarded by Briscoe merely as a prize to be picked up on the way to Aintree, an item in the horse's Grand National preparation. On paper he was, of course, absolutely right. Golden Miller had, in 1934, handsomely beaten all the best of the other horses in training both at level weights and in the greatest handicap of the year. It looked most unlikely that any of them would seriously take him on again at level weights in the Gold Cup, or if they did, that they would get near enough to make him go.

The name of Thomond II appeared in the entries for the Gold Cup, and Thomond II the year before had, as has been seen, beaten Golden Miller with a pull at the weights of only 7 lb. He had also finished second to him shortly before that, and third to him in the National. Thomond II was a brilliant horse, and Briscoe knew this, but he reasoned that Mr Whitney's objective was assuredly Aintree, as was his own. Thomond II was small, light framed and impetuous. With his light physique he was difficult to train in that he could not stand a lot of work. Briscoe, therefore, reckoned it to be unlikely that Thomond II's owner would risk him against Golden Miller. Besides, Mr Whitney had another good horse, Royal Ransom, entered in the Gold Cup. It was assumed, not only by Briscoe but by the public, that Royal Ransom would carry Mr Whitney's colours in the race and that Thomond II would run in the Coventry Cup the following day.

Miss Paget spent the winter in Germany and she did not see her steeplechase horses between the Grand National of 1934 and the Gold Cup of 1935. Briscoe kept in touch with her by letter and telephone, and he told her that, barring accidents, even with the 12 st and over which he was sure to get, Golden Miller would win his second Grand National. These sort of statements have a way of rebounding if not borne out, and perhaps Briscoe was not very wise in being so definite.

This season Golden Miller came out first on Boxing Day at Wolverhampton. The race was a three-mile steeplechase, which he won. He then won his next three races. The last of these was the Grand International at Sandown over three miles five furlongs, in which he carried 12 st 7 lb. Mention has already been made of this race. He won it, beating Really True and Delaneige, both of whom had been second in the National. Really True was receiving 1 st 4 lb and Delaneige 1 st – some weights to give away on the eve of a championship race! Golden Miller's next race was the Gold Cup.

As has been said, Golden Miller's preparation was aimed at bringing him progressively to his peak at Aintree on March 29th. The Gold Cup was to be his final winding-up race – a mere gallop on the racecourse, so to speak, or so his trainer thought.

No one amongst Golden Miller's connections was really taking that Gold Cup very seriously. Wilson had had a bad fall ten days earlier from a horse of Frank Brown's called D'Eyncourt. As a result of this he had badly torn his shoulder muscles and was out of the saddle until the National Hunt Meeting. On the first day he fulfilled a promise to Frank Brown to ride Lion Courage in the Champion Hurdle, but refused to take any other mounts.

Lion Courage was a very difficult horse to ride, but Wilson performed his task brilliantly and brought him home a winner by half-a-length. After the race he was in considerable pain. He cancelled all his rides for the next day and went up to London to see a specialist about his shoulder. Before leaving he announced that he would ride Golden Miller in the Gold Cup but no other horses at the Meeting. Like everyone else, he did not anticipate that the Miller would have anything other than a virtual gallop-over the next day.

Then, the situation changed dramatically. At about midday on the Wednesday Jack Anthony approached Bob Wigney, the Cheltenham racecourse manager. 'Bob,' he said to him jokingly, 'how much is it worth to you if I run Thomond in the Cup tomorrow?'

'About a monkey, I suppose,' Wigney replied with a laugh.

'Then read that,' Anthony said, handing Wigney a telegram. Opening it Wigney saw that it was signed by Mr Whitney. It instructed Anthony to declare Thomond II a runner in the Gold Cup since his owner would definitely be present to see the race.

A jubilant Wigney hurried off to the Press to release the news. Then he set about arranging for extra trains, racecards and staff to cope with the anticipated crowds. There were others, however, who had more serious problems.

Briscoe did not know that Thomond II was a runner until he met Mr Whitney the evening before the race. When he heard the news he was horrified. He had trained Golden Miller all along with a second National in view and no one knew better than he that his great horse was far from being fully wound up. He did all he could to persuade Mr Whitney to change his mind, pointing out that the hard race which was almost bound to ensue if Thomond II ran would do neither of their horses any good. He did not succeed. Mr Whitney had made his decision and refused to change it.

Briscoe, as well as all this, had the problem of his jockey to worry him, for Wilson's shoulder was obviously far from right. Even if the treatment was as successful as could be hoped it was clear that neither horse nor jockey was going to be one hundred per cent fit. No wonder Briscoe went to bed to face a sleepless night.

The field in 1935 was a classic one. As well as Thomond II there was Kellsboro Jack, who was very little, if anything, behind the other two. Kellsboro Jack was still not subjected to a specific preparation for any given race. He was kept fit and allowed to take his chance. He was again to be ridden by Danny Morgan, who had been given the ride the year before when Dudley Williams had been hurt in the New Century Chase, and who partnered Kellsboro Jack in all his races thereafter. The other two horses were Avenger and Southern Hero. All the starters except Southern Hero were worth and had carried 12 st 7 lb in handicaps, and Southern Hero had carried and won with 12 st 3 lb.

As Wigney had anticipated, once it became known that Thomond II was taking on the Champion the public flocked to see the race. It was the Gib–Easter Hero battle all over again with the prospect, this time, of there being no anti-climax. An hour before the first race all the roads were blocked. Trains from London, Birmingham and other centres were duplicated, but even these were crammed to capacity and at Paddington there were violent scenes as people fought for places. The specially large stock of racecards was soon sold out, and the turnstiles became jammed. As a result the crowd turned to the hedges bordering the course which they began to break down. Police, sent to the gaps, gave up trying to contain the rush and instead became collectors, returning to the stands with their helmets full of silver preferred to them as payment for entry!

To add a final touch of drama to the whole scene Miss Paget flew back from Germany in

Jock Whitney's Thomond II – one of the Miller's great rivals.

a private aeroplane and landed on the racecourse only half-an-hour before the race was due to be run. Apparently she was not in the best of tempers, and her expression did not become any more beatific when she learnt that her cousin was taking on Golden Miller with Thomond II.

Miss P, as has been said, liked a plunge every bit as much as her trainer did, and that news told her she was far from being on the certainty she had been led to expect.

It had been a splendid National Hunt season and this clash was a fitting climax to it. The weather, too, smiled on the Meeting and it was a beautiful, balmy spring day. The going was on the firm side which was held to favour Thomond II, who liked it that way, as against the Miller, who did not.

Billy Speck, Thomond II's rider, was, like Wilson, right on the top of his profession. Each knew all that was to be known about his own horse and that of his opponent. Speck and Thomond II had given the Miller one of his few beatings. Speck and Thomond II were a formidable combination. Thomond II may have been small, but he had courage enough for three ordinary horses. Billy Speck was a rider placed in the same class as Dick Rees. He had brains, dash and courage. 'If there was ever a better jockey than Billy Speck, I never saw him – except Dick Rees,' one who rode against him for many years has declared. Golden Miller, there is no doubt about it, was facing the test of his life, and he was not really fit, the going was not to his fancy, and his rider was lacking the full use of one arm.

For the first time the race was run on the last day of the meeting, Friday, March 15th. Golden Miller was favourite at 2 1 on. Here is the rest of the betting, and it is worth looking at: Thomond II 5–2 against, Kellsboro Jack 100–7, Avenger and Southern Hero 20–1. It shows the class of the field that Southern Hero could start at 20–1. Horse for horse, this was undoubtedly the best field seen in a steeplechase in England since the century began.

Southern Hero set the gallop, and it was a good one. The small field kept together, and with the strong gallop they presented an unforgettable sight, every one of those class horses striding out, and every one of them jumping perfectly. Avenger lay up with Southern Hero; Golden Miller and Thomond II were next and Kellsboro Jack last. At the third last the two fancied horses had begun to close on Southern Hero. The pace they were going was now terrific. Southern Hero had enough of it. He cracked and dropped out. Golden Miller and Thomond II came on side by side. Behind them Kellsboro Jack was making up ground. The leaders were two utterly different horses, the one big and lazy, the other small, free-running and impetuous. They both were perfectly ridden. Wilson was driving the Miller for all he was worth, kicking and pushing him and making his whip rattle down the horse's shoulder. Speck was doing that most difficult of all things – restraining the tearaway Thomond II from running himself out and yet keeping his place, giving nothing away and swapping strides with the champion. There was nothing at all between them jumping the second last. Coming into the last the Miller's great stride had begun to tell. He was, perhaps, half a length in front. Speck then went for his whip. It has been said of him that no one of his day and age could ride a horse into the last fence like Billy Speck. He drove Thomond II into it with such strength and dash that he landed him over it all but level with the champion. Locked together, they stormed up the hill.

Every man on the stand was on his toes, and every mouth was roaring encouragement. Neither horse would yield an inch. Slowly the Miller's great strength and staying power began to tell. At the crossing of the courses he was just in front. Thomond II hung on to him, fighting all the way, but he could make no further impression. The Miller won by three parts of a length. Kellsboro Jack, who had been close on the leaders at the last but who was not ridden out when it was seen that he could not join them, was a further five lengths away, third.

For the first time the Miller had had to give of everything he had to win. The going was not to his liking, nor was he really ready. It was a tremendous performance, a wonderful exhibition of strength, staying power, jumping ability and the will to win. He was not distressed after the race, but he was as near to it as he ever had been or was to be. He was blowing; it was obvious that he had had a hard race and that he knew it.

As for Thomond II, gallant in defeat, heart and courage had done all they could, and it was not for the lack of either of them he was beaten. He met a bigger and a better horse who, too, had these qualities in abundance. It has been said that a good big 'un will always beat a good little 'un. That is what happened in the best race ever run for the Gold Cup at Cheltenham, on March 15th, 1935.

And one must not forget the riders. Wilson, in considerable pain and without the full use of one arm, had ridden a second superlative race in three days to land both the big prizes of the Meeting. Speck had coaxed and driven Thomond II with such skill and dash that he almost brought down a very great champion. No wonder, then, that while they were drinking champagne in Sir John Grey's box afterwards Speck raised his glass to his conqueror and said: 'It was a grand race, mate. And, don't forget when we are old we can sit back in our chairs and tell them that we did ride at least one day of our lives!'

It is sad to relate that Speck never saw the day he could sit back and talk of old times, for he was killed at Cheltenham shortly afterwards.

Both Thomond II and Golden Miller went on to run in the Grand National on March 29th, and as this race marked the turning-point of the Miller's career, some attention must be given to it. After the Gold Cup he was firmly installed as favourite for the National. Big and little gamblers all over the country rushed to back him. He was everywhere coupled in doubles with Flamenco, the winner of the Lincoln. He was finally to start at 2–1 against, the shortest-priced favourite in the history of the race.

An escort comprised of two private detectives, a veterinary surgeon and stable employees accompanied Golden Miller from Briscoe's stables at Newmarket to Liverpool. This entourage surrounded him also on his way to the parade ring before the race. There had been rumours of an attempt to nobble him, and Briscoe was leaving nothing to chance.

In the opinion of many the horse looked lighter than was usually the case before his races. Captain Lyle, for one, noticed this and put it down to his hard race at Cheltenham. 'I do not think,' Captain Lyle had written about Golden Miller and Thomond II after the Gold Cup, 'that the chance of either horse at Aintree will be improved by this hard race.' He was to stick to this opinion firmly through the fracas that was to follow, saying that, as far as these two horses were concerned, they had left the National behind them at Cheltenham.

The story of Golden Miller's part in the race is soon told. Coming to the second fence after Valentine's, he faltered and appeared to be about to refuse. Driven into the fence with great determination by Wilson, he bucked over it anyhow and put his jockey out of the saddle.

Golden Miller in the paddock before the 1936 race. E. Williams up and Dorothy Paget on the right.

Thomond II, again superbly ridden by Speck, actually landed first over the last fence, but the four-and-a-half miles was beyond his physical powers. He was easily mastered on the run in by Reynoldstown. Speck eased him when he was beaten, and he finished third.

Briscoe and Miss Paget were naturally dumbfounded by Golden Miller's extraordinary behaviour. Apparently relations between owner and trainer were strained even before the race was run. It apppears from a statement issued by Briscoe the following Monday that when Miss Paget came to Aintree for the National and saw Golden Miller she told Briscoe that she did not like the look of the horse, that he did not look himself and that she considered that he had been thoroughly overgalloped on the hard ground at Newmarket.

It seems that there was at least some foundation for this statement since there were rumours circulating to the effect that this was just what Briscoe had been doing, and the lightness of Golden Miller's looks gave substance to them. Briscoe's answer to this was that if Miss Paget held that view she must send Golden Miller to another trainer. This was not a very amicable interchange to take place on the eve of a great race between the owner and trainer of the shortest-priced favourite in its history.

Briscoe was no doubt keyed up at the time. We have his own word for it that he had backed the Miller to win him £10,000 and that he was confident that, barring accidents, he would win. Accidents are an occupational hazard in any steeplechase and commonplace in the Grand National. He could not have been anything other than strained and on edge. There was the possible effect of the Cheltenham race to worry him, and the hardness of the ground and the rumours of nobbling. Yet, taking all this into account, it does seem that, on this occasion, a soft answer would have served him better.

Wilson, Briscoe and Miss Paget held a consultation when the Miller came back to his stable. Wilson expressed the opinion that the Miller was going short and had actually gone lame before the fence at which he went out of the race. Thereupon Briscoe called in two veterinary surgeons, who examined the horse and passed him sound. It was decided to run him in the Champion Chase the next day. Wilson was again engaged to ride him. This decision to run in the Champion was subsequently much criticised, but it is easy to be wise after the event, and there was a precedent for letting the Miller run, for Easter Hero had been knocked down at Becher's the second time round in 1931 and had come out and dead-heated in the Champion Chase the following day.

Only even money was asked and taken about the Miller in the Champion Chase, which in itself shows how much his performance of the day before had shaken public confidence. The Champion Chase is a race at level weights and there was no horse of Gold Cup quality in the field. Had the race been run at the time of the Gold Cup, Golden Miller would have started at least 7 or 8-1 on.

The Miller galloped to the first fence with the rest of the field, took off in a half-hearted fashion and hit it very hard half-way up. No jockey this side of paradise could have stayed in the saddle, and Wilson went. The Miller in his miraculous and majestic way somehow contrived to arrive at the far side of the fence and to stay on his feet. Even Aintree fences treated with contempt could not succeed in bringing him completely down. He proceeded to canter easily and by himself to the chair fence, which was the second fence on the Champion Chase course. There he was caught by a stable lad who was standing by. The lad got up on him and rode him back slowly towards the stands.

Then the fur began to fly. Disappointment, failure and financial loss in human and equine endeavour lead almost inevitably to frayed tempers and recrimination. That is what happened here. Golden Miller's antics - there is no other word to describe them - were to bring about a parting between the owner and trainer whom, up till now, he had served so well.

It is impossible to withhold sympathy from either of the protagonists in what, at this distance of time, seems to have been rather a sorry squabble. No one who has ever owned a horse who has started favourite and fancied in a race, however small, can fail to sympathise with Miss Paget in her disappointment when her great horse let her down so badly. Nor can one fail to feel for Briscoe, who had trained, schooled and watched over the Miller and had seen him come on from a backward and useless baby to spectacular greatness, who had backed him heavily and then seen him fail so wretchedly.

But, with temperamental people at any rate, it does appear to be true that those whom the Gods wish to destroy they first drive mad for Briscoe, having mentioned to Miss Paget before the race that he did not think he could continue to train the horse, now seemed determined to make certain that he would lose him. On Sunday he wrote to his owner telling her that her horses must be out of his yard within a week. He duplicated this letter, sending one copy to her London address and one to her Liverpool hotel, and he told the press what he had done.

Miss Paget, wisely, took her time about replying. When Briscoe was interviewed on Monday night he told the reporters that he had received no answer to his letters. He refused to comment further, saying that he wanted to see the motion pictures of the race before making any statement about Golden Miller's fall.

On Wednesday both owner and trainer issued statements to the press, the gist of which were that Miss Paget had accepted her trainer's ultimatum and that her horses were leaving his stable. On Thursday it was announced that the horses would go temporarily to Donald Snow, who was then training in Berkshire, and who had married a cousin of Miss Paget's. It was emphasised that their stay with Snow was to be purely a temporary one. Later Golden Miller was sent to Owen Anthony to be trained.

So, in sensation, ended the partnership between Golden Miller and Basil Briscoe. Each had brought fame and success to the other. It was an ending as unfortunate as it was unforeseen. The calm and placid part of Golden Miller's career was now over. In the future, sensation and he were never to be far apart.

No one has yet succeeded in satisfactorily explaining what did make the Miller try to refuse at that fence. Stories all different have multiplied and lengthened into legend and almost into mythology. One theory widely held at the time was that he was dazzled or unbalanced by flash bulbs or flares used by photographers. This was indignantly repudiated by a representative of the company which had the motion-picture concession. Another suggestion was that shadows might have affected him. Briscoe never, in public at least, put forward any explanation. Wilson thought the horse was not going right even in the canter before the race. One distinguished rider of the day has told the writer that he saw the motion picture of the race six times, and the only conclusion that he could come to was that no one except Gerry Wilson would have got the horse over the fence at all.

But might it not have been a cumulation of several different unrelated reasons? The Miller had carried 12 st 7 lb at Sandown on February 16th against good horses, and then had had a desperately hard race the fortnight before the National on ground which he did not like and when he was not really ready. The ground stayed firm between the Gold Cup and the National. It was more than firm, it was hard at Aintree on March 29th. The Miller was an exceptionally intelligent horse and an exceptionally lazy one. May it not have been that he decided that he had had enough galloping and jumping and landing over those big fences on iron-hard ground and that, having so decided, he stopped? Laziness and intelligence often combine to produce a streak of stubbornness in both horses and human beings. One thing, anyway, is undisputable. It has been said that the Miller never liked Aintree; he certainly hated it after March 29th, 1935.

Needless to say, Golden Miller's reappearance the next season was looked forward to with eagerness and a certain amount of anxiety. He would be nine on New Year's Day 1936, the year when a chaser is usually considered to be in his prime, but it was feared by many that his experiences at Aintree might have soured him. It was universally hoped that he would re-establish himself, for he was still a great favourite.

He came out first in a National Hunt flat race at Sandown on December 3rd. This was obviously just to give him the feel of a racecourse again. Ridden by Mr J. Gordon, he did a nice gallop and finished third. On December 30th, once more ridden by Gerry Wilson, he won a two-mile steeplechase at Newbury carrying 12 st 10 lb and without being troubled. He jumped and strode out in his own great style, and there were no hints of mistakes or refusals. Everyone breathed more easily. It looked as if Aintree had left no lasting effect.

But on February 26th, 1936, sensation struck once more. Golden Miller, again ridden by Wilson, was favourite and top weight in a three-mile steeplechase at Newbury. He never appeared to be going well, and five fences from home he ran out. That was bad enough, but his next race was the Gold Cup. What was going to happen at Cheltenham?

The first thing that happened was that the horse suffered yet another change of jockey. Strong and stirring words had passed between owner and rider after the Newbury race. It was shortly afterwards announced that Evan Williams, a young Welshman then attached to Owen Anthony's stable, would ride him in the Gold Cup. Williams, the son of Fred Williams the starter at Wolverhampton and the West Country meetings, had a great career before him, but he was not then well known. He had ridden as an amateur before turning professional, and had set up one most unusual record in that, at Cardiff on Easter Monday 1933, he had ridden the first winner, Mr Ghandi, as an amateur and the last, Vive l'Amour, as a professional. He had ridden at Cheltenham before, and at the National Hunt Meeting of 1935 had been beaten in the Broadway Novices Chase on Morse Code when that horse had been favourite. This is only worth mentioning because Morse Code is a horse we shall hear of again.

Williams rode Golden Miller in a gallop at Anthony's training-quarters at Letcome Bassett on March 4th and everyone expressed themselves satisfied with the way the horse went.

Wilson issued a statement to the press about the change of jockeys. 'I can only say,' he announced, 'that I had no say in the choosing of the jockey, but I consider the choice of Miss Dorothy Paget and Mr Owen Anthony a wise one.' At least, then, Williams knew that he had his predecessor's benison. It may perhaps be added that Wilson's words are reported to have been a trifle more informal when, after Newbury, he asked to be relieved of the task of riding Golden Miller in the future.

Golden Miller certainly could claim to have been ridden by a variety of jockeys, most of them the best in the land. Before the 1936 Gold Cup he had had thirty-nine races (three of them were under Rules of Racing). Wilson rode him in fourteen, Leader in ten, Stott in six, Lyall in two and J. Baxter, T. James, Mr Gordon, Mr Mount, H. Beasley, R. Kick and J. Leach in one each. By the time his career was over he was also to be ridden by Evan

Golden Miller (no. 4) in the lead in the 1936 Gold Cup.

Williams, Danny Morgan, H. Nicholson, F. Walwyn, A. Scratchley and George Archibald.

Despite the fact that Kellsboro Jack and Southern Hero were in the field in 1936, Golden Miller's task did not look anything like as difficult as that of the year before. Nevertheless, the plain facts stood out that he had all but refused in the National, had all but fallen in the Champion Chase and then had well and truly refused on a park course. He was, besides, to be ridden by a comparatively inexperienced jockey who had never ridden him in public before. Still, he had never run at Cheltenham except in the Gold Cup, and he had never been beaten there. There was little doubt in everybody's mind that he could win if he felt like it. The trouble was – would he feel like it? He started favourite, as he was, of course, fully entitled to do. The price, nevertheless, was a shade over evens, a long price indeed had it been certain that he was at his best.

The race was again run on the last day of the meeting. The going was holding and had been cut up by the earlier races. The day was one of spring and sunshine, and a big crowd had come to see the old champion run. He looked superb in the paddock. Physically he was in splendid condition. What was going on in his head? Everyone wanted to know, and no one did.

It must have been a nerve-racking experience for Williams getting up for the first time in public on this great horse in the race which, up till now, he had made his own. Were he to refuse, or to run out, or to get up to any of the quirks which had lately beset him, then it was any odds that his new jockey would be blamed. It was a tremendous test not only of Williams' horsemanship and jockeyship, but also of his coolheadedness and steadiness of nerve.

Southern Hero set out to make the running, followed by Royal Mail. Golden Miller lay behind them. He was fencing in his own tremendous, inimitable fashion, with all his old power and authority, and seemed to be giving his rider no trouble. Before the last open ditch Royal Mail took over from Southern Hero, and here Golden Miller moved up and passed them both. He was now on his own, and had three more fences to jump. He took the two plain fences down the hill confidently and in his stride.

A hush fell on the crowd as he galloped, quite alone and in silence, towards the last fence. Clear of his field by at least fifteen lengths, now, if ever, was the time for him to duck out or refuse if he were so minded. Williams took a slight steadier at him as they approached. What the jockey's feelings were with one fence and one only between him and a record never likely to be beaten may perhaps be imagined.

The Miller got up to none of his tricks. Cheltenham was his own ground, and he had never been beaten there. Every watcher on the stands was willing him to vindicate himself. Perhaps he knew it. He took the fence cleanly, pitched a little on landing and swept on.

The pent-up feelings of the crowd burst forth and a roar of cheering rose to the hills. The Miller passed the post galloping strongly on, alone and in majesty, with Royal Mail toiling twelve lengths behind. Kellsboro Jack was again third.

Kellsboro Jack and Danny Morgan had now been third in three successive Gold Cups. Whether, had his owner allowed Kellsboro Jack to be hard trained for this race, he would have gone nearer to troubling the Miller is a matter of conjecture. He was a very good horse indeed, but Liverpool was probably his spiritual home. His owner weakened this year and allowed him to be started in the Champion Chase, which he won without very much trouble. After his victory, a paper came out with the apt headline: 'How to Jump Liverpool, by Kellsboro Jack'. Besides being a good horse, he was a good-looking one. A popular story in his stable at the time was that statisticians came to measure him to see if they had at last found the perfect horse. They had to fail him because he was half an inch too thick in the jaw! He was, too, a Jackdaw horse, as Grakle was, and Jackdaw horses were very much inclined to temperament. It is probable that, handled as he was by a master of his profession, Ivor Anthony, Kellsboro Jack went as near to winning the Gold Cup as he ever could have done.

Golden Miller returned to Aintree that year. Sad to relate, he was knocked over at the first fence. Williams remounted him and he went as far as the second fence after Valentine's, where he had got into trouble the year before. Here he refused and was out of the race, which he had, in any case, no chance of winning.

There was no Gold Cup in 1937, due, as usual, to the weather, and the race was not reopened. But Golden Miller was sent to Aintree again. Danny Morgan was given the ride

(OPPOSITE) The scene by the winner's enclosure after the Miller's fifth successive Gold Cup win.

this time and the Miller delighted his friends and admirers by jumping all his early fences beautifully. Then he came to the fateful fence after Valentine's. As soon as he saw it his rider knew that he was going to refuse. Refuse he did, running out into the left-hand wing. Morgan drove him up to it again with the stragglers, and this time Golden Miller, to use his rider's own words, 'jumped down instead of up'. That was the end of it. Whatever happened at that fence in 1935, the Miller was never to jump it again. He never returned to Aintree.

He was back at Cheltenham, however, for the Gold Cup in 1938, and strongly fancied to win for the sixth time. He had won two of the four steeplechases in which he had been started before the race. The horse who had beaten him on both occasions was Macaulay, a good young horse who was to break down and be destroyed during the war years. Macaulay had been receiving 15 lb in the first of these races, but in the second he had beaten the champion at level weights. This was an impressive performance for a horse who had been originally bred as a hunter from an Irish hunter mare.

Again Owen Anthony brought the champion to the post looking as well as ever. But the Miller, after all, was not as young as he had been. He was now eleven years old, and although his wonderful constitution and placid temperament had enabled him to stay sound over six and a half seasons of hard racing, his age and the fact of his failures at Liverpool had to be taken into account when assessing his chances. There were, too, those two defeats by Macaulay.

This year the Miller was ridden by H. Nicholson. There were other changes of jockey, too. Ivor Anthony had a very good horse called Morse Code in the race. Evan Williams, who was to ride Morse Code, broke a collar-bone schooling Royal Mail about a week before the race, so Danny Morgan, who also rode for the stable, was given the ride.

It was not by any means a bad field. Macaulay was in it. He was to start second favourite at 3–1 to the Miller's 7–4. Southern Hero was back again, and Sir Francis Towle ran his brilliant and spectacular front-runner, Airgead Sios.

Morse Code started at 13–2, but he was quietly fancied as having a better chance than most of beating the champion. He was nine years old, he had won over three miles and he was a splendid jumper over park fences. He was a horse who galloped over his fences, and his owners, Lt.-Col. D. C. Part and Captain Bridges, and his trainer knew that, good as he was, he would have little chance of getting round Aintree. As a result of this he was specially trained for the Gold Cup. So was Golden Miller, who also was not to be started that year at Aintree. This is probably the first year that two top-class horses at or near the top of the handicap were exclusively trained for this race.

Ivor Anthony, then, had been able to concentrate on bringing Morse Code to his peak for the Gold Cup, undistracted by thoughts of Aintree at the end of the month. It must have been a task after his own heart, for he was a near genius at getting a horse ready on a certain day to win a certain race. It was he who sent out Brown Jack six times in succession to win the Queen Alexandra Stakes at Ascot.

It was again weather of spring and sun. A tremendous crowd had come, most of them again drawn to see if the old champion could make it six in a row. The going was very hard. That, and his years, were against him.

Morgan's instructions were that he was not to hit the front before the last fence. Airgead Sios, as usual, set out to make the running. He was followed by Golden Miller. Morgan on

Morse Code jumps the last in the 1937 race to win from Golden Miller.

Morse Code sat in behind the Miller and tracked him. Three fences out, Airgead Sios made a mistake and was finished. The two others came on alone. Morgan followed the Miller down the hill into the second last. Both horses jumped this well. Coming round the bend, Morse Code was half a length behind the favourite. But Nicholson was now pushing the Miller hard, whilst Morse Code was going easily on the bridle.

They were all but level at the last fence. Morse Code landed over it half a length in front. Nicholson had his whip out now, and he was using it. The Miller would not give in. Up the long straight he struggled to overcome the younger horse. At the crossing of the courses he drew level. But he was under hard pressure and Morse Code was going easily. Morgan then knew that he and Morse Code were going to be the first horse and jockey to beat Golden Miller at Cheltenham. When he asked him to go, Morse Code drew away. The Miller's great heart had got him to the other horse; it could do no more. The edge of his splendid speed was gone. He lost to a horse two years younger, specially trained for the race, and beautifully and stylishly ridden.

The Miller lost nothing in defeat but the race. The crowd, as ever, rose to him. The public as a rule do not love a beaten favourite, yet in his defeat he did not forfeit their affection. He was cheered and cheered again as he came for the first and only time at Cheltenham into the second horse's stall.

So, sadly and in defeat, we must leave him. He was a truly great horse. He was bred for chasing and built for it and everything was big about him including his heart. He was called

Ivor Anthony (*left*) and Lt Col D.C. Part, the trainer and owner of Morse Code.

upon to give good horses what seemed almost impossible weights and did so and won his races. He is the only horse to win five Gold Cups. In those days it was not re-opened. Had it been in 1937 he would almost certainly have won six. He is the only horse to win a Gold Cup and a Grand National in one year. After over forty years these records still stand. Here are the figures: fifty-five races (three of them under Rules of Racing); won twenty-nine, placed in thirteen. Winning stakes £15,005.

Apart from being a great horse he was also a good-looking one, though it might perhaps have been said he was a shade heavy in his shoulder. This was held in some quarters to be a possible explanation of his latter poor performances at Aintree and his dislike of the course. He was also, as Wilson, the man who probably knew him best of all, has said, a terribly sound horse. He had to be to stand up to the testing questions that were constantly demanded of him and to answer them so triumphantly.

It is only fair, too, to recall that it was Briscoe who taught him and schooled him and made him. Briscoe turned him out to win four out of his five Gold Cups and his only National. Besides his triumphs with Golden Miller, Briscoe had many other successes during those years. He completed the Gold Cup–Champion Hurdle double twice in succession with Golden Miller and Insurance, and was the only man to do this until Vincent O'Brien came along.

Nowadays Briscoe is, perhaps, largely forgotten, but as a young man at the start of a spectacular career, he smashed records all around him. He came to a tragic end, but it can still be said of him with truth that brave men were living before Agamemnon, and that Briscoe was one of them.

5

Pre-War and Post-War

MORSE CODE WAS confidently expected to win the Gold Cup again in 1939 and to become the third horse to win it in successive years. He was again trained specially for the race, and this increased the confidence felt in him. The dividing of the paths between the Gold Cup and the Grand National was now becoming apparent. It was beginning to be recognised and to be said that the Gold Cup was the grave of fancied Grand National horses, and there had been some surprise expressed at Sir Francis Towle running his National contender, the free-jumping and spectacular Airgead Sios, the year before. This year, although entered, Airgead Sios was taken out and did not start.

It was, too, a sign of the times that the field was small and, on the whole, undistinguished. In 1939 the Cup was suffering from a sort of adolescence. It had left behind its childhood, but it had not yet come to maturity as the main objective of the National Hunt year. Its prize money was still puny compared to the National, although it increased with a jump this year to a value to the winner of £1,120, as compared to £720 the year before. This was the first year that the race was worth over £1,000 to the winner.

It was fairly obvious to informed onlookers that, with National horses dropping out, the race had to go on to become a race of supreme importance, an objective all on its own for owners and trainers to aim at, or else to sink gradually into relative unimportance and obscurity. But races rise and fall, and it is a great tribute to the Cheltenham management that the Gold Cup has climbed steadily to supremacy.

But to return to 1939. The race was run on March 9th of that suspense-ridden spring, just a few days before Hitler occupied Czechoslovakia. Morse Code started at 7-4 on, as he had every right to do. He was again ridden by Danny Morgan. It would have been interesting to have seen their respective prices if Golden Miller, at twelve years of age, had been started in his seventh Gold Cup. The Miller had, in fact, been trained for it. He had had one outing before the race, at Newbury, and been badly and sadly beaten. It was not, however, until March 7th that Owen Anthony announced that he had not got him as fit as he would have liked, and that he had received Miss Paget's permission not to run him. He never ran again, and after six years the entries looked empty without him.

Morse Code's preparation had been interrupted by frost and he had missed a couple of races, but about a week before the Gold Cup he had been taken to Kempton and galloped

Mrs A. Smith Bingham's Brendan's Cottage, winner of the 1939 Gold Cup, leads Morse Code over the last fence.

there three miles over fences with two others from Ivor Anthony's stable. Morgan had ridden him, and the horse had appeared to go very well. The going was heavy, but he had won in the deep before. On paper there was nothing to beat. Everyone connected with Morse Code was brimful of confidence.

Bel et Bon, ridden by Gerry Wilson, was second favourite at 11-4, Brendan's Cottage was 8-1, and it was 25-1 the others, who were Embarrassed and L'Estaque.

No one seemed willing to set a gallop. The first time round they crawled past the stands, with Embarrassed in front. Long before this, Morgan realised that he was most unlikely to win. Morse Code would do nothing right. He was galloping like a dead horse and scratching over his fences. Down the far stretch of the course Brendan's Cottage and Morse Code went past Embarrassed, but it was obvious that Brendan's Cottage was going far the better of the two.

At the second last, Morgan had his whip out and was using it. They came to the last together, but Owen on Brendan's Cottage had not moved. In the straight Owen asked his horse for his effort, and he went away to win by three lengths from a tired and labouring Morse Code.

There were no excuses for the favourite, nor was there ever any explanation for his performance. Like many another horse, he could not have been beaten, but he was.

In a way this race underlines the immensity of Golden Miller's performances. Morse Code was a very good horse prepared by a brilliant trainer to win this race twice in succession, yet he failed. Golden Miller survived training vicissitudes, hard races, ground he didn't like and last-minute changes of jockey to win it five times. His conqueror's failure is, in itself, a tribute to the Miller's soundness, consistency and greatness.

Brendan's Cottage was a nine-year-old gelding by that great sire of steeplechasers,

Cottage, out of a mare called Brendan's Glory. He was owned by Mrs A. Smith Bingham, a daughter of a Mr Charles Garland, an American who lived near Rugby and raced under both rules. He was ridden stylishly and with complete absence of fuss by George Owen, who was later to train Russian Hero to win the National. He was the best horse on the day, but he met what must be universally accepted to be a better horse on an off-day and must be written down as a lucky winner of the Gold Cup. He was, incidentally, the only winner of the Gold Cup to have won as a two-year-old on the flat.

The National Hunt Meeting of 1940 was curtailed to two days owing to war-time restrictions. The National Hunt Steeplechase course was under plough, and this race and the hunter chases were abandoned. As a result of the plough the Gold Cup course had to be shortened by two furlongs. The start was moved forward across the racecourse and the horses started with their tails to the second fence.

The days fixed for the meeting were March 13th and 14th, the Gold Cup being scheduled to be run on the second day. Racing took place as arranged on the 13th, Miss Paget and Owen Anthony taking both the Champion Hurdle and the National Hunt Handicap Chase, the hurdle with Solford and the chase with Kilstar. They were expected by almost everybody to win the Gold Cup the following day with Roman Hackle, a seven-year-old whom Miss Paget had bought in Ireland the year before, and so to annex all the principal prizes of the meeting.

Roman Hackle had been a good horse as a six-year-old. He had won the Broadway

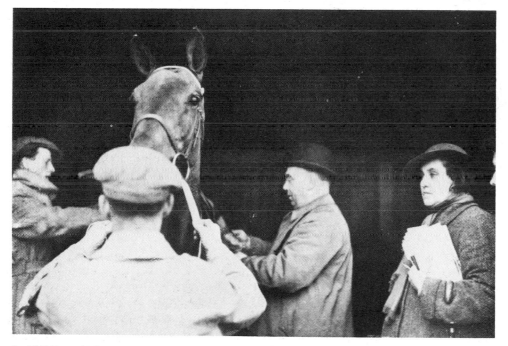

In 1940 Dorothy Paget won the Champion Hurdle with Solford (seen here with trainer Owen Anthony saddling up), and the Gold Cup with Roman Hackle.

Novices, that nursery of Gold Cup horses, at Cheltenham the year before.

He was not, this year, being opposed by any previous winners, for Morse Code had been retired and Brendan's Cottage had suffered a leg injury and would race no more. Despite the absence of these two it looked, just the same, as if Roman Hackle was going to have quite a bit to beat. Airgead Sios was back again and said to be a certain runner, as was Professor II, who had been one of the favourites for the Grand National at the last call-over. In the field, too, were Hobgoblin, a five-year-old who was thought to be brilliant, and the old stagers Royal Mail, Bel et Bon and Rightun. The last-named was, like Airgead Sios, a front-runner who liked to set the pace. It was thought that if they both started taking each other on out in front they might run the rest of the field off their legs and the result might be spectacular.

Moreover, apart from what he had to beat, there was to be set against Roman Hackle's chances the fact that he had only had one race since the previous season. Altogether it looked like being an uncommonly interesting Gold Cup.

Then the weather intervened, as it has a habit of doing at Cheltenham. Snow fell on Wednesday night and the course was unfit for racing the following day. Fortunately it was now recognised that the Gold Cup was one of the two chief events of the National Hunt season and it was not abandoned, as had happened in 1931 and 1937. It was impossible to move the racing forward one day to Friday, since Windsor had been granted a two-day meeting on the Friday and Saturday, but a date was found on the following Wednesday, the 20th. This was only a postponement of six days, but it changed the whole aspect of the race.

In the first place the breathing-space was seized upon by Roman Hackle's connections to give him the race he was thought to require. He was sent to Windsor on the Saturday to run in a two-mile chase. He was giving weight away all round, the distance was believed to be too short for him, and no one would have been surprised if he had been beaten. In fact, he put up a most impressive performance, coming from behind and running the two placed horses out of it on the flat. This confirmed in most people's minds the opinion that he would win the Gold Cup if he could beat Airgead Sios.

Then Airgead Sios, along with Professor II, went to Wolverhampton on Monday. Between the last two fences, when the two of them were racing together clear of their field, Airgead Sios broke down. That put paid to his chances at Cheltenham, and the following afternoon he was struck out of all his engagements. Professor II won this race, but it was obvious that he would not be subjected to another hard race so soon before the National, so he, too, failed to accept. The way was thus left clear for Roman Hackle, and the race looked at his mercy. He was allowed to start at the surprisingly good price of even money.

Rightun, as usual, went away in front of Hobgoblin, Royal Mail and the favourite. Hobgoblin met the fate usual for novices, however brilliant, in this race, for he fell at the fence nearest the stands. Rightun, Roman Hackle, Black Hawk and Royal Mail, in that order, were all there or thereabouts three fences out. Here Williams let the favourite go. Galloping strongly up the hill, he won as he liked by ten lengths. Williams said afterwards that he was laughing at the opposition all the way round. It certainly looked like it.

Roman Hackle was far from being a handsome horse. He was a big, raw-boned, ugly bay. But he could gallop and jump, and he won Miss Paget her sixth Gold Cup and Owen Anthony and Williams their second. There was talk at the time of his being a second Golden

Miller, which the coming years were to show he most emphatically was not.

National Hunt racing in 1941 was, as was to be expected, even more curtailed than in 1940. Cheltenham was, however, one of the courses which were granted dates. There was no Grand National. A suggestion for holding a substitute race at Cheltenham was said to have been opposed by the Cheltenham Town Council, but in any event the Home Secretary vetoed it. That being so, the Gold Cup now reigned supreme and unchallenged as the chief event of the National Hunt year. The date for the race was fixed for March 20th. The distance was still reduced to three miles, and was to remain so until 1946. The value of the race to the winner had, of course, tumbled during the war years. In 1940, 1941 and 1942 it remained constant at £495, the lowest figure since the inception of the race. In 1945 it was still further reduced in value to £340. Thenceforward, it has climbed rapidly and substantially in value.

Despite the curtailments and interruptions (there were only eleven days racing in February and eight in the first three weeks in March), the field for the Gold Cup was numerically strong, for there were ten runners. Although in quality it could not be said to match up to some of the classic fields of the 'twenties and 'thirties, it did not look to be a poor-class one. One name was missing, that of the gay and gallant Airgead Sios. Early in the season it was thought that he had come completely sound from his leg injury, but late in January he broke down once more and irremediably in a training gallop, and had to be destroyed.

Roman Hackle was back in the field again, and again expected to win. But Roman Hackle had been having his ups and downs. In February he had been beaten into fourth place by a horse called Sable Marten. It was true that he had been giving Sable Marten no less than 2 st, but he had been expected to have been able to do it. However, at Plumpton on the Saturday before the Gold Cup he appeared to redeem himself at the right moment by reversing this result, and giving Sable Marten the same weight and a beating by three-quarters of a length. He was, therefore, firmly installed as favourite.

The rest of the field were newcomers to the race. Ivor Anthony had two from Wroughton this year to pit against his brother's favourite. These were Red Rower, bred by Lord Stalbridge out of his famous mare Red Maru, and Mr David Sherbrooke's Poet Prince. Both of these horses had been running well, and Red Rower had been an outstanding novice. Red Rower was to be ridden by Danny Morgan and Poet Prince by his owner. Unfortunately for him, Mr Sherbrooke had a fall the day before and could not take the ride, which was given instead to R. Burford. Red Rower had been leased from Lord Stalbridge by Lady Sybil Phipps and ran in her colours.

The best of the remainder was probably Savon, a nine-year-old who had been a good novice but who had had long absences from the racecourse owing to unsoundness. Professor II was also a starter this year.

Two furlongs from home it was obvious that Roman Hackle was not going to win a second Gold Cup. It then seemed that the race lay between Ivor Anthony's pair, Poet Prince and Red Rower. These two came over the last fence together, but Poet Prince stayed on better up the hill to win by three lengths from Savon, who ousted Red Rower from second place by a short head. Roman Hackle, tired and well beaten, finished eighth out of the ten runners. Once again Ivor Anthony had brought out one to beat a fancied horse of his brother's. Burford came from a family who had been faithful servants to the stable. His father, also R.

Burford, had been second in the National of 1920 on a Wroughton-trained horse, and had ridden Brown Jack in his early hurdle races. It was fitting, therefore, that he should get and take the chance that Mr Sherbrooke missed. It was, just the same, extremely bad luck on Mr Sherbrooke, who was a practising veterinary surgeon, that he could not become the second amateur to ride the winner of this race. Mr Sherbrooke had bought Poet Prince for only forty guineas and had sent him to Ivor Anthony to be trained. The horse was touched in the wind and at first was regarded by the stable as being very moderate indeed. The first race he won was a small hurdle at Colwall Park. Like many another horse, after winning his first race he soon showed improvement. The following year, owner ridden, he won the Stanley Steeplechase at Liverpool. Finally, as has been seen, wind or no wind, he was good enough in 1941 to beat Miss Paget's warm favourite and to win the championship. He was operated on for his wind the following year and, although he does reappear in the Gold Cup, it is not, unfortunately, amongst the placed horses.

There were only eighteen days' steeplechasing in 1942. This was partly due to Government restrictions and partly due to the weather, which closed in and made racing impossible between January 10th and March 14th. Again the Gold Cup was the highlight of the season, such as it was.

The National Hunt Committee had voted to continue with the sport only after a statement by Lord Rosebery that every member of the Cabinet from the Prime Minister downwards was in favour of racing. But there was a good deal of adverse comment in the press, it being felt in many quarters that this decision was not in accord with the demands of total war. A letter appeared in *The Times* when the date of the National Hunt Meeting approached suggesting that the Cheltenham executive should cancel the fixture and give the prize money to Cheltenham warships week. Although this drastic suggestion was not adopted, it showed the way the wind was blowing, and most people connected with steeplechasing realised that it was unlikely that the sport would be allowed to continue during another winter of war.

The National Hunt Meeting took place on consecutive Saturdays, March 14th and 21st. On the first day most of the fancied Gold Cup horses turned out for a dress rehearsal, as it were, in the Grand Annual Steeplechase. This was won by Danny Morgan on Red Rower from Médoc II and Mr J. V. Rank's Broken Promise. Savon, the probable Gold Cup favourite, fell on this day's racing and was destroyed.

The weather was bad on the following Saturday. It was damp and foggy and there was a very small attendance. In the absence of Savon, Red Rower was made favourite. Médoc II and Broken Promise, as well as two former winners in Poet Prince and Roman Hackle, were in the field. There were twelve runners and the race was run at a very fast pace. The race was marked by one of those mix-ups involving the favourite, most unusual in the Gold Cup and much more typical of Aintree than of Cheltenham.

The incident happened at the last open ditch, the same fence which plays such an important part in so many of these races. Here Solarium and Broken Promise were far ahead of the rest. Solarium was the leader by about half a length, but Broken Promise was going particularly easily. At this stage, in fact, Broken Promise looked all over a winner. But Solarium fell, and Broken Promise fell over him. Red Rower, the leader of the second

(OPPOSITE) Poet Prince with Roger Burford up after winning the 1941 race.

division, who was moving up to make a challenge, all but fell over both of them.

Nicholson, on Médoc II, arrived on the scene after the tangle had sorted itself out and found himself left in command of the race, much as Leader had been on Golden Miller seven years before. Two fences out, Médoc II was eight lengths in front of Red Rower, whom his rider had somehow kept on his feet, rallied and re-collected. Red Rower had no hope of narrowing the gap. Médoc II went on to win by the same distance. Asterabad, a good-looking horse of Lord Bicester's, whose name thus appears in the placings of this race for the first time, was third, and Schubert, a horse of whom we shall hear again, fourth.

Médoc II thus reversed the Grand Annual placings with Red Rower, but he may have been lucky to have done so. He did, however, give Reg Hobbs, his trainer, compensation for the loss of Savon, who had also been in Hobbs' stable. There were a few hard-luck stories after this race. Broken Promise was going particularly well when he was brought down and might well have given Mr Rank his first Gold Cup; Red Rower was interfered with; Roman Hackle fell and broke the collar-bone of his rider, Ron Smyth, the then champion jockey.

As this was the last appearance of Danny Morgan in the race, a word may perhaps be said about his amazing record in it. He first appeared 'in the money' when he was third on Kellsboro Jack in 1934, and thereafter was never out it. Here is the record in detail, for it is worth looking at: third on Kellsboro Jack 1934, 1935, and 1936; won on Morse Code 1938; second on Morse Code 1939; third on Royal Mail 1940; third on Red Rower 1941, second on Red Rower 1942 – seven years and never out of a place.

There was not to be another Gold Cup until 1945, when the end of the war was in sight. On September 10th, 1942, a notice appeared in the *Racing Calendar* and put an end to much speculation and heart-searching on the subject of continuing steeplechasing. The notice read as follows:

The Stewards of the National Hunt Committee have received notification from his Majesty's Government that they are unable to sanction National Hunt Racing during the season 1942–43.

On December 10th of the same year the Stewards of the Irish National Hunt Committee partially lifted a ban which had been imposed by them some years earlier and allowed horses which were not in Ireland on June 15th, 1941, to run there, subject to certain qualifications. Roman Hackle was one of the few horses who took advantage of this. He went over to Miss Paget's Irish trainer for the duration. Médoc II was also sent to Ireland.

Steeplechasing in England started again on January 6th, 1945. There were meetings arranged for Cheltenham and Wetherby, but Wetherby could not be held, so, appropriately enough, Cheltenham ushered in the new era alone.

After a lapse of almost three years it was no wonder that newspaper correspondents advised their readers to exercise caution in their betting and, if they must bet, to stick to horses who had shown before the break that they could jump fences. This advice was not difficult to follow, for many of the old campaigners turned out once more to try to earn the cost of their long lay-off. In one race at Cheltenham there was one horse aged sixteen, two aged fourteen and one thirteen. This race was won by Schubert, the Gold Cup fourth of 1942, who was now eleven.

H. ('Frenchie') Nicholson and Médoc II who won the 1942 race by 8 lengths from Red Rower.

Major Lord Sefton with Médoc II after his horse's win.

Danny Morgan learning to ride army style when he joined the Household Cavalry during the war.

There was to be no Grand National in 1945, so the Gold Cup still reigned alone as the chief aim for owners and trainers. Former Gold Cup horses, too, were still about. Schubert was out again on February 14th at Windsor in a three-mile chase which was one of no less than eleven races on the day's programme. Poet Prince was in the same race, as was Paladin, a horse who had been expected to run well in the Gold Cups of 1941 and 1942 but had had to be taken out in both these years due to injury. He had, apparently, forgotten how to jump in the interval, for he got stuck on top of the first fence at Windsor, leaving Schubert and Poet Prince to fight it out. Schubert beat the former champion by a length, but Poet Prince ran such a good race that it was thought his operation must have been successful. A little later another old friend, Red Rower, now, like Schubert, eleven, won under 12 st 7 lb at Windsor, having Asterabad in third place behind him.

It was probable that the champion this year would come from one of these horses, and the pundits picked Red Rower as the likely one. Red Rower was now back in Lord Stalbridge's colours, which had been carried to victory once before in this race when the Hon. Hugh Grosvenor won on Thrown In. He was now trained by his owner, who had also owned and trained the last National winner – Bogskar in 1940. D. L. Jones, a light-weight jockey who had to put up no less than 3 st deadweight in order to do the 12 st, was engaged to ride him.

The race aroused immense public interest. The end of the war was in sight and victory was in the air. Everywhere there was a feeling that war-time burdens were lifting. This was the first big steeplechase to be run for almost three years. Vast crowds thronged to see it.

The race was run at a one-day meeting, on Saturday, March 17th. As if in harmony with the general upsurge of relief from the grimness of war, the weather held good. It was a clear, bright day and the going was perfect. It was not a high-class field. That was not to be expected in the circumstances, but the number of starters – sixteen – was a record.

Although Rightun was in the field, he was now fifteen and his years did not allow him to make the pace. It was Schubert, ridden by his trainer, C. Beechener, who set off in front. As they went into the country for the second time Schubert still led from Paladin, Rightun and Red Rower. Three fences out Schubert and Paladin were in front. Red Rower had not been jumping too well and he was some lengths behind the leaders. Overhauling Red Rower and making up ground with every stride was old Poet Prince, moving again like a winner and a champion. He jumped level with Red Rower and went on after the leaders. Then, suddenly and tragically, his run ended. His wind came against him and he dropped back, beaten, out of it.

At the last Schubert and Paladin were still together. They were being shouted home when Red Rower appeared on the scene. He came at them, caught them and jumped past them. Then he went ahead up the hill to win by three lengths.

It was an extremely popular win. The horse had started a well-merited favourite; his owner was a great supporter of steeplechasing and a member of the National Hunt Committee. Apart from owning and training the winner, he had also bred him, so it was a great personal victory.

Red Rower was not an impressive horse to look at, but he was game and consistent. If he had been unlucky in 1942, the Fates certainly relented in 1945. It is not often that a horse gets three chances to win a high-class steeplechase and wins at the third attempt at the age of eleven, although Royal Tan's record in the National is somewhat similar. But Red Rower's record of third, second and then first after an interval of three years is unique in this race.

So, with Red Rower's victory, the war years of the Gold Cup ended. Only two races had been missed, and these were the years when there was no steeplechasing in England. During the curtailment, the existence of the race proved of immense value to steeplechasing. It meant that the championship was still there as long as there were horses to run for it. It provided an objective to be aimed at by owners and trainers struggling to keep going during those dark days. Looking back, it is surprising how well the quality of the fields was maintained. The Gold Cup emerged from the war firmly established and with its prestige enhanced.

Appropriately enough the post-war era was to be ushered in by a victory for one of the great horses of the race. He was unable, through having reached his maturity during the

Third time lucky for Red Rower seen here after his win in 1945.

war, to run in the great open steeplechases in England when in his prime and there to prove his greatness once and for all. He was past his best when he won the Gold Cup and ran in the National, but he did enough at least to put him amongst the aristocrats of the race. Despite his having won only one Gold Cup, his other achievements make it essential that more space be devoted to him than that one easy victory would at first sight appear to merit.

6

Prince Regent and Fortina

MR JAMES V. RANK, as far as the great races went, was an unlucky owner. He was another striking example of luck in racing not going to the most deserving. His three ambitions in sport were to win the Derby, the Waterloo Cup and the Grand National. He died in 1952 without having won one of them. When he died, he had been an owner for more than thirty years and he must have spent vast sums in his attempts to fufil these ambitions. Moreover, he was an owner who adorned the turf. The form of his horses was there for all who ran to read; betting played no material part in his racing; his object was to win races, and winning them was for him reward enough.

It was cruel luck that, owing to the war, the best steeplechaser he ever owned had no chance to attempt to win a series of Gold Cups, nor to run in the Grand National in his prime and at a reasonable weight. It was in a line with this luck that, the year after his death, his horse Early Mist should win a Grand National for an owner whose colours had been registered for a mere two years.

In his search for a champion, ill-luck dogged Mr Rank. He owned Southern Hero, and Southern Hero was good but not good enough; he owned Broken Promise, and Broken Promise fell when he looked all over a winner of the Gold Cup; he wanted to buy Reynoldstown as a young horse and was dissuaded by a friend's advice that Reynoldstown would never be any good. However, he would not allow himself to be discouraged, and instructions were issued to his agents that any young horse by My Prince who had possibilities was to be looked at with a view to purchase.

In 1936 Mr Livvock of Newmarket bought at Goff's Sales a yearling by My Prince out of a mare called Nemaea. News of this yearling came to Mr Harry Bonner, who was then buying horses for Mr Rank, and he bought him as a two-year-old. The colt was sent to a man called Paddy Power to be broken. Power was killed in a motor accident going to the Dublin Horse Show and the horse then went to T. W. Dreaper, Mr Rank's trainer in Ireland, with whom he was to remain for the rest of his racing career. He was named Prince Regent and was not raced until the autumn of 1939.

It was as a seven-year-old, in his second year of serious steeplechasing, that Prince Regent really began to give away weight and to show what he was made of. It is this year, 1942, and the one following upon which his claims to greatness most firmly rest. The weights which he was called upon to give away and the races he ran under these great burdens are reminiscent of Golden Miller in his prime, although Prince Regent's performances under weight are not quite so impressive as those of Golden Miller, nor were the horses to whom he gave weight of the same class as most of Golden Miller's opponents.

In the year 1942 Prince Regent had seven races. He won four and was placed in one. The lightest weight he carried was 11 st 10 lb, the heaviest 12 st 12 lb. He carried 12 st 7 lb in four races, including the Irish Grand National which he won.

In 1943 he ran in seven steeplechases and one weight-for-age flat race, which he won. He won three of the steeplechases and was never unplaced. He never carried less than 12 st 4 lb in the steeplechases. With one exception the horses who beat him or ran up to him carried less than 10 st. The exception was the Irish Grand National, in which he was beaten by four lengths by Golden Jack, who had been second to him the year before. Médoc II ran unplaced in this race carrying 12 st. Prince Regent carried 12 st 7 lb and gave Golden Jack, who incidentally was by Golden Miller's sire, Goldcourt, 18 lb. But this was an unsatisfactory race and the Stewards of the I.N.H.S. Committee held an enquiry after it into the running of the winner.

In 1944 Prince Regent failed again in the Irish Grand National, going under by a length to Knight's Crest, who was receiving 3 st. He had only four steeplechases that year and won two of them. He carried 12 st 7 lb in them all. He did very little racing in 1945, having fallen in a steeplechase at Baldoyle early in the year and being off work for a long time. When he came back, he failed by a head to beat no less than Roman Hackle over 3 miles 160 yards at Leopardstown. Roman Hackle was receiving exactly 3 st. Even though Roman Hackle had tumbled in the handicap, he had a touch of class about him, and this may well have been one of the best performances of the Regent's career.

In 1946 the big English chases were open again. By this time Prince Regent had become the idol of Irish steeplechasing. His reputation was enormous. Even at eleven he was confidently expected to repay Mr Rank for all his former disappointments, and to become the first horse since Golden Miller to win the Gold Cup and the Grand National. His claims in both were undeniable, and it is not surprising that he found few contenders willing to take him on at level weights at Cheltenham.

Schubert, now twelve, did not accept again, nor did Chaka, a horse who had once been held to have had possible classic steeplechasing claims and who had fallen in 1945. A rising hope, Poor Flame, was, however, considered to be better than both of them, and Poor Flame was a runner in the Gold Cup. He was an eight-year-old, a tearaway type and a wild jumper. Although he had won all his races in England this season, he could not really be considered anything other than a novice, for the previous year he had won the lightweight race at the Carlow point-to-point in the hands of Mr J. R. Cox. Red April was also entered, and a French horse, Jalgreya, but altogether the opposition to Prince Regent was pretty thin. This was not to be wondered at, considering the immediate post-war difficulties under which English trainers were labouring. There were shortages of labour and of fodder, and, not least, of courses on which to run their charges. Newbury, Sandown, Kempton and Hurst Park were, amongst others, denied to them. There were even doubts about Aintree being ready for the National.

Cheltenham was, however, back in its pre-war state. The plough had gone and the Gold

Cup course was restored to its original distance of three miles and a quarter. The start was once more behind the stands and the former first fence was back again. The race was worth £10 more than it had been to Brendan's Cottage – £1,130 to be exact – so it was the most valuable Gold Cup up to that date.

The Regent came to Cheltenham in state, for he was attended by an entourage which included a special guard. He had had only one previous race in England and, as was to be expected, his appearance in the parade ring attracted enormous attention. His looks fulfilled the expectations of those who had heard so much about him. He was, they found, a bay horse nearly seventeen hands high, full of blood, bone and quality. Those whose memories went back to the 'twenties and 'thirties may have thought him a trifle more the 'Aintree

Mrs J. V. Rank leads in her husband's Prince Regent.

type' than either Easter Hero or Golden Miller, for he had in appearance just that little bit more of power and strength and just that little bit less of the racehorse than the other two. All were agreed, at any rate, that his looks gave him entry into the ranks of the great if his performance could live up to them.

He could do no more than win, and win in the most convincing fashion is what he did. He simply strolled away from the opposition. Poor Flame, no easy horse to ride in that company, courageously and brilliantly ridden by Fred Rimell, tried to take him on two fences out and paid the inevitable penalty of a bad mistake. Coming round the top bend, Prince Regent slipped and all but fell on the flat. It made no difference. In the straight, Hyde was looking over his shoulder to see where the other horses were. The Regent sailed over the last fence and won majestically by seven lengths. Poor Flame was second and Red April third.

Hyde has since put it on record that in this race he realised for the first time that his mount was past his best, and that the edge had gone from his great speed. 'It took me a minute or two to beat that fellow today, Tom,' he said to his trainer after the race. It is undeniable that in this Gold Cup Prince Regent had everything in his favour but his years, and to offset them he had the experience which his years had given him. He came from a peaceful Ireland full of good Irish corn to an England recovering slowly from her wounds, not yet a year out of war. It was an England where steeplechase horses were looked on by the Government in power as anachronisms from the feudal system, toys of the privileged classes it was pledged to destroy, where fodder and help were hard to get, transport and accommodation hard to find, and licences for the restoration of stabling and yards dreams of the future.

When facts are faced, it remains clear that Prince Regent beat nothing in that Gold Cup. Poor Flame was a novice and Red April never good enough to challenge a champion. Nor did he appear in the Gold Cup again. He went to Aintree and started a raging favourite under the top weight of 12 st 5 lb. He ran a most gallant race, but could only finish third to Lovely Cottage and Jack Finlay. His best distance may always have been something less than the four-and-a-half miles of the Grand National. Which is not to say that the gallop he could go might not have enabled him to win that race, had he run for it in his prime.

From the viewpoint of history it is a thousand pities that Prince Regent did not take on Fortina in the 1947 Gold Cup. The 1946 race is no criterion by which to judge greatness. His claims to greatness must, it is suggested, rest on his years in Ireland; for his performances at Aintree, though gallant in the extreme, were failures, and not even such successful failures as those of Easter Hero.

Irish form in the war years was probably far above its usual standard, there being no English market for the best young horses to go to; the weights he gave away were such as would surely have broken the heart of anything less than a horse of superlative class and courage. Bearing these things in mind, it seems that the mantle of greatness cannot be denied him, even if he never acquired it in open competition.

The position of the next year's winner, Fortina, is by no means so easy to assess. He was a flash in the pan, but a singularly brilliant one.

The National Hunt season of 1947 was bedevilled by the weather. An appallingly bad winter led to more days' racing being lost than almost anyone could remember. As usual, the National Hunt Meeting suffered. Frost and hard weather made racing on the original

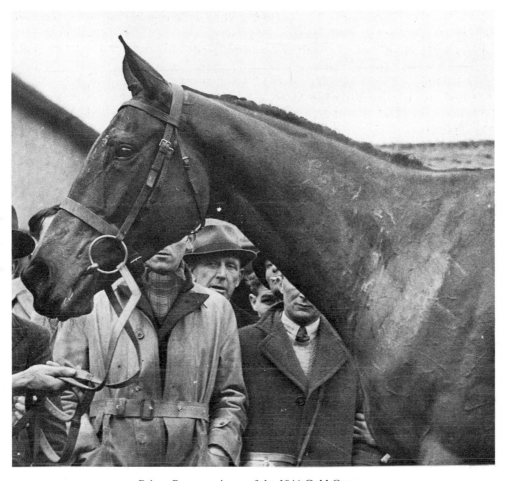

Prince Regent, winner of the 1946 Gold Cup.

days fixed out of the question and the whole meeting was postponed for a week. Then the snow came down and the postponed meeting could not take place. However, by this time it was realised that the Gold Cup must be run if it was at all possible, and arrangements were made to tack on an extra day's racing to the April meeting. Accordingly, the chief events of the National Hunt Meeting were put down for decision for Saturday, April 12th.

Prince Regent was not entered for the 1947 Gold Cup. At the age of twelve he had another cut at realising one of Mr Rank's ambitions for him – to win the Grand National. Again he ran a most gallant race, but in heavy going and carrying 12 st 7 lb he could do no better than finish fourth, light weights at long prices occupying the first three places.

There were twelve runners in this year's race and, in a most open market, Happy Home and Coloured Schoolboy were considered the most likely to win. There was, however, also in the field a big handsome chestnut, an entire horse called Fortina, who had been bought in France for Lord Grimthorpe earlier in the season. Before the Gold Cup he had only one race in England, the Lancashire Chase, which he won. Of the rest, the only ones worth mentioning are Chaka, who had accepted again this year, Prince Blackthorn, an old opponent of Prince Regent's in Ireland, and Bricett, a Grand National horse.

It was a warm sunny day and racegoers had the unusual experience of watching the Gold Cup without their overcoats. The race was run at a very strong pace, which was set by Chaka. Passing the stands the first time, Chaka was eight lengths in front of Fortina, who was ten lengths ahead of the rest. Fortina was closing the gap all the time, and coming down the hill Chaka tired. Here Fortina passed him and drew farther and farther away. That was all there was to it. Fortina eventually won an uneventful race by ten lengths. He was ridden by Mr R. Black, who thus became the second amateur to win this race. Happy Home toiled in second and Prince Blackthorn third. Coloured Schoolboy fell, giving Fred Rimell a bad fall and ending his riding career.

Before going on to deal with the successes of Cottage Rake which were to fill the next three years of the Gold Cup's history, it is worthwhile to take a look at the general background of steeplechasing at this time, for by now the post-war era was getting under way.

The sport had never been so prosperous, nor had public interest ever been so intense. Attendances, where the weather allowed them to be, were high, and where flat race meetings were held at the same venue they often rivalled or excelled attendances in midsummer for the flat. Runners were numerous and ready money was plentiful, for the post-war boom was on.

Over the next few years go-ahead executives were quick to take advantage of this state of affairs, and races over park courses with prizes undreamt of before the war were soon established. The first of these in time was the Emblem Chase at Manchester. This race was named after Lord Coventry's famous mare who won the National in 1863 and was, from its inception, worth over £1,000 to the winner. At Kempton Park in 1947 the first King George VI Steeplechase, worth no less then £2,286 to the winner, was run. In 1949 the late Sir John Crocker Bulteel inaugurated the Queen Elizabeth Steeplechase at Hurst Park. After Lord Mildmay's tragic death in 1950, Sandown Park founded the Mildmay Memorial Chase worth over £1,000. The Great Yorkshire Chase at Doncaster completed the 'top-line' steeplechases. These races, together with the great all round increase in prize money, provided inducement for the best park chasers to come and do battle against each other far more frequently than in pre-war days. They also provided a spectacle for the public and a series of tests for horses in, or nearly in, Gold Cup class. The culmination of these tests was, of course, the Gold Cup itself, which also, to keep pace, steadily increased its prize money. In 1954, the thirty-first year of the race (or twenty-ninth, if one does not count the two blank war years), it was worth £3,576, just over five times its value in the year of its inauguration. Thus, in post-war years, helped by these important semi-championship races run at intervals throughout the season, the Gold Cup grew both in prize money and prestige.

Other things were changing, too. Steeplechasing was becoming less of a sport and more of a business. The old-time 'clubbable' atmosphere was vanishing. There were more horses running, a higher-class horse was being put to steeplechasing and, numerically, there were far more runners. But the new owners coming in were, most of them, of a different type to those of the 'twenties and 'thirties. With the existence of penal taxation, there were none of the possessors of vast fortunes like Miss Paget and Mr Whitney coming along, and even these were beginning to cut down their interests. The septuagenarian Lord Bicester stood his ground and increased his string, with the result that successes began to come more frequently to his colours, but he was an exception.

Businessmen who wanted a bet were, however, entering the sport in some numbers. Many of these were the owners of one or at the most two horses, for which they had often paid a fancy price in Ireland or elsewhere. Their earnings cruelly cut by taxation, they searched everywhere for tax-free increments. Betting was one of these. Indeed, with the Stock Exchange depressed and dormant under a Socialist Government, it was practically the only one. But, since betting was part of their business, it became necessary for them to make as sure as could be that when the money was down the horse came up. One result of this was that good horses began to appear at the smaller meetings in the West and elsewhere, where they would romp home at money on. One of the old brigade was heard to remark of this state of affairs that, formerly, if he had a bad horse for a good owner he could go down to the West and pick up a little race with him, but now, if he did that, he came up against one of Mr X's five-thousand pounders!

The soldier owners and soldier riders, the 'cutaway captains' of former years who had brought the cavalry spirit and carefreeness and a certain amount of glamour to many a raw December day, had all but disappeared. Many of the old sporting owners were killed stone dead as far as chasing was concerned by rising costs and went out of the game altogether, though a few struggled on with very much reduced commitments. But, fortunately, with the increase of prosperity on the farm, a new class of sporting owner who loved horses and knew racing sprang up immediately after the war to take the place of the old. This was composed either of young prosperous farmers riding their own horses, often graduated from point-to-points, or older men fulfilling an ambition nursed through the doldrums of the inter-war years of seeing their colours carried under Rules. They were indeed a welcome influx of sporting blood to take the place of the soldiers and the sprigs of the nobility.

There was, as always during such times, a great deal of ready money about immediately

after the war. The volume of betting increased enormously and the ring strengthened. The big flat-race bookmakers found it worth their while to attend chasing meetings, and in some cases reported a turnover bigger than corresponding meetings on the flat.

On the whole, the public benefited. There were more horses running, which provided a better spectacle; the big races newly established on park courses brought out the good horses earlier and fitter; there was a stronger ring, so that it was easier to have a bet; and, with money flowing in, accommodation could be improved.

Lord Bicester who was for long a leading owner.

All this had a favourable effect on the Gold Cup. This race, with its comparatively small field and level weights, was a far better betting medium than the Grand National. It provided a substantial if not enormous stake with small risk of injury, and a horse who ran in it was not likely to have his physical resources so taxed that he could not be pulled out again early next season to have a go at the big park prizes already mentioned. It was a race exactly suited to the changing conditions of the day. No wonder it prospered.

A new generation of jockeys had also arrived. As the Welsh had largely dominated the inter-war years, now it was the turn of the Irish. Three young Irishmen were to figure largely in the races for the Gold Cup over the next six years. They were the brothers Tim and Martin Molony, and Aubrey Brabazon. These men had learnt their trade in Ireland during the war. A little later, for he served throughout the war in the 5th Inniskilling Dragoon Guards and was delayed in getting going until demobilisation, Bryan Marshall came to the fore.

Tim, the elder of the two Molony brothers, started riding as an amateur when in his teens. He turned professional in 1940 and came to England in 1945. He first topped the jockeys list in the season 1948–49 and remained there or thereabouts for the following five years. Aubrey Brabazon, the son of a famous father who had a powerful stable of mixed flat and jumping horses at Ranger's Lodge, The Curragh, first rode as an amateur at the ripe old age of thirteen! However, at fourteen he was apprenticed to his father and went through the full hurly-burly of a jockey's apprenticeship. This served him well, for he was as good on the flat as over fences. Brabazon's ability to ride a flat-race finish not only with his hands but with his brains played a large part in the victories of Cottage Rake in the Gold Cup.

But there is little doubt that, without any disparagement of Brabazon or the elder Molony, the genius to be thrown up in steeplechasing during the post-war era was Martin Molony. His career in the saddle was cut short by a bad fall, but by that time he had proved himself supreme amongst the jockeys of his generation.

Martin Molony was often compared to Dick Rees. Each was supreme in his day. Although Molony was not, perhaps, quite the stylist Rees was, he must have been very, very near to him as a jockey. In a finish he was every bit as brilliant as the former champion. In fact, their methods of bringing a tired horse successfully home were very much the same. There was in each the same downthrust purposeful head, the relentless driving into the last, the timing which only genius can give when the driving stopped and jumping began, then the combination of strength and artistry which gathered the horse together and brought him home on the flat – in front. To see Martin Molony come from between the last two fences on an apparently hopelessly beaten horse and win his race must, to many of those who could remember him, have been like seeing Rees reincarnated.

Bryan Marshall took over the throne vacated by Molony as the supreme rider of his day. It may seem strange that no further account of him is given in these pages, but Marshall was never so much as placed in the Gold Cup.

So much for the changing steeplechase scene and the actors who were to grace it for the next few years. It remains now to look at one of the great horses who won the Gold Cup.

7

The Reign of the Rake

COTTAGE RAKE, WHOSE three successive victories in the Gold Cup give him claims to rank in the same class as Easter Hero and Golden Miller, was, like the other two, born and bred in Ireland. Unlike the others, he was, however, kept in Ireland and owned and trained there.

He was by that great sire of chasers, Cottage. Cottage had already one Gold Cup winner to his credit in Brendan's Cottage. As a matter of interest, that year, 1939, he sired the winners of both the big races, for Workman, who won the National, was also by him.

Cottage Rake was bred by Dr T.J. Vaughan, and first raced as a six-year-old in a 'Bumper' flat race on March 1st, 1945, when he was unplaced. His next appearance was in a Maiden Hurdle at the Limerick Christmas Meeting of the same year, which he won with ease. In February 1946 he won a 'Bumper', and was then put by until October. His next three races were all on the flat. He ran unplaced over two-and-a-half miles at Limerick Junction, unplaced in the Irish Cesarewitch won by Finnure, who was later to beat him again over fences, and then won the Naas November Handicap. It will be seen that during his formative years Cottage Rake was very lightly raced, and also that he was a high-class long-distance horse on the flat.

Before that Naas meeting he was sold to Mr F.L. Vickerman, in whose colours he was to race for the rest of his career. And the story of how the sale came about is worth telling.

Vincent O'Brien was then only twenty-nine years old and at the threshold of a career which, still far from finished, is already one of the most famous and spectacular in the annals of racing both over fences and on the flat. Mr Vickerman was his very first owner. A Dublin wool-merchant, he was both a loyal and important patron.

In 1944 O'Brien had run two horses, Dry Bob in the Irish Cambridgeshire, and Good Days in the Irish Cesarewitch. Both he and Mr Vickerman had an each-way double on the horses, O'Brien's stake being £2, and Mr Vickerman's £10, both each way. Dry Bob deadheated and Good Days won. As a result O'Brien drew £1,000 and Mr Vickerman £4,500. The figures might have been twice these amounts but, even so, they were substantial enough sums to take out of the ring at that time. Mr Vickerman then told O'Brien that he wished to use his winnings in buying a horse likely to carry his colours prominently in high-class steeplechases.

By this time there was considerable interest, naturally enough, being displayed in Cottage

Rake by prospective purchasers. There was also a persistent rumour going round that he made a noise. The first person who almost had him bought was Major 'Cuddy' Stirling Stuart. He asked the late Maxie Cosgrave, the well-known vet, to examine the horse. Cosgrave refused to pass him owing to his being a whistler and Stirling Stuart left him. By one of those ironies that always seem to crop up in racing Major Stirling Stuart was the owner of Cool Customer, later to be defeated decisively by Cottage Rake in two Gold Cups.

A little later the Rake was again almost sold. Another leading vet examined him on this occasion, and reported that although he made a noise this should not affect him unless he were to get a bad cold. But the purchaser declined to take the risk, and Cottage Rake remained where he was.

Shortly afterwards rumours reached O'Brien's ears that Dr Vaughan was making en-quiries about having the horse trained in England. Already O'Brien's flair or genius, call it what you will, for spotting champions in embryo was fully developed. He discussed the matter with Mr Vickerman, told him exactly what the vets had said, and added that in his opinion the horse had tremendous potential, and that he did not think they should let him go. They then met Dr Vaughan at Mallow and a deal was made, the price being £3,500. Mr Vickerman gave Vaughan a cheque for £1,000, intending this to be security pending a further examination. Yet a third vet was then called in. At this moment Cottage Rake suddenly began to give evidence that he was not one hundred per cent right in front. The consultant, quite rightly, took notice of this fact and warned that there might be a tendency to rheumatism in his joints later on. O'Brien, desperately worried that he might be saddling Mr Vickerman with a thoroughly unsound horse, discussed the whole matter with him in the light of this new situation and they resolved to see Dr Vaughan again. The doctor maintained that the cheque had been given to bind the sale and had not been made subject to a further examination. After a few words had passed the deal went through, fortunately indeed for Mr Vickerman, as it was to turn out.

Cottage Rake took to jumping immediately. He soon proved to be what he remained throughout his career, a quick, brilliant, facile jumper. O'Brien's system of training has always been founded on making horses happy and feeling that they are enjoying themselves. When he was training jumpers he never asked them to do at home as much as would be demanded of them on a racecourse. The schooling fences, though sufficiently stiff so that no liberties could be taken with them, were smaller than regulation racecourse fences. In O'Brien's stable a horse learnt to enjoy his jumping without being over-taxed at home, so that he came to the racecourse fresh and ready to run for his life. This system preserved for the horses in O'Brien's care both their courage and spirit, and kept intact their keenness for racing. Moreover, by making them happy at home they knew that on their return from racing they would come back to a place where they were accustomed to thrive, prosper and be content. In this way their racing careers were prolonged, and by the maintenance of their eagerness to race they could be switched with ease from fences to hurdles and to the flat.

All this was doubly important in the case of a horse such as Cottage Rake who possessed brilliant speed. He was going to be asked in his races for all that speed from the last fence to the line. The power to produce it must therefore be conserved, and not dissipated by stress and strain at home.

Cottage Rake came to his first race over fences on Boxing Day 1946. The place was

Leopardstown and the race The Carrickmines Steeplechase, then the most important novice steeplechase of the first half of the Irish season. Ridden by Aubrey Brabazon, who was later to partner him in all his Gold Cup triumphs, he won as he liked by twenty lengths. It was his first steeplechase, yet unquestionably the thing was done in the style of a future champion. Park fences at any rate, were no trouble to him. He slung them behind him in his stride and galloped away from the last fence with a burst of speed for which he was later to become famous. His next steeplechase was the important Maiden Chase at Fairyhouse, the chief novice event in Ireland. This he won by three parts of a length, and eleven days later, carrying the formidable burden of 13 st, he won the 'Mickey Macardle' Memorial Cup, another conditions race. This initial steeplechasing season ended for him on April 26th, when, again carrying 13 st, he was beaten into third place in The Champion Novice Chase at Naas.

Cottage Rake going down to the start of his first Gold Cup, 1948.

At this time Cottage Rake was not particularly impressive to look at. He appeared to be a shade on the small side for a high-class chaser, there was not much middle piece to him, and then and always he was, Brabazon says, narrow in front of you when you sat on him. In many ways, in fact, he looked more of a flat race horse than a chaser. As if to emphasise this and certainly as proof of his and his trainer's versatility, he came out next back-end and won the Irish Cesarewitch carrying 8 st 2 lb.

Then, at the Leopardstown Christmas Meeting he won the December Handicap Chase in the most brilliant fashion, beating that year's Molyneux Cup winner, no less a horse than Cloncarrig, ridden by Martin Molony, into fourth place. It was apparent, now, that he was something very much out of the ordinary. It remained to be seen how he would fare were he to be sent to do battle with the cross-channel cracks.

These, in 1948, were a fairly formidable lot. There was Major Stirling Stuart's Cool Customer; Miss Paget's Happy Home, runner-up to Fortina; Coloured Schoolboy; and, last but by no means least, Fortina himself.

It was expected that these would be the chief contenders for the Gold Cup – no mean opponents for a horse so lately out of the novice class that he had only run in one handicap steeplechase. One danger, and probably the greatest one was, however, quickly removed. Fortina was beaten in the Emblem Chase by Silver Fame, a brilliant chestnut of Lord Bicester's of whom we shall hear again; he then ran down the field in the King George VI Steeplechase and was immediately retired. As a stallion he went to The Grange Stud at Fermoy, County Cork, where he proved himself a prolific and successful sire of National Hunt winners.

In the absence of Fortina it seemed likely that Cool Customer would start favourite for the race. He won the Princess Margaret Chase and the Great Yorkshire Chase, both at Doncaster, but there were doubts in some people's minds whether he would get the three-and-a-quarter miles at Cheltenham.

Cottage Rake, in the meantime, disappointed everybody by falling in the Leopardstown Steeplechase, a £1,000 race in Ireland. Nevertheless he came from Ireland to Cheltenham with a good deal of quiet confidence behind him. He had built up and filled out enormously since the previous year; the only criticism which could be levelled at him now was that he had not, perhaps, the substance of some of the greater of his predecessors. There was, too, felt to be a doubt about his ability to jump with the vastly more experienced horses with whom he was matched, and he was allowed to start at the very nice price of 10-1.

It was a really high-class field, both in looks and on performance. As he watched them in the paddock, one observer noted with what seemed to be an air of some surprise that they all looked hard and fit with nothing left to work on. They looked, in fact, trained for this race and nothing else. The old idea of regarding the Gold Cup as a Grand National trial was not yet dead, and was dying hard. But die it did in the years to come. The fact that the Gold Cup field all appeared to be specially trained for the race would not be a matter for comment today.

Despite the long price and the disappointing Leopardstown result O'Brien had faith in his horse. But he was very much keyed up and on edge. This was his first great chance to win a classic steeplechase and to establish himself beyond doubt in his chosen profession. He left the enclosures and walked down to watch the race from the last fence, quite alone with his anxieties and his hopes. He knew Happy Home, runner-up the year before, to be a really useful horse. Indeed he had good reason to know all about him.

In 1933 O'Brien's father asked a friend called Frank Flannery who was going to the Newmarket sales, to buy him a mare. Flannery bought him Golden Emblem, then in foal to Tetrameter, for 35 guineas. Golden Emblem produced two filly foals and subsequently was sold cheaply in Dublin to Michael Magnier of the Grange Stud, Fermoy. The great Cottage, who was also, of course, the sire of Cottage Rake, was then standing at the Grange Stud, and Magnier mated Golden Emblem to him. The result of this union was a colt foal subsequently named Happy Home and sold to Miss Paget. This was the horse that O'Brien, rightly as it turned out, put down as the greatest danger to Cottage Rake.

It was a clear bright day, and the twelve horses made a fine sight going down to the start. Cool Customer was favourite at 7–2, but the question of his stamina was not to be decided this year, for he fell at the very first fence. This was the first and only time that Cool Customer fell during the whole of his racing career. He simply did not look at the fence and took it by the roots. His connections were dumbfounded.

Passing the stands Klaxton led from Happy Home, Coloured Schoolboy and Cottage Rake. At the last open ditch Happy Home and Cottage Rake had drawn clear and had the issue between them. They made for home galloping strongly and jumping fence for fence. Happy Home's jumping appeared a shade cleaner and faster; Cottage Rake had the edge for speed between the fences. With Happy Home on the rails they came together round the last bend and into the straight. Martin Molony, knowing his opponent's blinding burst for speed from the last fence, for he had seen it and been left standing by it at Leopardstown two months before, drove Happy Home into the last as only he could do it. He gained the advantage he sought, for he landed at least a length and a half in front. But Brabazon was not to be hurried or flurried.

Here, as in the Golden Miller–Thomond II duel, were two brilliant jockeys each riding a very different race exactly suited to the horse under him – Brabazon, perhaps not too confident of his horse's jumping under pressure, holding up the Rake, relying on his speed from the last fence; Molony, taking the other on, hoping the less-experienced horse would blunder, striving to get the advantage that would offset the other's speed.

Brabazon's coolness and the Rake's courage did the trick. The Rake, in fact, did not jump the last fence too well. Brabazon let him recover himself and got him balanced. Then – and it was not until they were half-way towards the post – he asked his horse to go. The response was electrifying. In a matter of strides the Rake overhauled Happy Home, passed him, and drew away. Molony's great strength and finishing power could do nothing against this sudden burst of speed pulled out on an uphill finish after three-and-a-quarter miles of a championship race run at a strong gallop. The distance was a length and a half. Coloured Schoolboy was third, but once the other two had started to make the best of their way home he might as well not have been at the races, for all hope he had of winning.

But O'Brien, then, knew nothing of this. Standing beside the last fence he had seen the horses come hurtling at him out of the sun. He knew, of course, that they were Cottage Rake and Happy Home, and he saw Molony land in front and get first run on his horse. Then they went thundering away from him up the hill and into the cheers and the shouting. From where he stood it was impossible to tell which was the winner. All he knew was that Happy

Home had been in front when they passed him. Walking disconsolately back to the stands he reflected on the irony of the fact that he had probably been beaten by the colt foal from his father's mare and his first great chance snatched from him.

At the unsaddling enclosure he could not bring himself to ask anyone the result but stood, quite alone, waiting for the horses to come in. The first to enter was Happy Home and his heart sank still further. Then Cottage Rake came and a great cheer went up. Molony rode Happy Home into the second stall while Brabazon confidently entered the first. O'Brien then at last knew that the great prize was his.

Cottage Rake next went to Fairyhouse for the Irish Grand National. In this race he failed to give 3 st to a goodish horse called Hamstar. This raised doubts in some minds whether the new champion had the strength to give away weight in long-distance races. It was going to be interesting to see what would happen in 1949.

Cottage Rake's objective in 1949 was a second Gold Cup. On his way to that prize he was sent over to contest the big English chases. The first of these was the Emblem Chase at Manchester. Here he was matched against Silver Fame, ridden by his old opponent, Martin Molony. He was set to give Silver Fame 7 lb and 1 st to Cromwell, third in the 1948 Grand National. He did it all right, but he had to run for his life to do it.

Silver Fame and the champion jumped the second last abreast and all out. Again Molony employed the same tactics against Cottage Rake as he had done in the Gold Cup. He drove Silver Fame into a lead of a length coming into the last, and landed over it two lengths to the good. This time Cottage Rake made a definite blunder. Brabazon lost his whip, a new silver-mounted one given to him by a well-wisher. Silver Fame seemed to have the race won.

But once more the champion's courage and finishing speed and his rider's coolness turned the trick. Cottage Rake, ridden out by Brabazon with his hands, came and caught the other and won by a neck.

At Kempton in the King George VI Steeplechase yet another horse landed over the last in front of Cottage Rake, and once more the champion's finishing speed defeated the challenger. This time the horse was Roimond, another of Lord Bicester's handsome chasers. On this fast course Cottage Rake's great speed was shown to its true advantage and, in effect, he won as he liked. But his jumping here lacked cleanness, and his jockey had to make use of his speed between the fences to make up for this. In this race, the previous year's Gold Cup runner-up Happy Home, could do no better than finish a bad third, even though he was receiving 12 lb from the champion, instead of meeting him at level weights. But Happy Home was now suffering from an enlarged hock and was probably nothing like as good as the year before.

Thus Cottage Rake had well established his claims to be considered likely to become the third horse to win more than one Gold Cup. Moreover, it was improbable that any of those whom he had already met and beaten when giving away weight would trouble him when they met on even terms in the championship. The danger, if any, was likely to come from last year's fallen favourite, Cool Customer.

Cool Customer was trained in the North by Jack Fawcus, who had ridden Southern Hero for Mr Rank, and his preparatory races did not bring him across the champion's path. He won four of these races in the most convincing style, so he was obviously ready to make up for his fall the year before – if he could.

The Irish would not hear of anything beating Cottage Rake. Mr Vickerman was said to have refused a five-figure offer for him after Kempton. He was in his tenth year, and he now had the experience of jumping with and beating top-class chasers to set beside his brilliant speed. There is little doubt that this was the year when he was at his best. It was going to take something extra-good even to live with him.

Then, in February, he was found to have a slight discharge from the nose. This held him up in his work for a few days. It was not a serious stoppage, but enough, nevertheless, to cause worry with the big race so near.

The day of the race was March 10th. On the night of the 9th, after the first two days of the meeting had taken place as arranged, the weather turned and a hard frost set in. Next morning the ground was like iron and the day's racing was abandoned. The race was reopened almost immediately to the original entries and again a date in the Cheltenham April Meeting was fixed – this time April 11th.

This was put down as a stroke of luck for Cottage Rake. The infernal 'Cheltenham weather' may well have done him a good turn, even as it may have done for Roman Hackle seven years before, but it is worth pointing out that Hatton's Grace and Casteldermot, also from O'Brien's stable, had the infection at the same time, and both won on the first two days.

There were six runners, a good-sized field considering the postponement. Of these it seemed that old Red April and Royal Mount, who had been third in the National, could be ruled out straight away. Finnure, too, did not seem yet to be in Gold Cup class, and Coloured Schoolboy had had training interruptions. It was generally agreed that the race lay between Cool Customer and the champion. Cottage Rake was 6–4 on, and Cool Customer 7–2 against.

The pace was poor throughout the first circuit. At this slow pace Cool Customer did not jump too well and he made a bad mistake at the water. At the top of the hill the second time round Cool Customer was ahead and beginning to go on. Coloured Schoolboy was second, and Cottage Rake third. Here Brabazon moved up, jumping past Coloured Schoolboy at the last open ditch and joining Cool Customer. The pair then began to race.

This was a repetition of last year's battle, with Cool Customer in the place of Happy Home. Only it now looked as if the champion was in trouble. With the improved pace Cool Customer was jumping brilliantly and gaining ground at every fence. As they rounded the last turn into the straight Cool Customer was on the inside and a length and a half in front. Brabazon went for his whip.

Cool Customer still held his advantage at the last fence. He was going, it seemed, far the better of the two for the champion was hard ridden and under punishment. Once more the Rake had a horse land in front of him on the flat, and this time defeat stared him in the face. But once more his finishing speed, courage and his rider's brilliance all told their tale.

It looked from the stands as if Cool Customer had got the better of them, and northern throats were shouting victory. Yet neither Brabazon nor Cottage Rake would give in. Slowly, up the hill, the gap narrowed. The Rake drew level, and the two horses ran on together. Then it was seen that the Rake was indeed a champion. Eighty yards from the post, whatever extra it is that makes a worldbeater told. The Rake began to draw clear. He was two lengths ahead at the winning-post. The Irish roar nearly split the heavens.

It was a great victory and stamped the Rake as a great horse. He was ridden with outstanding brilliance by Brabazon, who, on this occasion, had availed himself of the interval caused by the postponement to get married, and had shown that matrimony had not interfered with either his judgment or his dash.

Cottage Rake was back at Kempton at the end of the year for the King George VI Steeplechase. This time he was opposed by Finnure, who was said to have made great improvement since the previous season. Cool Customer had tendon trouble and did not run this season. Finnure was receiving 11 lb from Cottage Rake, and in the event he beat him by three parts of a length. This led to a good deal of talk that Cottage Rake, now all but eleven years old, had passed his best and that Finnure, a nine-year-old in his prime, would beat him in the Gold Cup as Morse Code had beaten Golden Miller. Finnure was a most taking,

Jumping the second fence in the 1950 race are *left to right* Cottage Rake (A. Brabazon), Clarendon (A. Mullins) and Nagara (R. Black).

handsome horse, like most of Lord Bicester's. Obviously he had at least a chance of beating the champion, who in the meantime did nothing to enhance his reputation, for he was brought down in the Leopardstown Steeplechase, in which he had also fallen two years before.

But Brabazon was of the opinion that the Kempton race had been run at too slow a pace for his horse, and that had the gallop been a stronger one the result might have been different. Also, there was Finnure's pull at the weights to be remembered; 11 lb in the deep is a fair steadier, especially to a light-framed horse like Cottage Rake.

If the Gold Cup is ever dull, this one was. The presence of the champion and the challenger frightened off everything else in near-championship class, and the other horses might just as well have stayed at home. For the first mile and a half the race was run at a mere crawl, moving Michael O'Hehir, the Irish commentator, to remark on the air that the runners were moving at the pace of 'a slow bicycle race'.

Presumably Molony, on Finnure, had orders to slow down the pace in an effort to repeat the Kempton victory. At any rate he lay determinedly behind the champion, who had to set his own pace down the far side of the course.

Due to Brabazon's quick thinking, Finnure was caught in his own trap. At the top of the hill for home the jockey gave Cottage Rake one down the shoulder. Before anyone else realised what had happened, they were into a six-length lead and away. Molony on Finnure set off in a pursuit which was hopeless from the start. Covering the ground in those long, raking strides so peculiarly suited to his name, Cottage Rake swept farther and farther into the lead, and won in a canter by ten lengths. Finnure was second and the Marquis de Portago on Garde Toi, both of whom were having their first experience of English fences, third.

This was the easiest of Cottage Rake's races for the Gold Cup. He had now more wins to his credit than Easter Hero, and ranked second only to Golden Miller. Brabazon became the second jockey to ride three winners of this race, thus equalling Dick Rees's record. Cottage Rake confirmed the form with Finnure, for when the 11 lb advantage was taken away, Finnure could not live with him.

Brabazon had a wonderful meeting, for he won the Champion Hurdle on Hatton's Grace. The following Saturday he went to Hurst Park and, riding a 7–1 odds-on favourite, was caught on the post by an unconsidered outsider to make the race a dead-heat. The story which follows is told with Brabazon's permission. He was called before the Stewards and fined £25 for careless riding. After the race a newspaper came out with a headline 'Caught Napping'. The horse's trainer was, however, sympathetic. 'Ah, poor Aubrey,' he commented. 'It was the only sleep he had during the week!'

It was thought that Finnure might not have shown his true form in this race, for he was sweating freely before it and ran and jumped listlessly in it. In the light of later events it is more likely that the Kempton race flattered him and deceived on-lookers into thinking that he was better than he was, for he was not of much account afterwards. The following year he was kept for Liverpool, where he slipped up at the first fence, but before that he had only been able to win a little race at Ludlow and a three-horse race at Sandown. He did not run the next year, but returned to the racecourse at the age of twelve in 1952–53, and failed to win in four outings.

Many were of the opinion that Finnure's stable companion, Silver Fame, though he was two years older, would have given the champion a better run for his money. Silver Fame, a lion-hearted horse, won the National Hunt Handicap Steeplechase at that meeting and the Golden Miller Steeplechase at the April meeting just over a month later. At the time he was thought to be a most gallant horse, but not quite of the highest class. The following year, at twelve years of age, he was to show that if Finnure had been over-rated, he had surely been under-rated.

This was the last of Cottage Rake's Gold Cups. He had landed the odds for the second time, for he started at 6–5 on. He went on to fail once more to give away lumps of weight in the Irish Grand National.

Aubrey Brabazon and Cottage Rake jump the last to win their third Gold Cup, 1950.

Fairyhouse never really suited him. It was then a twisting track which had, as it were, grown up from the original natural course, and it contained, too, an amount of ridge and furrow. Cottage Rake was above all a racehorse. To give of his best he wanted a galloping track where he could display his brilliant speed. Also, being light of his middle, he was not built to carry and give away big weights in handicaps. He was never sent to Aintree, and it is unlikely he would have survived a Grand National, certainly with the weights that he would have been asked to carry there. Although he was a very different horse from Golden Miller, like Golden Miller Cheltenham was his spiritual home.

At this time he was only eleven years of age. He had lost nothing of his speed and brilliance. There did not seem anything about likely to beat him or even get near him at level weights, and his connections had hopes of equalling or even surpassing Golden Miller's record.

Then tragedy struck. At the end of each season Cottage Rake was let out every morning into a field with a donkey as his companion. He was fond of the donkey and once in the field with him he settled down quietly to graze. Cattle used the field overnight, but the man in charge had strict orders to move them before the horse and donkey came out.

Shortly after he had retired from his 1950 campaign something went wrong with the arrangements. The cattle were left in the field and the donkey got in amongst them. Cottage Rake threw up his head and looked for his old friend. Failing to find him he went mad, and began to gallop wildly round and round the field. In the course of this he got too close to a corner, turned sharply and, on the turn, gave himself a leg. Although treatment was immediately applied he was off the racecourse for twelve months, and ran only once or twice again. He ended his days in quiet retirement on the farm of a friend, near Fermoy in County Cork.

The stakes won by Cottage Rake are an interesting example of how enormously prize money had increased since the war. His three Gold Cups brought his owner £7,724. Golden Miller's five netted Miss Paget £3,350 – less than half!

In his long racing career Golden Miller won £15,005 in stakes, which included £7,265 for a Grand National. Cottage Rake's three Gold Cups, his Kempton Park and Emblem Chase victories alone brought £11,826 to Mr Vickerman.

There can be no question but that Cottage Rake was a great racehorse. The chief weapons in his armoury were his blinding speed from the last fence and his quickness in getting away from his fences. His failures in handicaps may perhaps have slightly marred his reputation in some quarters, but it must be remembered and repeated that he decisively defeated two of the best fields ever seen in the Gold Cup, and in his third victory beat out of sight a horse strongly fancied against him, and whom bookmakers and public ranked within two points of him in the betting. He comes high amongst the immortals of Cheltenham – or anywhere in steeplechasing.

8

Upsets and surprises

THE SEASON 1950–51 was once more badly hit by the weather. The Gold Cup was again postponed, and again postponement changed the whole aspect of the race. This was doubly unfortunate, as there were several good horses due to run and one that showed promise of greatness.

There was no Cottage Rake and no Cool Customer. These two stout-hearted battlers had gone from the acceptors. Cool Customer did attempt a comeback. He was entered for the Cup and ran in the Great Yorkshire Chase, a race which will require a word to itself in due course.

The first part of the season was graced and dignified by a win of the Royal horse, Manicou, in the King George VI Steeplechase at Kempton Park. Manicou was a smallish, chestnut entire horse. Ridden by A. Grantham, he defeated Silver Fame by two lengths. This win made Manicou a very live candidate for the Gold Cup, and it goes without saying that there could have been no more popular victory than a win in the Royal colours.

But the horse to emerge this year who appeared to have the touch of greatness upon him was Arctic Gold. Winner of the Broadway Novices at Cheltenham the year before, Arctic Gold was owned by Mr J. H. Whitney, who thus made a welcome reappearance in top-class English steeplechasing. By Iceberg II, Arctic Gold was a six-year-old, a chestnut and a hard puller like Easter Hero, Mr Whitney's great horse of twenty years before. At this time he showed signs of being just such another as Easter Hero and, like him, was entered in both the Gold Cup and the Grand National. There was some speculation whether it would be wise to run a headstrong young horse in the National so early in his career, but when the weights came out and it was seen that he had only 10 st 13 lb to carry, the bait proved too tempting to be refused. It was then announced that he would be a definite starter in both races. He was, therefore, going to be asked to complete a double which not even Golden Miller achieved, for the Miller had been seven when he won them both. That he had every chance of doing it he showed when, immediately after the publication of the Grand National weights, he won his fourth steeplechase in succession. This was no less a race than the Great Yorkshire Chase. In it he galloped a high-class field into the ground, beating Lockerbie and Freebooter by five lengths and ten lengths. Cool Customer was also in the field and was well beaten, so this performance had indeed the stamp of a champion about it. Cool Customer had run once before that season, but after this race his leg came against him again and he was scratched from the Gold Cup, and the racecourse saw him no more.

As a result of these performances Arctic Gold became – and stayed – a raging favourite for the National. He almost certainly would have started favourite for the Gold Cup had the race been run as originally intended.

The acceptors were as follows: Manicou, Silver Fame, Freebooter, Finnure, Bluff King, Coloured Schoolboy, Norborne, Lord Glenfield, Arctic Gold, Royal Tan, Lockerbie, Cillie Dolly.

Of these, Freebooter seemed an unusual entry, for he was something of a Liverpool specialist and had top weight in the Grand National. Moreover, he was believed to be suffering from a 'Cheltenham bogey'. Certainly his record there was a dismal one. He had never won a race at Cheltenham and, for a usually safe jumper, had the surprising record of having fallen twice in six starts on the course.

If Freebooter hated Cheltenham, old Silver Fame loved it. It was his happy hunting-ground. As has been seen, he had won two good races on the course the previous year. On his last appearance there before the National Hunt Meeting in 1951 he defeated Freebooter by three lengths at level weights. He was now in his twelfth year, but he was one of the few horses who retain their speed until late in life. No one could say that he had been lightly raced. His first victory was at Naas as a four-year-old in a 'Bumper' flat race. Since then he had run in forty-seven races and won twenty-four of them, eight of these wins being at Cheltenham. By now the old warrior knew every blade of grass on the course and exactly what he could do to every fence and still remain standing. He was a popular favourite and rightly so, for no gamer horse or greater trier ever raced at Cheltenham. He might, however, have missed his great partner, Martin Molony – and he responded ideally to Molony's strong handling – had the race been run on its original date, for Molony was in bed with a chill and did not ride at the meeting. Molony, commuting between Ireland and England in an aeroplane, was then riding with unparalleled brilliance and had the astounding average in England of one winner in every three rides.

The first two days of the meeting took place as arranged. Tim Molony, substituting for his brother on Hatton's Grace, won the Champion Hurdle to make yet another record for M. V. O'Brien. Then the rains came. All night there was a downpour, and when the stewards came to inspect the course next morning it was obvious that no racing could take place. The hurdle course was under water and much of the steeplechase course was unusable. The rest of the meeting was abandoned, and the Gold Cup tacked on to the April fixture.

If it was not one thing it was another. Of the last ten Gold Cups, snow had caused postponement in 1940, frost in 1947 and 1949, and now flooding. If the expedient of reopening the race had not been adopted, four out of the ten Gold Cups during the immediate pre-war, wartime and post-war period would have been lost. Snow and ice were perhaps to be expected in the Cotswolds in early March, but flooding did seem to many people to be an avoidable risk and there was some criticism. But, lying as it does in the heavy ground at the foot of Cleeve Hill, Prestbury Park is by no means easy to drain, though later extensive improvements have largely cured this defect.

The Grand National this year was on April 7th, and, because four of the original Gold Cup acceptors ran in it, a word must be said about what happened to them. April 7th was unusually late for the National, so that had the Gold Cup been held as intended a horse probably never had or will have a better chance of repeating Golden Miller's feat and winning both of them, for he would have had just over a month to recover from Cheltenham and get ready for Aintree. This may or may not explain why the unusually high proportion, for modern times, of four out of ten of the original Gold Cup acceptors were also engaged in the National.

The fact that the reopened Gold Cup was to be run only eighteen days after the National also made it most unlikely that a horse who had had any sort of a hard race at Aintree would come out again in the Cup. And that is what happened.

The National was the famous – or infamous – 'ninepins National'. The thirty-nine starters were sent away to the worst start in the long history of the race. One young amateur whose horse was facing the wrong way when the tapes went up said afterwards that he did not know that the race had started until he heard 'They're off!' on a spectator's wireless!

The field rushed at the first fence like a rout of disorganised cavalry producing Balaclava-like scenes of disorder and disarray on the far side. Finnure slipped up here and went out of the race. Freebooter, who despite his top weight was second favourite, was knocked over at the second fence. Arctic Gold survived until the Canal Turn, where he fell when in the lead. He then ran loose, made a general nuisance of himself, and finally crashed into the rails beneath the stands. The rails, fortunately, smashed. Arctic Gold rolled over, got to his feet and proceeded towards the paddock. Royal Tan did the best of them. Along with Nickel Coin he was the only runner left standing after Valentine's the second time round. The two jumped the last fence together, but Royal Tan blundered, and that year had to be content with second place.

Freebooter, whose trip to the second fence had not been enough to tire him, and whose fall had left him unhurt, alone of these horses stood his ground for the Gold Cup on April 25th. When the runners were published, they bore a very different look from the first list. They were: Manicou, Freebooter, Silver Fame, Lockerbie, Mighty Fine and Greenogue.

Manicou had not been trained on as had been hoped, and had been beaten into third place by Bluff King at Lingfield the Saturday before the National Hunt meeting. Silver Fame, too, had slightly blotted his copybook, by failing to give 13 lb to Lockerbie on March 31st at Manchester. Still, Silver Fame, against this weak field and with Martin Molony in the saddle, was expected to win, and he started at 6–4 against. Lockerbie was not far behind him at 3–1, whilst Freebooter was third in demand at 5–1.

The Queen and the then Princess Elizabeth came to see the Royal horse run. Unfortunately Manicou hit the fence after the second water very hard, and dropped out of the race. Three fences out, Lockerbie was leading, but here, one after the other, they all came at him – Silver Fame, Greenogue, Freebooter and Mighty Fine. Freebooter blundered, and the others, going on at a great pace, left him as if he were standing still. Lockerbie, Silver Fame and Greenogue jumped the last abreast, as good a spectacle as one could wish to see in steeplechasing. Lockerbie could not tackle the hill, and Silver Fame and the outsider were left to fight it out. Fight it out is what they did, all the way to the winning-post. Five yards away Silver Fame got his head in front and kept it there long enough to win. The distance was a short head.

Even now, over twenty years after the race, there are some who were there who say that

Manicou, a runner in the 1951 Gold Cup, and owned by HM The Queen, had previously beaten Silver Fame in the King George VI Chase on Boxing Day 1950. He is seen here jumping the last in that race with Brian Marshall up.

the verdict was wrong, and that Greenogue was the true winner. But Bob Wigney, the course manager, who was in the stewards' box right on the line, had no doubt that the decision was the correct one and that the judge was right. In those days, of course, there was no photograph. Had there been one it would have unquestionably have endorsed the decision.

Molony's brilliance from the last fence home was never seen to better advantage, and the old horse may well have owed the crowning achievement of his career as much to his jockey's strength and genius as to his own courage and refusal to admit defeat. The race was run at a tremendous pace throughout on going which was officially returned as firm. The time, 6 minutes 23⅘ seconds, was a record.

The winner was owned by Lord Bicester and the runner-up by Mr J. V. Rank, so two of the best supporters of steeplechasing were rewarded by one of the greatest races for the cup. Sad to relate, this was Martin Molony's last appearance in the saddle at the National Hunt Meeting.

The shape of things to come in 1952 began to be apparent at Leicester on January 7th. Here Silver Fame and Arctic Gold contested a five-horse chase and were backed down to 9-4 on and 9-4 against respectively. Neither the old champion nor the young contender distinguished himself. Between the last two fences it was apparent that Arctic Gold would win no race that day; Silver Fame, who might have been expected to have known better, clouted the last fence so hard that he knocked all the steam out of himself. They were then

Lord Bicester's Silver Fame, winner of the 1951 race.

both run out of it by an outsider, Walvis Arch. Those, therefore, who had marked those two as the likely aspirants for the championship began to think again. There had, prior to this race, been whispers that all was not well with Arctic Gold, and after it it seemed evident that the years were at long last taking their toll of Silver Fame.

Earlier in the season there had been a rumpus about the riding arrangements of Miss Paget's horses. Fulke Walwyn trained for Miss Paget two high-class half-brothers bred in France. The elder of these was Mont Tremblant, an uncommonly handsome chestnut horse bred by M. M. Hennessy, son of the owner of Lutteur II the one and only French winner of the Grand National and bought for Miss Paget as a four-year-old by Mr M. Stacpoole. Mont Tremblant, now six, was making a name for himself in a quieter and less spectacular way than Arctic Gold the year before. He graduated with honours from novice to handicap class finishing his novice career by beating Devon Loch and Filon D'Or at Hurst Park, and beginning his efforts in handicaps at Kempton on February 21st by slamming a high-class field, to all of whom except Cromwell he was giving weight. Lanveoc Poulmic, his half-brother, an enormous horse, was a year younger. After Lanveoc Poulmic had been beaten at Sandown Park in November 1951 by Daytime, D. V. Dick was given the honour of riding Miss Paget's horses, including Mont Tremblant. This was a tremendous chance for Dick, who had been riding with quiet competence for some years, and, as will be seen, he made full use of it.

Probably, however, the most surprising thing about the 1952 race was that Freebooter was the ante-post favourite. Apart altogether from his poor record at Cheltenham and the fact that he was said to hate the place, his performances over park courses, taken as a whole, were scarcely inspiring. In 1950–51, out of ten starts, he could only win one little race at the beginning of the season with odds of 7–1 laid on him. His record in 1951–52 did look much better. By December 1st he had run in four races and won all of them, including the Grand Sefton. But, on examination, these results are not as impressive as they look at first sight. The three races which he won over park courses were all minor ones, and with the exception of the last he beat very little in them. In his last victory he defeated Silver Fame at level weights by six lengths at Haydock Park. But, as Silver Fame showed a month later in the Leicester race, his powers at last appeared to be on the wane. Despite his decline, however, he took his revenge on Freebooter at Sandown on January 18th, beating him once more, and once more at level weights, although in fairness it must be said that the winning margin was only a neck. Still, this did not look good enough form on Freebooter's part to win the Gold Cup. Yet he stayed favourite in the ante-post lists, and started favourite at the short price of 7–2.

Freebooter was a very good Liverpool horse, though whether we should be hailing him as quite such a horse as we do now had Cloncarrig not fallen three fences out in 1950 is a matter of conjecture. He looked like a Liverpool horse and he jumped like one. His jumping was too deliberate for the pace at which the top-class horses now jumped park courses, and, unlike Kellsboro Jack, he seemed unable to adjust himself to jumping at Gold Cup pace. This year's field was a better one than the year before and many considered that he was unlikely to live with them. But he started favourite just the same.

Arctic Gold did not win a race this year. He had three races. In each he ran prominently and then appeared to weaken. It seemed clear that all could not be well with him. His nerve

Gold Cup day 1952, the field at the second fence; *leading left* Greenogue, *centre nearest* E.S.B., with the winner Mont Tremblant; the grey on the right is Shaef (Fred Winter up) who broke his bridle at the water first time round and yet finished second.

may well have been affected by going through the rails at Aintree. Later he was operated upon for his wind, but he was never again a force in top-class chasing.

Of the other of last year's stars, Lockerbie was not started and Greenogue had been disappointing, but there were newcomers to the race with the highest qualifications. The most interesting of these was undoubtedly Knock Hard. Like Cottage Rake, Knock Hard was a good horse on the flat and possessed of great speed. His only previous appearance in England had been in the King George VI Steeplechase at Kempton the previous season. Here he fell three out when appearing to hold a great chance, and his jockey, Dowdeswell, thought that he must have won had he stood up. He was said by some not to like jumping, and by others to be a clumsy fencer, either of which, if the case, boded ill for his chances at Cheltenham.

In a way Knock Hard's detractors were right on both these counts. In conformation he was a shade too short in the back to be a natural jumper. In addition, despite all O'Brien could do with him by way of education and persuasion, he never really liked leaving the ground. Jumping did not come easily to him, and he had no natural aptitude for putting himself right or for recovering from his mistakes. It was O'Brien's opinion that, in many if not most ways, he was more of a high-class horse on the flat than a jumper. Indeed, he proved himself as such before he went on to compete with the best over fences. In 1949 he was the medium of a big stable gamble in the Irish Cesarewitch. On the flat, over a distance, Knock Hard's brilliant speed needed conserving for one run. They went a great gallop that year and his jockey may have hit the front too soon. His unfancied stablemate, Hatton's Grace, winner of that year's Champion Hurdle, came and caught him almost on the post, winning by a length and a half.

In the following year, 1950, Knock Hard won the Irish Lincoln, carrying 8 st 12 lb, by five lengths from twenty-five runners. That he had both speed and ability there was no doubt, and the fact that he came from Vincent O'Brien's stable alone made him worthy of respect. E.S.B., second to Statecraft in the King George VI Chase, and Shaef, a game little grey, completed the most fancied candidates.

The race was run in very heavy going and at a terrific pace. There were no less than thirteen runners. It was considered to be one of the best-looking fields which had contested the race.

Freebooter fell coming down the hill the first time. The pace at which the race was run may have had something to do with this. Certainly his position as favourite had not enabled him to lay his Cheltenham bogey. Silver Fame was done with going out into the country the second time, and Greenogue dropped out here, so that was all of last year's runners out of it.

Meanwhile E.S.B. and Mont Tremblant were going on through the mud at a great pace. At the second last Mont Tremblant was clear and, bar a fall, seemed to have the race won. Shaef, who had lost his bridle at the first water and whose rider was keeping the bit in place with the reins, passed E.S.B. to take second place. Then, suddenly, a challenge materialised. Out of the mist, seemingly from nowhere, hurtled the form of Knock Hard and his rider. Making a late run and going great guns, they were closing the leader with every stride. Then they hit the second last and came down, and that was the end of that.

Mont Tremblant, keeping up his strong gallop, went on to win by ten lengths. He went through the top of the last fence and must have given Dick an anxious moment, but it did not check his gallop. Shaef was second and a late-running Galloway Braes was third. This was Miss Paget's seventh Gold Cup victory.

The name of Shaef's rider was then little known. It was F. T. Winter. His feat in keeping the bit in his horse's mouth has already been referred to. This was Winter's first appearance in the placings of the Gold Cup. A born horseman if ever there was one, Winter, next season, was to sky-rocket to fame by riding more winners in a season than had ever been done before. Difficult horses would go for this young man when they would go for no one else. Horsemanship and race-riding were bred in him, for he was the son of a flat-race jockey who had won the Oaks in 1911. The qualities of courage and determination were his own. In 1948 he had broken his back in a fall at the first fence at Wye and was told he must never ride steeplechases again. Five years later he topped the jockey's list with the then largest numbers of winners in history. There will be more about Winter later in this book.

By the time the National Hunt meeting of 1953 had come round, the Gold Cup situation was uncommonly interesting. Mont Tremblant, now seven, had early in the season been strongly fancied to repeat his victory. He had, however, been fired during the summer, and subsequent events seemed to show that something, whether it was this operation or not, had taken the edge off his speed. A keen, cold wind of competition now blows hard across the heights of top-class steeplechasing, and a champion cannot afford to lose or to allow to become blunted any of the weapons which have put him on his pinnacle. Although he was to run many other good races, Mont Tremblant never again quite touched the heights he had done in 1952, nor did he achieve the greatness which his promise then forecast for him. In the King George VI Steeplechase he failed to give 7 lb to Halloween. He did not fail by

Mont Tremblant clears the last fence to win the 1952 race.

much, but he made a mess of the last two fences, and on his Gold Cup form he should have won.

Not that Halloween was not a doughty opponent. He was a horse who had come up the hard way, and come up fast. Now eight years old, he had been hunted, point-to-pointed and then become the champion hunter-chaser of the 1950–51 season. After that he had been introduced to chasing proper, and made his mark on it. A small, tough, courageous horse, he was not by any means everybody's ride. During his point-to-pointing and hunter-chasing days he was ridden by his owner, Captain R. B. Smalley of the Royal Marines, for whom he went admirably. Captain Smalley sold him for a long price to the Contessa di Saint Elia, in whose colours he came to open chasing. In his first two races when ridden by professionals he fell, and Captain Smalley was recalled to ride him again and to give him back his confidence. After that Winter rode him and won on him. Wightman, Halloween's trainer, then gave Winter a special retainer at £250 to ride the horse in all his races. This step was immediately successful. Halloween responded to Winter's horsemanship, and rocketed in no time at all into championship class.

It was thought by most people that the Gold Cup lay between these two. Both critics and public chose to ignore the chances of Knock Hard. They did so at their peril, for Knock Hard that year was specifically aimed at the Gold Cup. The story of his adventures and misadventures during his preparation is so extraordinary that it merits retelling in some detail.

His campaign was aimed to commence on Boxing Day at Kempton in The King George

VI Steeplechase. At the commencement of his preparation he was being schooled over hurdles. Meeting one of them wrong, with his notorious inability to put himself right, he went straight through it. In doing so he dragged his hind legs across the top of it and tore a flap of skin away from the front of the leg below the hock. This had to be stitched, and although it mended quickly O'Brien was very conscious of the mental effect it might have on his jumping, quite apart from his concern about the possibility of the wound re-opening during a race.

Tim Molony was engaged to ride him in all his races in England that year. At Kempton he hit the first fence very hard and almost came down. Recovering, he ran on in Molony's hands to finish third, five lengths behind Mont Tremblant – who, in turn, was beaten a length by Halloween. As he watched him it became obvious to O'Brien that his dislike of jumping had, if anything, taken a turn for the worse. On his return Molony confirmed this. The horse had landed so spread-eagled over the first, he said, that had he moved an inch either way he was gone. Thereafter he jumped like a frightened horse, stopping and propping, and having to be driven into all his fences.

The obvious and urgent task then was to get his confidence back, and there was not much time to do it in if he were to take on the best on March 5th at Cheltenham. He was brought home, and everything possible was done to bring back his enthusiasm for racing and fluency to his jumping.

His next appearance in public was in the Ticknock Handicap Chase at Leopardstown on January 24th. Carrying 12 st 7 lb, he jumped the last fence upsides with Mariner's Log, to whom he was giving 1 st 6 lb. Mariner's Log ran away from him on the flat, and in the end he was beaten into fourth place by Carey's Cottage and Amritsar, who were getting, respectively, 3 st and 3 st 1 lb. At least he had not made any bad jumping errors, but it seemed to O'Brien that he had run a listless sort of race, and O'Brien was worried about him.

The Great Yorkshire Chase in a fortnight's time was his next objective, and after much thought O'Brien decided to let him take his chance. With 11 st 7 lb on his back and giving 2 lb to Teal, he beat the 1952 Grand National winner by five lengths. It did not escape the eyes of the knowing, however, that his jumping had been far from perfect, and that he had made a bad mistake at halfway. Moreover, Teal had not been on the racecourse since his National Victory, yet he had jumped the last alongside the winner. Teal's performance was held by many to be the more impressive. He was announced as a certain runner in The Gold Cup. His Northern supporters claimed that he was going to succeed where Freebooter had failed and be the first horse to win the Gold Cup and Grand National in reverse, as it were, and also the first horse to bring the Gold Cup north.

Molony reported to O'Brien that Knock Hard was still scared of jumping. By this time, however, O'Brien was wondering if there might not be another, physical reason for the horse's reluctance to jump. It seemed to him that a heart condition might provide the true explanation, and he resolved to have him expertly examined. On his return home he arranged for a cardiogram to be taken.

The expert had arrived with the cardiograph and carried out his examination. As a result he warned O'Brien that there might well be something wrong with the horse's heart, but that he required further time to consider and prepare a full report. Time, however, just then, was what O'Brien and the horse's connections did not have. A decision had to be made whether or not to run in The Gold Cup. O'Brien believed that he had by now, at least in some part, succeeded in re-establishing the horse's confidence. After consultation, debate and discussion, it was decided to let him take his chance.

Molony was told there was some doubt about the horse's heart. One of the bravest riders in the business, Molony expressed himself to be not in the least concerned, and as events and the race he rode were to show, this was indeed a true statement.

The Gold Cup that year looked a most open race. Neither Halloween nor Mont Tremblant had distinguished himself between Kempton and Cheltenham. But there were other aspirants too. Peter Cazalet trained a brilliant horse in Rose Park, a front runner and hard puller who had first flashed out of the fog to win a Bumper race one murky afternoon at Leopardstown. Since coming to England Rose Park had proved a champion at two-and-a-half miles. He had never run over the Gold Cup distance, but those who knew said he would stay. In addition there was Lord Bicester's Mariner's Log, the brilliant novice who had beaten Knock Hard at Leopardstown, Galloway Braes, last year's third, and Lanveoc Poulmic, Mont Tremblant's huge half-brother.

On the day the going was firm, and that was said to be the way Knock Hard wanted it. Dick was on Mont Tremblant, Winter on Halloween and Pat Taaffe from Ireland, one of the finest riders ever to sit in a steeplechase saddle on Mariner's Log. There was a last-minute change in the riding arrangements for Rose Park. Bryan Marshall had been engaged to ride, but he was injured in an earlier race, and the mount was given to T. Cusack.

The race was in foggy weather and, as was now becoming customary, at a tremendous pace. The first three horses who could be discerned from the stands as they came for home were Rose Park, Mont Tremblant and Galloway Braes. These three, going great guns, were in front, and it seemed certain that the winner must come from one of them. Tim Molony, some way behind, was hard at work on Knock Hard and, it appeared, not getting much answer. Halloween was not dealing too well with the hill and appeared to have no chance.

Then, at the second last, in an instant, everything changed. Rose Park, hard held, looking all over a winner, over-jumped and came down. All at once the other two leaders were seen to be labouring. And, behind them, Molony had at last got the response he was looking for. Knock Hard, once apparently hopelessly out of it, began to accelerate in an amazing fashion. Up the hill, coming into the last, he had closed with the leaders. Here he made the most splendid leap, which put the result of the race beyond all doubt and, incidentally, supplied one of the best photographs in steeplechasing history. Halloween, changing the downhill for uphill, ran on to pass the toiling Mont Tremblant and Galloway Braes to take second place. The distance was five lengths. Galloway Braes was third again, and Mont Tremblant fourth. Lanveoc Poulmic got rid of his jockey at the last.

It was probably the most extraordinary race for the Gold Cup ever to be run – two horses apparently hopelessly out of it at the second last occupying first and second places. Molony said afterwards: 'I was driving hard at the top of the hill and, for a while, making no impression.' What Molony said to O'Brien was: 'This horse simply doesn't want to jump any more. Once he jumped the last and saw nothing in front of him he just ran away with it.'

It was a tremendous triumph for both jockey and trainer. There can be no doubt that

Knock Hard ridden by Tim Molony taking the last to run on and win from Halloween ridden by Fred Winter, 1953.

Molony's opinion was right, yet O'Brien had somehow succeeded in instilling sufficient confidence into Knock Hard that in this race, despite his dislike for it, his jumping had been perfect for he had not made a single mistake. He was ridden with the utmost courage and determination by a jockey who understood his weaknesses and knew that his strength was his speed. Molony drove him into his fences and, at the same time, conserved his speed for the final brilliant burst up the hill.

The winner was trained by M. V. O'Brien – his fourth Gold Cup in six years. There is, of course, only one word to describe O'Brien's feats as a trainer, and the word is genius.

There was a tragedy in this race. Teal failed to break the northern hoodoo. In fact, he added to it. He hurt himself at the water, was operated on for a ruptured bowel, and died some days later.

'Four Ten is a remarkable seven-year-old marked for distinction,' wrote the anonymous chronicler of the jumping season in the 1953 edition of the *Irish Horse*. He may have written better than he knew, for all Four Ten had done at that time was to defeat the very moderate Irish three-miler, In View, in the National Hunt Handicap Chase. Four Ten slammed the Gold Cup field in 1954 every bit as convincingly if not more convincingly than Knock Hard had done in 1953. Moreover, every one of the horses whom he beat had run the year before, except Shaef, who had run prominently in 1952. All this, however, is to anticipate. It is necessary to go back and look at some of the significant events of the season.

One of these events took place at the first fence of the first race of the first day of the new

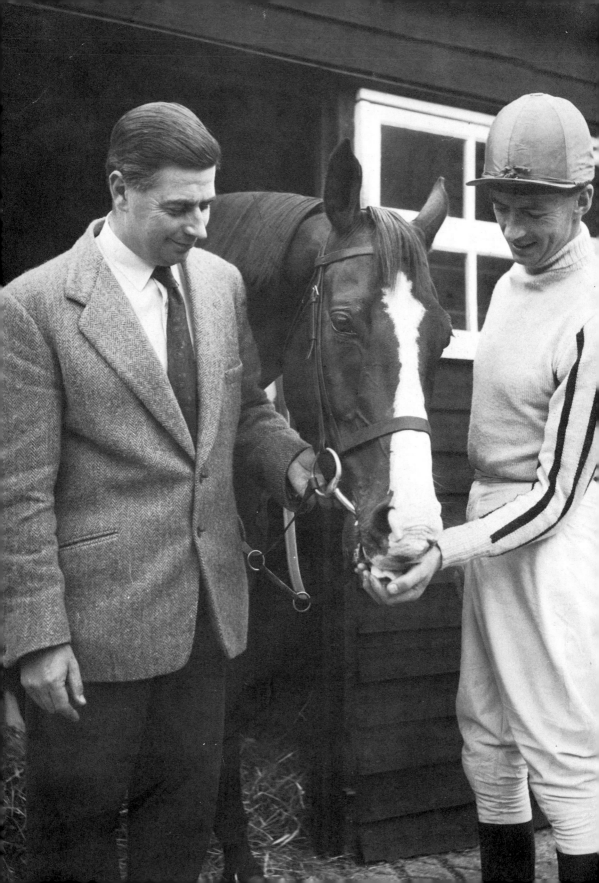

season. Here Winter's mount fell and broke his rider's leg. Winter was out of the saddle for the rest of the season. Nobody could describe Winter's career as one of easy success. A graph of it would show a violent alternation of ups and downs – in 1948 a broken back and the probability of never riding again, in 1953 champion jockey with the record number of 121 winners, now, in 1954 an injury incapacitating him for the whole season. This injury may well have had an effect on the result of the Gold Cup. Halloween, now with the experience of a full and successful season in top-class chasing behind him, was deprived of the services of his regular rider. In 1953–54 he had eight races and could only win one of them – a little race at Wincanton worth £136, his first race of the season. This little race was complimented by the appearance in first and second places of a Gold Cup runner-up and a former winner. Halloween, at level weights, in it defeated Cottage Rake, now fourteen, by five lengths. In his eight races this season Halloween was ridden by four different jockeys, all of them top-class. It is no disparagement to any of them, nor is it intended to be, to say that he went for none of them as he went for Winter.

Meanwhile the old brigade had been having at each other in the usual way throughout the season. At first Galloway Braes looked like being the champion. He gave a terrific exhibition of jumping to win the King George VI Steeplechase, beating Mont Tremblant at level weights. Mont Tremblant had had more veterinary attention during the summer, this time for sinus trouble, but he won his next two races after Kempton, and started favourite for the Gold Cup. He may have been entitled to do so, for although it is unlikely that a horse would come back to the winner's enclosure after being displaced, and he would have made history had he done so, there were black marks against most of the other runners. Halloween and Rose Park had lost their form; Galloway Braes was said to have stamina limitations which would find him out at Cheltenham; Knock Hard had not come over for the big races and his form in Ireland gave him no chance in the championship; and Mariner's Log had not quite lived up to his early promise. No one bothered much about a horse called Four Ten, quietly and most capably trained by J. Roberts at Prestbury – almost on the course.

Yet, had one looked at the record, it would have been seen that Four Ten had won three out of his last six races and had only been out of the money once, and that through a fall. Also, when one looked at him, it was to be seen that he had looks enough for a champion and matched Mont Tremblant as the most handsome horse in the race.

The story of the race is soon told. Galloway Braes fell at the last open ditch when in the lead, and once more Mont Tremblant appeared likely to win coming to the second last. Between the last two fences Mariner's Log caught and passed Mont Tremblant and the Irish horse was then being shouted as the winner. It was then that Four Ten came with a rush to challenge. Mariner's Log and Four Ten jumped the last together and under pressure. Four Ten, driven right out by Cusack, went on to win by four lengths. Halloween again faltered coming down the hill, and again ran on up to the finish and was third. The going was very heavy and the race was once more run at a great pace. Four Ten, like Halloween, was a promoted hunter and ex-point-to-pointer. He had obviously great strength and power, and he went through the deep and won this race like a really good horse. At 100-6 he was,

(OPPOSITE) J. Roberts and T. Cusack, trainer and jockey of Four Ten photographed in John Roberts' yard at Prestbury.

until then, the longest-priced winner in the history of the race. Having looked at him again, one and all pronounced Four Ten to be a worthy winner and a horse fit, in his looks and on his performance on the day, to be champion. Subsequent events, however, seem to have shown that this was not a very good Gold Cup.

Four Ten started favourite for the race in 1955. His preparation did not include running him in the top-line chases, so he did not meet his fancied rivals before the race. He started the season inauspiciously, too, by falling in his first race at Cheltenham.

From the point of view of the weather the 1954–55 season was the worst for many years. Not only did the usual enemies, frost and snow, cause cancellations, but flooding, too, made racing impossible on many occasions. The weather played havoc with trainer's plans and disrupted training programmes. Whether the remarkable upset in form in the Gold Cup was a result of all this, it is impossible to say. It is, however, at least possible that the weather and the consequent difficulties with which trainers were confronted had some effect on the race.

It had promised to be a really interesting Gold Cup. Fred Winter was back in the saddle again and, so far from suffering any ill effects from his injury and his absence, was riding more brilliantly than ever. As if to celebrate his return, Halloween won the King George VI Steeplechase for the second time, beating Galloway Braes by six lengths. Halloween, with Winter on him, seemed back to his form of two seasons ago, and his jockey was said to be extremely sanguine of their chances in the Gold Cup. Bramble Tudor, the first mare to come into Gold Cup class for a very long time, was being tipped in the north, and was strongly fancied elsewhere to be the first of her sex to win since Ballinode.

Early Mist, the 1953 winner of the Grand National, was held in Ireland to have a great chance, and on the day started third favourite. Crudwell, Pointsman (winner of last year's Grand Military), Galloway Braes, Rose Park and a rank outsider called Gay Donald completed what looked like a very high-class field.

Snow and frost nearly prevented the race being held. Snow caused the cancellation of Tuesday's racing. Frost came down on Wednesday night, and definite decision to race was not taken until after midday on Thursday. The public were not admitted until 1.30, and the start of racing was put back an hour.

The going was once more very heavy. This, and stories of training interruptions, may have warned some observers that the form was unlikely to work out, but few were prepared for the turn-up which followed.

Gay Donald, the outsider of the party (his starting price was 33–1, eight points longer than that of his nearest rivals, Crudwell and Rose Park at 25 to 1), took command of the race from the fourth fence, and won as he liked. The distance was given as ten lengths, but Gay Donald was only hacking coming home, and found time to deal very cursorily with the last two fences, which caused speculation in some minds as to what would have happened had anyone been there to race with him over them. Halloween was second and Four Ten a lucky third, Pointsman falling when in third place. But Four Ten never looked like making a race of it with the winner.

(OPPOSITE, ABOVE) Four Ten (*left*) taking the last fence with Mariner's Log who finished second, 1954.
(BELOW) Mrs A. Strange leads in Four Ten after his win.

The explanation of Four Ten's running was thought to be that his training had suffered much from interruptions; Bramble Tudor had been coughing, and had had to be given a very hurried preparation, and this explained why she had run so indifferently. One way or another, most people thought that the result was a freak one, the only such result in the history of the race, and that it had been brought about by the weather and training mishaps and interruptions which prevented the fancied horses from showing their true form. Gay Donald was the longest-priced winner in the history of the race, and some held that he was flattered by the result.

But two things happened after this Gold Cup which, it is suggested, may go to show that the 1955 winner was a better horse than at first thought and the 1954 champion not quite such a good one.

Four days after the Gold Cup, Four Ten came out in a three-mile chase at Windsor. This was the course over which he had done one of his best Gold Cup trials, and odds of 13–2 were laid on him to beat his three opponents, even though the least he had to concede to them was 1 st. In the event, he was beaten a head by Bacchus, a moderate horse who had not run since October.

Mont Tremblant presumably was not considered to be Gold Cup class in 1955, for he was not started for the race. He went instead for the Mildmay of Flete Challenge Cup, and won it by two lengths from Wise Child, to whom he was giving 8 lb. This was an impressive victory, and the race was run on the same day as the Gold Cup. On March 19th at Sandown Mont Tremblant and Gay Donald met. Gay Donald was set to give the other 2 lb. Those – and they were many – who held that Gay Donald's win in the Gold Cup was a fluke made Mont Tremblant favourite at 5–4 to beat him. Gay Donald repayed them for this slight by presenting Mont Tremblant with the 2 lb and a four lengths defeat.

In one week before Christmas 1955, disaster struck at three horses in or about Gold Cup class. Gay Donald and Mont Tremblant broke down badly, and Halloween suffered a leg injury in a race with Pointsman. The loss of Gay Donald was a blow to the season's racing, for he was confidently expected by his admirers to prove, once and for all, that the 1955 race was not a flash in the pan. Limber Hill, however, made himself a live candidate and the ante-post favourite by winning the King George VI Steeplechase. It was not so much the fact of his winning, for the Kempton race has not in the past been a good guide to the Gold Cup, but the way he did it. He came from a long way behind and, running on with great stoutness and courage, pegged back the free-running and bold-jumping Galloway Braes, who was brilliantly ridden by the irrepressible Winter.

There were rumours from Ireland that Quare Times would attempt the Gold Cup-Grand National double and that he was fancied to succeed. Then there was a rumour that Quare Times would be kept for the Gold Cup and would not enter the Grand National at all. Had this rumour been a fact, it would undoubtedly have made the Gold Cup into a race of extraordinary interest since Limber Hill the year before had given Quare Times 2 lb and beaten him by a length in the National Hunt Handicap Chase when it was fair to assume that Quare Times was not at his peak. However, all speculation on this subject ended when it was announced in March that Quare Times would not run in the Gold Cup, but would

(OPPOSITE) Gay Donald (A. Grantham up) clears the last to win the 1955 Gold Cup.

attempt to win a second National, and that Sam Brownthorn would represent the O'Brien stable at Cheltenham. Four Ten, now trained by Kilpatrick, had been taken out of the National, so that no horse was left with the double engagement. The complete divergence of the two lines of form was thus becoming more and more apparent.

There is little doubt that the injury to Gay Donald and the withdrawal of Quare Times robbed the race of much of its interest. Nor did the weather help matters. Frost and snow set in early in February, and no less than forty-six days racing were lost just at a time when Gold Cup horses would be coming out for their winding-up races. The Great Yorkshire Steeplechase had to be abandoned. This not only meant the loss of one of the new steeplechasing 'classics', but also that Limber Hill, a firm 5–2 ante-post favourite for the Gold Cup, would have no outing in public between Boxing Day and the race itself. Limber Hill, though a big horse, was said to require very little work, and to run his best races when fresh. Even so, those who supported him would perhaps have been happier had he had the spoils of the Great Yorkshire Chase under his belt before he went to Cheltenham.

Pointsman, another live candidate, even if his jumping was far from being above suspicion, had had a change of jockeys. He, like Four Ten, was in Kilpatrick's stable. At the beginning of the year his owner, Sir Percy Orde, had given Tim Molony a retainer to ride all his and Lady Orde's horses. But in a gallop on the racecourse shortly before the Kempton race Pointsman had not appeared to go at all well for the champion jockey, and in the big race on Boxing Day he ran lamentably.

The entries were enlivened by the appearance in them of Sir Ken, the former champion hurdler, and Cruachan, another hurdler well in championship class. Molony resumed his partnership with Sir Ken, but after looking a champion in the making Sir Ken disappointed his admirers in his last race over fences before Cheltenham. In the event he was taken out of the Gold Cup and ran and won on Wednesday instead. This was, however, the first time that two top-class hurdlers put to fencing had appeared in the Gold Cup entries.

Sam Brownthorn, from O'Brien's stable, remained second favourite at 6–1. Any horse trained by O'Brien automatically commanded respect. Sam Brownthorn's form, too, looked good. He had won three three-mile steeplechases in Ireland off the reel. But this form did not stand up to critical examination. He had beaten the very moderate mare, Nibot, twice, and at Gowran Park on January 19th the elderly Air Prince and the novice Brenair II. T. Taaffe, his rider, came to the meeting with the stamp of success upon him, for he had just equalled Martin Molony's record of riding six successive winners.

It was generally thought that Irish horses might well scoop the pool at the National Hunt Meeting, for Ireland had not suffered anything like so badly from the weather as had this country, and O'Brien's gallops were said to have been open throughout the cold spell. Things seldom, however, turn out as expected in racing, and, as it happened, the Irish have seldom had so unsuccessful a meeting.

The weather turned fine at exactly the right moment. The sun shone brilliantly on the day of the Gold Cup, and Prestbury Park looked at its loveliest. Limber Hill stayed a firm favourite. Looking at him in the paddock before the race, it was clear that he had all the appearance of a champion. It remained to be seen if his running would live up to his looks.

The going was perfect, and one might have expected a fast-run race, but in fact it was run at a slow pace with Cruachan, the novice, at the head of affairs. Pointsman was all but down

Mr J. Davey's Limber Hill (J. Power up) jumps the last followed by Vigor (R. Emery up) to become first and second in the 1956 race.

at the third, and Morrow did exceedingly well to stay on. Coming down the hill the second time, it was pretty obvious that Limber Hill was in charge of proceedings. Here Sam Brownthorn made his challenge on the outside, but he was soon done with.

Two fences out it seemed clear that Limber Hill had the race won bar a fall, and he had jumped so perfectly that a fall appeared at least unlikely. Cruachan actually jumped the last fence with him, but once Power said go, it was all over. Stretching out up the hill, the favourite went away to a most impressive victory by four lengths. The unconsidered Vigor ran on to take second place, and once more Winter and Halloween appeared from nowhere to run Cruachan out of third place. Halloween was thus placed in this race for the fourth year in succession. The fences had been stiffened this year, but there was no grief, possibly due to the slow pace in which the race was run.

Limber Hill was the second horse to win the big race at Kempton and the Gold Cup. He had a romantic history. He was bred by his owner and named after his owner's farm. His sire was the virtually unknown Bassam, whom Dutton, oddly enough, had also had in his care, and whom he had trained to win a few small steeplechases. His dam, the Gainsborough mare, Mindoon, was bought cheaply by Mr Davey during the war. She was mated to a cart horse to get her in foal the year before she bred Limber Hill. Dutton, his trainer, when a practising solicitor, had won the Grand National on Tipperary Tim. In that year, 1955, he also trained Papa Fourway, the champion sprinter, so he had in his stable the leading sprinter on the flat and the champion long-distance steeplechaser. It was no mean feat to win the Gold Cup with a horse that had not had an outing in public since Boxing Day.

As well as breeding him, Mr Davey had broken, schooled and hunted Limber Hill. This was indeed an achievement, since Limber Hill was a massive and powerful horse – he had nearly ten inches of bone – and Mr Davey was not in his first youth. He was, however, undisguisedly and justifiably jubilant after the event. When a friend came to congratulate him on his win, saying that in the winner he had got a right good horse, he replied: 'I've got a good horse? I've got a horse and a half!'

Three weeks later Limber Hill was beaten by a head at Manchester, but as he was giving his conqueror no less than 2 st 6 lb and the distance, two miles four furlongs, was thought to be too short for him, this defeat was not held against him.

With his size and scope, his great stride and power of acceleration from the last fence, it seemed probable that Limber Hill, then only nine years old and in his prime, might well run up a series of victories and prove to be the drawcard that steeplechasing was looking for.

Sadly, this was not to be. He appeared to summer well, and came back to the racecourse to start favourite in the Emblem Chase at Manchester on November 17th, but the race was run in desperately deep going which he never liked, and he could only finish fourth to a good horse, Dizzy, trained by Tom Dreaper in Ireland. Next time out, at Kempton, favourite once more, he ran so badly that Power had no option but to pull him up. A veterinary examination disclosed an injury to his back, and he was retired for the season. He was the first horse to bring the Gold Cup north.

9

Changing Times

THE SEASON 1956-57, which ushered in an era of change and progress in the world of Steeplechasing, was bedevilled by injuries to good and promising horses. Dizzy, who had appeared to be on the threshold of a great career, broke a bone below his knee and never raced again; Halloween strained his heart and was retired; and Galloway Braes, tragically, was killed in the King George VI chase on Boxing Day.

But virtually unnoticed while all this was happening, another horse was quietly and unobtrusively making his mark. He was called Floral Tribute, and he was to play a considerable part in the next three Gold Cups under a new name – Linwell.

Standing barely over sixteen hands, Linwell was a compact, well-made horse, full of personality. By the Irish classic winner Rosewell, he was out of a mare called Rubia Linda, whose pedigree had already produced no less than twenty-eight jumping winners in the previous two generations.

In 1953 David Brown, the rich industrialist whose corporation produced Aston Martin cars, asked his racing manager, Ivor Herbert, to go to Ireland and buy him a couple of likely chasers. Herbert had already spotted the horse in the form book. He liked both his breeding and the fact that he had stepped up a place in each of the bumper flat races that he had contested. Linwell was then owned by Paddy Quinn of Fethard, County Tipperary, the same man who had bought Golden Miller as a yearling, and whose young horses were always well done and cared for like children.

Despite the fact that, when he saw him in Paddy Quinn's field, the horse had curby hocks and his fore feet were none too good, Herbert immediately sensed something about him, and recognised his quality. Eventually a deal was done for £750, which was the maximum Mr Brown had allowed Herbert to spend. He returned home well pleased with his purchase though, as he himself would be the first to admit, he then scarcely knew just what he was getting. The plan was to run him in point-to-points and, for a start, his original name of Floral Tribute was changed to Linwell.

His maiden effort under his new name was at Crowell. It was not a particularly encouraging beginning, for he took the first fence by the roots and put Herbert on the floor. But his next effort was more satisfactory. At the Oxford University Meeting at Lockinge he came with a late run to finish third in a high-class field. This was, in fact, the pattern for all his future races. He was a slow starter, and liked to swing along behind before coming with a late, and, in most cases, devastating run for the post. Herbert gave him plenty of time, and it was not until the 1955 season that he really started serious steeplechasing.

This began at Kempton in March. Another jockey who had come over from Ireland to school him and ride him cried off at the last moment, and Herbert engaged Scudamore in a hurry. He could not have made a more fortunate choice. Michael Scudamore was an ex-amateur, a horseman who set himself to learn about and understand the horses he rode, and who possessed, besides, great dash and courage. He rode Linwell in most of his formative races thereafter, and the horse and his connections owe much to Scudamore's skill and patience. That year Linwell won six of his fifteen races, and was only out of the money twice.

During the season, however, Herbert, a man of many parts, for as well as being an owner, rider and trainer of racehorses he is an author, playwright, television writer and journalist, decided that he could no longer hold the licence as he was writing for a London newspaper, and it was transferred to the head lad, Charley Mallon. A former rider himself – he had ridden over two hundred winners in his day – Mallon had learnt his job under Tom Coulthwaite, and later had been head lad to Hector Christie. He and Herbert were to form an admirable partnership.

In January 1956, carrying only 9 st 9 lb, Linwell won the Mildmay Memorial chase from Wise Child and Devon Loch and, later the same year, in November, he beat Kerstin by a short head in the Grand Sefton Trial Chase at Hurst Park. Kerstin, the mare, 'the crack from the North' was known even then to be a live Gold Cup prospect, so Linwell's connections had every reason to be pleased. It was pointed out against him, however, that the distance had only been a short head, and that he was receiving 8 lb from the mare. It was generally assumed that the handicapper had not yet caught up with him, and that when he did the weight would stop him. Be that as it may, three weeks later he beat Hall Weir at Cheltenham, won at Warwick and then went back to Cheltenham to beat Hall Weir again. This made it four races in a row, and already it was apparent to Herbert and Mallon that he was one of those high-spirited, courageous horses who really love Cheltenham and who give of their best on its testing track. On December 5th Kerstin had made this form look particularly good by winning the Christmas Cracker Chase at Liverpool convincingly, with 11 st 13 lb on her back.

Herbert now realised that he had a very live Gold Cup prospect on his hands, though amongst the racing writers only the sapient Francis Byrne of *The Times* appeared to agree with him. Herbert conveyed his confidence to his family and friends and between them they backed Linwell to win them a substantial sum at long prices.

After his second Cheltenham win early in January 1957, Linwell was knocked over in the Mildmay and beaten into second place by Pointsman at Kempton. He did not like Kempton; it was much too sharp for him; but by now the handicapper had him at 11 st 9 lb and, as a result of these defeats, both public and press largely discounted his chances of carrying level weights against the cracks.

On paper, indeed, it looked a useful enough field for that Gold Cup. Rose Park was back again, having won the King George VI on Boxing Day, and thus shown that he could stay at least three miles. He had also won his last two races convincingly, though these were over shorter distances. Gay Donald, too, was a runner. He was now eleven, but he had a recent good win at Windsor to his credit. In addition there were Sir Ken, the former champion hurdler, Pointsman, Lochroe and E.S.B. But Kerstin, despite the fact that she had shortly before fallen in the Great Yorkshire Chase, was the public fancy. She was backed down from 11–1 to 6–1 to start joint favourite with Pointsman. Linwell was 100–9.

Although the going was soft the presence of Rose Park ensured that a strong gallop would be set, as indeed it was. He dashed off into the lead with old Gay Donald at his heels and jumping every bit as fluently. The rest of the field were strung out behind them.

All this exactly suited Linwell. Scudamore had received no riding instructions from Herbert before the race, for he knew the horse and his ways so well that by now none were needed. Dropping him in at the back, he allowed Linwell to gallop along at his own time, taking the fences without effort and as they came. He was enjoying himself and conserving his strength, while up in the van the leaders were busy cutting their own and each other's throats. Things, in fact, were going just as Herbert had hoped.

On the second circuit the pace set by Rose Park showed no signs of weakening. Gay Donald was the first to crack. He hit the fence after the water, lamed himself and was pulled up. Here, too, Sir Ken gave Bryan Marshall a crashing fall, continuing Marshall's history of ill-luck in this race. Rose Park went galloping remorselessly on, but others, now, were beginning to make their moves. Kerstin, who had never been far away, closed perceptibly on the leader, and shortly afterwards Scudamore began to move Linwell up towards the fighting line.

At the third last, Kerstin had got to Rose Park and Scudamore had brought Linwell up to them both with one long, perfectly timed run. Pointsman was a length or so behind these three. They were now, all of them, going hard for home.

Two from home, as they came into it. Linwell showed the quality that makes a champion. Here Scudamore took Kerstin on. Linwell flung it behind him with a tremendous leap. Kerstin checked, screwed sideways and interfered with Pointsman. Landing a length to the good, Scudamore had got first run and he kept it. Linwell was over the last with another length in hand, and up the straight he showed no signs of faltering. Kerstin most gallantly came at him again. She got to a length of him but could do no more, and the little horse held his advantage to the line.

As Linwell came into the winner's enclosure Mallon showed Herbert proof of the confidence he had in his horse, for he had left the rug and stable gear by the winner's stall!

It was a tremendous achievement for a small stable and a small horse bought for a modest price, to pull off this supreme prize of steeplechasing. Unlike though they were in conformation, for Kerstin was a big mare full of scope and quality, the first and second were in fact cousins, for they had the same grand-dam in a mare called Toi Fish, by Yutoi.

After this race Linwell was retired for a summer's rest. The lad who did him was glad enough to see him go, for it was one of his peculiarities that, calm and placid on the racecourse, in his box he became steadily more bad-tempered as the season progressed. By the end of it he would lunge at and try to bite anyone who came into it. At grass he was self-contained and kept away from other horses – a manifestation of his solitary character which led him, too, to run his races from behind, away from his field, preferring, as it were, to race always by himself.

He was back again at Fontwell on October 8th, when he ran second to Crudwell at level weights. Three weeks later this result was repeated at Ludlow.

That year Madame Hennessy of the famous French brandy family had presented a Gold Cup for a top-class steeplechase of over three miles to be run during the first half of the season. A handicap worth over £5,272 to the winner, it was aimed to attract the best staying steeplechasers in training, and this was what it did. It was to be Linwell's first real objective in the new season. He was set to carry 12 st 2 lb, and give lumps of weight away to almost all the field.

Madame Hennessy herself owned a small French bred horse called Mandarin, who resembled Linwell not only in size but also in his qualities of stoutness and courage. He had won the Broadway Novices Chase, that nursery of Gold Cup winners, the previous season, and he looked like a coming champion in doing it. At Cheltenham, in the first running of the Hennessy, Linwell and Mandarin came over the last fence together. But up the hill the task of conceding 16 lb to one of the class of Mandarin was too much for the champion. He was beaten three lengths, fighting back gamely under his big weight. Subsequent events were to show that, in defeat, he may here have given one of the finest performances of his career.

It was a most appropriate victory, for the Hennessy family were no strangers to steeple-chasing. Lutteur III, owned and bred by Monsieur James Hennessy, had won the Grand National in 1909.

Meanwhile other events were taking place, which were to lead to the shaping of the Gold Cup field.

At the previous National Hunt Meeting a big horse trained by Vincent O'Brien and called Saffron Tartan had displayed an astounding power of acceleration to win the second division of the Gloucestershire Hurdle. Many watchers wondered then if they were seeing a future champion. Such was the power and authority with which he won his first steeplechase, the Maiden Chase at Fairyhouse a month later, that they became convinced of it. But Saffron Tartan, when he reappeared in the autumn, ran listlessly. Clearly he was not 'right in himself' as it were, and after his troubles had been diagnosed as equine flu he disappeared – though only temporarily – from the arena of top-class steeplechasing. Neither Kerstin nor Pointsman opened the season auspiciously. Old Gay Donald was, however, back again, enjoying himself and apparently jumping with all the abandon of his youth. Limber Hill, too, had returned to the racecourse and was said to be aimed at regaining his crown, though his performances gave little hope of success.

The King George VI Chase, notorious as it is as an unreliable guide to Gold Cup form, nevertheless produced a great race amongst the contenders for the Championship. Mandarin, Lochroe and Kerstin jumped the last together. Mandarin, in soft going, giving away weight and on a course considered too sharp for him, displayed every ounce of that unyielding courage which was later to bring him to an immortal niche in the annals of steeplechasing, to win by a length.

Pointsman broke down in this race, and was out for the rest of the season, but before they lined up at Cheltenham a new contender had pushed himself into the limelight. Mrs Pleydell Bouverie's Polar Flight, though in many quarters regarded as more of a National horse, put

(OPPOSITE) Linwell comes in after winning the 1957 Gold Cup.

himself into at least serious consideration for the Gold Cup by winning the Mildmay Memorial, and then beating Linwell at Newbury, though to achieve this latter feat he was in receipt of 13 lb.

At Newbury Linwell was not in fact fully wound up, for he had been rested in readiness for the big race. He showed, however, that he was coming back to his best just when it was wanted by giving Lochroe 8 lb at Kempton and only going under by three lengths. Here, too, owing to the sharp course, different riding tactics were tried with him and he had gone to the front four out. Everyone who saw it agreed that this was a good Gold Cup trial.

There were certain alterations at Cheltenham that year. For some time the course authorities had been worried about the weather and the wear on the track. They had, therefore, begun to contemplate constructing an entire 'new course', on which certain races could be run or switched to as and when the state of the going required. A start on this work had been made, and there was then a separate course coming down the hill having four entirely new fences on it. The top bend, too, had been altered and widened. This was, of course, made-up ground, and, since there had been an unremitting deluge for a day before the meeting took place, it became very heavy and cut up, and caused the clerk of the course no little anxiety. The Gold Cup course itself was altered that year too. The $3\frac{1}{4}$-mile start coming down the hill, with the runners in full view of the stands, being used to start the race.

On the day Mandarin was favourite to win from Linwell, with Polar Flight and, surprisingly, Gay Donald, well backed. Kerstin was at sevens. The unconsidered Game Field set off in front with Gay Donald, Kerstin and Mandarin, in that order, in close attendance. Just before the eighth fence from home Linwell moved up to Mandarin. Then sensation and disappointment struck. Mandarin had already made one dreadful mistake at the first open ditch. Here he hit the fence, screwed sideways and shot Madden up his neck. Linwell, taking off perfectly, hit him as he screwed, and the next thing Scudamore knew he was on the ground and out of the race with a gash on his forehead and an eye that was rapidly swelling and closing. Both the favourites had gone at the same fence.

Immediately afterwards Polar Flight put his hind legs into the water and all but stopped. At the top of the hill, turning for home, it looked, unbelievably, that old Gay Donald, jumping with all the speed and fluency that he had displayed three years ago in his prime, might be going to get back into the winner's enclosure and set up a record. But then Hayhurst sent Kerstin on. Slack too, had by now got Polar Flight going again. Down the hill he caught Gay Donald and closed on the mare. They fought it out fence for fence all the way home. Kerstin just held on to her advatange, and won by three-quarters of a length. Hayhurst, who was only having his third ride round Cheltenham, displayed admirable coolness and judgment throughout the race, to bring the Championship north for the second time. Gay Donald gallantly struggled into third place. Kerstin, the second mare to win, was fully entitled to her victory but it could hardly be called a satisfactory race with Mandarin and Linwell, the best-backed horses in the race, gone at one fell stroke. It has often been

(OPPOSITE, ABOVE) The 1958 field taking the second fence led by *right* Game Field (J. Boddy up) *left* Gay Donald (F. Winter up) and Kerstin (S. Hayhurst).
(BELOW) Kerstin clears the last fence to win from Polar Flight.

said that the fences are there to be jumped. Kerstin jumped them and won; she could do no more. The time, 6 minutes 53 seconds was, oddly enough, an exact repetition of Linwell's time the year before. Kerstin, like many another good horse, was bred in County Tipperary and had been bought by her owner, Mr G. H. Moore, as a four-year-old.

Before the new season had far advanced it was obvious that a fresh star had arrived on the steeplechasing scene. The great, or near-great winners of the Gold Cup in the late 'fifties were, one after the other, plagued by ill-fortune or bad luck, and this horse, Pas Seul, was no exception.

Pas de Quatre, dam of Pas Seul, had been bred by Fred Darling, and she had already bred one Gold Cup winner in Gay Donald. She was, however, a shy breeder and her owner, Harry Frank, lent her to Mr P. J. Burt, owner of Gay Donald, to see if he could get her in foal. She was put to Erin's Pride, who was by Fairfax. It was believed that the union had been unfruitful and, that spring of 1953, Mr Burt's girl groom rode her in two ladies' point-to-points and three hunter trials. When Mr Burt died the mare was returned to Harry Frank. Bob Turnell, who had not long retired from a successful career as a jockey and was carving out another, equally successful, as a trainer, saw her there and asked Mr Frank what he was going to do with her. 'Shoot her, unless you want her,' was the uncompromising reply.

Turnell took the mare away and sent her to the Littleton Stud, where she was covered by Royal Tara. A week later, to his great astonishment, the stud groom telephoned him that she was going to foal. That foal was the future Pas Seul.

As might perhaps have been expected after all these vicissitudes, at first the foal was not a particularly prepossessing specimen. When Turnell took Mr Frank to see him the owner asked him: 'Whose foal is that?' 'He's yours,' Turnell replied, 'but I want first refusal of him.' This was given, and subsequently Turnell bought him as a yearling for £600 on behalf of Mr John Rogerson, for whom he trained. As events were to show it was a singularly shrewd purchase, and a great tribute to Turnell's eye and flair for a horse.

Pas Seul first saw the racecourse as a four-year-old, when he had a quiet start with a couple of runs, unplaced, over hurdles. Soon, however, he was doing enough at home to show them that he had brilliant potential. Unfortunately with that brilliance went what often accompanies it – uncertainty. The following season in his first three chases, when he was maturing from five to six, he was twice on the ground. He then proceeded to run up a sequence of six wins over fences and hurdles. These victories were not, however, accomplished without his making some really horrifying mistakes, from which his speed and strength only just combined to save him. It was now obvious that, could these mistakes be eliminated, the seeds of greatness were there within him and, despite the fact that he was only six, it was decided to let him take his chance in the Gold Cup.

In a way it was a brave decision to make, for that year the field looked a classic one. Saffron Tarton, fully recovered, it was said, from his indispositions of the previous year, was back again. He was eight years old and in the hands of Vincent O'Brien he looked fully prepared to fulfil all his early promise, having won his last three races convincingly under big weights. There was another representative from Ireland, too, in Lord Fingall's Roddy Owen, a handsome Owenstown gelding trained by Danny Morgan on the Curragh. As in the case of Pas Seul, Roddy Owen, also, had his problems. Like the great rider after whom

Roddy Owen ridden by Mr J.R. Cox, Kempton Park, Boxing Day 1958 where he came second in the King George VI Chase. He went on to win the 1959 Gold Cup ridden by Bobby Beasley.

he was named he had something of a wayward disposition. Captain Rodcrick Owen, one of the finest amateur riders of all time and the only serving infantryman ever to ride the winner of the Grand National, was a gay and unpredictable character who was no respecter of persons. It was he who, when gently rebuked by his General for spending too much time on the racecourse, made an answer which must go down in history as one of the masterpieces of controlled impertinence. 'Captain Owen,' the General said. 'I have been here two months and have not had the pleasure of making your acquaintance.' 'My loss, General, not yours!' was the classic reply.

Roddy Owen, the horse, was also greatly given to the unexpected. He had come over on top of Danny Morgan when he went down to try him for Lord Fingall, and, in a race, when he wanted to jump, he jumped. That was that, and woe betide any rider, however skilful, who tried to interfere with or alter his ideas about the time and place of taking off. That year Mr J. R. Cox, one of the best amateurs ever to come out of Ireland, had been asked to ride him in all his races. They were desperately unlucky not to win the King George VI Chase, being brought almost to a standstill four out, and even then only losing by a head to Lochroe. Roddy Owen was at his headstrong worst in the Leopardstown Chase, however, and ran and jumped badly. Just before the Gold Cup, Bobby Beasley, who had ridden him in nearly all his races previous to that season and who knew him better than anyone else, suddenly became free. Mr Cox most generously offered to stand down, and Beasley was given the ride in the Gold Cup.

Linwell was also in the field, and here, too, there had been a change of riders. That season Mr Brown had taken a second claim on Winter's services, and Winter, now approaching the very peak of his fame, for he had been champion jockey for the past three seasons, was free on the day and he had the ride. Linwell had been a model of consistency that year, having won twice and been placed twice in four starts, the last defeat being at the hands of Taxidermist, winner of the previous season's Hennessy and also a runner in the Gold Cup. Kerstin was back again, too, but Polar Flight suffered injury and was taken out, as was Neji, winner of £90,000 in stakes in America, who had been brought over to Ireland to be specially trained for this race.

More and more stable confidence appeared to be behind Saffron Tartan, and he was made a very strong ante-post favourite. On the morning of the race, however, when doing his pre-race workout he coughed badly. The horse, as has been said, had already suffered badly from equine influenza. To run him might have finished him forever. Vincent O'Brien had no option but to strike him out. This he did, and as a result all the betting was thrown into disarray. In the end Taxidermist, astonishingly enough, started favourite at fours.

Heavy rain had turned the new course, which had now been extended, into a terrible morass, and the stewards directed that the race be run over the old course which, however, was not in a much better state.

The race itself needs little description, save for the finish. Pas Seul, who had been beautifully ridden throughout by W. Rees, son of L. B. Rees and nephew of the immortal Fred, came to the last a clear length and a half in front. He had jumped perfectly, without making the semblance of a mistake, and he was full of running. Linwell, however, driven by Winter, was coming at him with that long run of his, and looking more dangerous every moment. Over on the left and a length or so behind, Roddy Owen was bearing down on them both, though he was being hard ridden by Beasley at the time.

Rees on Pas Seul had no option but to go for the last as if it was not there, and this is just what he did. The roaring from the crowd was continuous and massive as the three horses came at the fence. Distracted by this – or by something – Pas Seul never looked at it. Down he came – slap in the path of Linwell. Roddy Owen, who was free from trouble,

(OPPOSITE, ABOVE) Taxidermist (Mr J. Lawrence up) was amongst the leaders at the second fence, 1959.
(BELOW) Pas Seul falls at the last in the 1959 race.

jumped it perfectly and was away up the hill with three lengths in hand.

Linwell had been to all intents and purposes stopped dead in his tracks, and he in his turn hampered Lochroe. Winter got him going again, but it was then a hopeless chase. Roddy Owen held his advantage to the line.

Taxidermist had knuckled over in the mud after landing five from home, and Kerstin failed to stay in the desperately heavy going.

Afterwards, of course, the post mortems began. Linwell, here, was surely the unlucky one. Through no fault of his own or his rider he was stopped in his run just when it was reaching its culmination. In the history of this race Linwell must go down as one of the unlucky horses. Small in stature, perhaps on the whole unprepossessing in appearance, he had the heart of a lion and, had the wheel of fortune turned even slightly his way after his first victory, he would almost certainly have figured in the record books as winner of three Gold Cups. But this is not in any way to decry the merit of the victor, who was a high-spirited horse of the highest quality, and ridden with both dash and brains.

Luck that year may have been on the side of Roddy Owen, but he had had his share of bad luck before and was to encounter more of it again, and no one could deny that it was a great National Hunt triumph. Lord Fingall had been an enthusiast in the cause of National Hunt Racing all his life. As a Gentleman Rider between the wars he had had his greatest success when he won the National Hunt Steeplechase for Mr Ambrose Clark on Sir Lindsay. A member of the Irish National Hunt Steeplechase Committee, he had served two terms as a steward and given generously of his time and experience to preserve and further the interests of all concerned with the jumping game. Danny Morgan had been a very distinguished rider indeed. He had won this race on Morse Code, as we have seen, and had, as well, ridden the winner of almost every big steeplechase and hurdle race except the Grand National. A jockey of great style and polish, some of his performances are still remembered and talked about to this day. Bobby Beasley came from the greatest of all Irish steeplechasing families. His grand-uncle, Tommy, the hero of countless episodes and contests, won the Grand National no less than three times and, in addition, beat Fred Archer in a welter race on the flat, while his grandfather, perhaps an even more accomplished horseman than his brother, won the Grand National on Come Away and rode in his last steeplechase at Punchestown at the age of seventy-three, and in his last flat race ten years later!

As has been said at the beginning of this chapter, times were changing in steeplechasing. The importance of the Grand National and Aintree in general was fading fast. The Gold Cup was now fully recognised amongst racing people as the ultimate aim of the high-class steeplechaser. But the greatest change of all was the coming of the sponsors.

The first and most important of the sponsored races was The Whitbread Gold Cup, instituted by Colonel Whitbread of the brewing family, and an owner of some magnitude himself. Others, sensing that they could benefit both themselves and the sport, were not slow to follow. Thus, prize money, promotion and publicity all increased with resulting benefits to sponsors, promoters, and steeplechasing. Sponsorship did not come to the Gold Cup itself, however, for another thirteen years. But the race was now to be contested by a series of horses who hovered on that knife-edge which separates the very good from the truly great.

10

The Almost-Immortals

IT HAS TO be admitted that Pas Seul did not start the following season as a potential champion should. He fell in the Hennessy in November. A week later, at Sandown, he started favourite, but a series of mistakes ruined his chances, though he showed his brilliance on the flat by getting up from nowhere to within three-quarters of a length of the winner, Oscar Wilde, to whom he was conceding 10 lb. At Kempton on Boxing Day he blundered his chances away at the open ditch to let Mandarin and Pointsman fight out a desperate finish. He was beaten at Kempton once more in January, this time by Plummers Plain, and more mistakes cost him a race at Lingfield a week later. It did not look at all good for his chances in the championship.

He sustained an overreach in the Lingfield race, and, while he was under attention for this, Dr Charles Barke, the nerve treatment specialist, rang Turnell to ask if he could try his method of 'impulse change' on the horse. This consisted of a course of massage of the nerve centres. When asked, Mr Rogerson gave his consent, and Dr Barke visited Pas Seul for twenty minutes each day for a fortnight. By this time, however, the critics had mostly written him off, and were looking elsewhere for a serious contender to occupy the champion's throne.

One challenger had been soon removed. Saffron Tartan, as a result of his respiratory troubles, had been operated on for his wind, and it had been decided to keep him to hurdling for the season. He had changed stables, too. O'Brien by now was turning his interests to the flat, and so Saffron Tartan's owners brought the big horse to England and entrusted him to Don Butchers. But things had also been happening to the other old stalwarts. Mandarin's hard-won victory over Pointsman finished him for the season, since he developed tendon trouble and, although he never actually broke down, it was considered wiser to fire him. Pointsman, too, disappeared from the scene shortly after that race. But Kerstin, who had shown tremendous courage and staying power in winning the Hennessy in which Pas Seul fell, was still there, as were Roddy Owen and Lochroe. In addition there was Knightsbrook, a newcomer recently imported from Ireland, who had been brilliant when winning the Emblem Chase and the Great Yorkshire, though in both cases under very light weights.

When the day came round it was, in fact, Knightsbrook who was made favourite from Kerstin and Lochroe.

In the race Kerstin tried to force the pace almost from the start. Whether this was a wise tactic is open to question, but, rounding the bend from home, to many on the stands it looked like succeeding. Here Kerstin was still in the lead and going, it appeared, the best of the lot. Pas Seul was, however, in close attendance, as were Roddy Owen and Lochroe. Knightsbrook was right out of it, proving that he did not really have the class for this sort of race - which is ruthless in exposing weakness in horse or man.

Kerstin's chances looked even better when Pas Seul made one of his characteristic blunders at the second last. But Rees sat tight and the horse recovered, and was into his stride again with hardly a check. Between the last two fences that stride had in fact swept him into the lead, a fraction in front of Lochroe, who had come through to deprive Kerstin of second place. Kerstin then began to show signs of distress, and Roddy Owen, hard driven, was closing on her. That was the order, but a length would have covered the lot as they came to the last.

Rees on Pas Seul was in a position to try the nerve and hardihood of any man. Pas Seul had just made his first mistake of the race. It was here in almost similar circumstances last year that he had fallen and thrown his race away. But a year *had* passed. Pas Seul had matured in strength, speed and staying power. Rees now knew him inside out, and knew, too, that he possessed the essentials of a true champion - acceleration and blinding speed from the last. Riding with consummate coolness he sat quite still coming into the fence. This allowed Lochroe to get to him and jump it almost abreast of him.

They landed all but level. Mould immediately set Lochroe alight. He shot to the front and for a moment it looked as if the little horse, at the age of twelve, was going to bring the championship to Fairlawne for the first time. But Pas Seul under Rees's hands had made a perfect jump. Rees, every bit as cool as Brabazon had been on Cottage Rake in much the same situation eleven years before, gathered Pas Seul up. Then he let him go. To those watching, it seemed as if, with the fence safely behind him, the big horse's stride and speed would soon settle the matter. But half-way up the hill little Lochroe, running on with the greatest determination, was still three parts of a length in front. Then Rees really sat down to ride. He got a hero's response. Pas Seul came to Lochroe's girths, caught him, passed him, and won, still accelerating, still pulling away, by a length.

It was one of the best races seen for years in the Gold Cup, and once again a good big 'un had beaten a good little 'un. It was, too, an immensely popular and appropriate victory, for Mr John Rogerson, a great supporter of steeplechasing, was that year senior steward of the National Hunt Committee.

Kerstin fell at the last in a collapse almost as spectacular as that of Pas Seul the year before. In so doing she went right underneath Roddy Owen. How she did not bring him down and how Beasley stayed on are steeplechasing mysteries, but she robbed him of whatever chance he had of fighting out the finish up the hill.

Pas Seul was then only seven, and there seemed no limit to the heights he might attain. In April he tried to give 28 lb to Plummers Plain in the Whitbread Gold Cup. They crossed the last fence together but the weight beat him on the run in, and he succumbed by a length and a half. The third horse was no less than twenty-five lengths away. Pas Seul lost no prestige in this defeat, for Plummers Plain was no mean performer, especially in a handicap with a low weight.

As has been said, the good horses of this period were unlucky. Pas Seul had made a slight noise all his life. After this race it became considerably worse, and it was clear that he would have to be operated on. Mr Braine, the Gloucestershire veterinary surgeon, hobdayed him and he spent the summer at Guildenhurst Manor in Sussex, Mr Rogerson's home. Bob Turnell's comment on him to Mr Rogerson at this period of his career is worth repeating. 'He's a funny horse,' Turnell said, 'really a brilliant jumper. There is no better performer over the Beaufort's stone walls.' (Turnell had hunted him.) 'But at odd times his faculties seem to desert him.' This was an apt summing-up. Though those moments of aberration were becoming fewer, they still made him a disconcerting horse to ride, for even now he seldom survived any race without at least one major mistake. It was a tremendous tribute to his strength and courage that those mistakes were so often overcome.

Rees, of course, knew him through and through, but in the following season Rees accepted a retainer from Peter Cazalet's Fairlawne stable, and another jockey had to be found. The choice fell on D. Dick.

There could not have been a better one. David Victor Dick, whose name has already appeared in these pages, had been in racing all his life. As an apprentice at the age of seventeen he had won the Lincolnshire Handicap in 1941. Increasing weight terminated his career on the flat. After war service he turned to jumping, and won the 'Devon Loch' National on E.S.B. in 1956, and many other big races. A natural horseman, the trouble he had with his weight limited his opportunities, but when they came his way he made the most of them. In a sport where brave men proliferate he was a sort of Marshal Ney – 'The bravest of the brave.' He was also a character in his own right. Some years later when he rode Dunkirk, the fastest jumper of fences since Clashing Arms and possibly even faster than him, Dick is said to have turned to the owner in the unsaddling enclosure after winning his race and uttered the one word – 'Blimey!'

From the very beginning of the season it was obvious that Pas Seul was going to have to fight to keep his crown. There was one obvious and very dangerous challenger. Saffron Tartan, this year, was being trained for and aimed at the Gold Cup. The previous season he had run third in the Champion Hurdle and then put up an impressive performance under 12 st 7 lb to win a two-mile chase at Cheltenham just over a month later. It was its only appearance over fences that year. These two runs alone clearly demonstrated that he was far from being a spent force. Dave Dick's lifelong friend and rival, the great Fred Winter, had been engaged to ride him in all his races. His first outing of the new season was in The Grand Sefton Trial Chase at Hurst Park. Here he only failed by three parts of a length to give a stone to a useful horse of Colonel Whitbread's called Mariner's Dance, which indicated that, if things went right for him, he would be the one they all had to beat by the time the National Hunt Meeting came around again.

But Saffron Tartan, like Pas Seul, had elements of the unusual in his make-up. Whether these were accounted for by the strange temperament of his dam it is, of course, impossible to say. She was called Kellsboro Witch and she did not belie her name, for she was described by her former owner, Mr Maurice O. Springfield, a Master of Hounds, as 'a holy terror, both in the hunting field and on the racecourse'. In all her racing career she succeeded in winning just once. This was at Hethersett in 1936. The only other runner, a thirteen-year-old called Two Royals, fell. Kellsboro Witch took fifteen minutes to get round, since,

according to her owner's account, she refused nearly every fence at least once before finally deciding to jump it. After the race, when she came back to his kennels, Mr Springfield, in telling the story, declared that if his hounds had been short of food that night Saffron Tartan would never have been conceived!

But from the very first Saffron Tartan had showed that he possessed both brilliant speed and powers of acceleration. Vincent O'Brien has said that his potential was tremendous, but that his tragedy was the virus that dogged him and the subsequent operation, both of which made him never the horse he just might have been. It is also, incidentally, a tribute to O'Brien's perception that when Saffron Tartan was first sent to him he was unbroken and in the rough. Before he saw him he was in two minds whether to take him, since even then his thoughts were turning towards the flat. Once he laid eyes on him, however, burly and unfurnished as he was, he knew he had to have him. Such is genius.

Whether it was the effect of his virus or not, his form since the infection appeared to be in and out. This year, for instance, after such a promising beginning, he never got into the race at all in the Mackeson Gold Cup, then won the King George VI brilliantly at Kempton, a course which may have suited him best of all, despite its sharpness and his size, since it enabled his rider to conserve his stamina and exploit his speed. Usually the safest of jumpers, he then proceeded to fall in a two-mile chase at Sandown. This was his last race before the Gold Cup and, despite what everyone knew he could do, there were doubts about whether he would do it. In addition there was a serious question mark against his ability to stay the stiff three miles and a quarter of the Gold Cup course. He had, however, the immeasurable advantage of Winter's assistance from the saddle. Moreover, Winter knew him now, recognised his brilliance, and believed in him. And when Winter believed in a horse, in the wonderful way he had, that confidence was communicated to the horse to the ultimate profit of them both.

Pas Seul's preliminaries were more impressive, though he, too, showed signs that his old characteristics were far from conquered. He won his first two chases easily under 12 st 7 lb. Then, on the same day that Saffron Tartan fell at Sandown, starting favourite like his rival and in the very next race, he threw his chances away by a series of blunders reminiscent of his very worst performances of two years before. After that, in the Stone's Ginger Wine Chase, he could do no better than finish a remote sixth to Pouding. He redeemed himself somewhat by giving 35 lb to King's Nickel, and slamming a useful field without the semblance of a mistake in the Manifesto Chase at Lingfield on February 18th. His next race was to be the Gold Cup. His connections had every reason to feel that he had come back to his brilliant best at just the right time, and that he would win them their second championship. The ebullient Dave Dick told Mr Rogerson that he didn't know they made horses like him. 'It's as if you were driving a Rolls-Royce against a lot of mini-cars!' he said.

It was generally conceded that the championship was a match between these two, though Mandarin, now aged ten, was back in the field. But Mandarin, apart from his leg trouble,

(OPPOSITE, ABOVE) The field on the first circuit in the 1961 race. *Right to left* Pas Seul (11) (Dave Dick), Olympia (4) (Mr Mark Hely Hutchinson).
(BELOW) Fred Winter leading at the last on Col. G. R. Westmacott's Saffron Tartan which won the 1961 race.

had had an appalling fall early in the season at Chepstow and seemed to have lost both his form and his confidence. Olympia, a handsome Irish mare, and Frenchman's Cove, then a promising novice, were the only other runners of any consequence.

The ground was good, which favoured Saffron Tartan's suspect stamina, and he started favourite at 2-1, with Pas Seul a strong second favourite at 100-30. Winter was just then in unstoppable form, for he had won the Champion Hurdle the day before on Eborneezer.

Although Mandarin tried to make all the running the forecasters were right in prophesying that the race lay between the two cracks. At the last open ditch Pas Seul had one of his unaccountable lapses. Having jumped perfectly until then, he proceeded to hit it an unmerciful crack and dropped back from amongst the leaders to fourth place. Immediately Winter seized his opportunity and sent Saffron Tartan on. Dick drove Pas Seul up to him again, and down the hill these two great riders on two superb horses fought it out stride for stride. Over the third they were still locked together, and there was nothing between them round the long bend for home. But that mistake had taken something out of Pas Seul, and against such a one as Winter on a horse like Saffron Tartan, even Pas Seul could afford to give nothing away. Between the last two Dick was at work on him. With Winter sitting still, Saffron Tartan drew a length or so ahead. Saffron Tartan jumped the last perfectly, and again Pas Seul blundered. The favourite came on up the hill with his race, it seemed, well won.

What no one then realised, but Winter knew only too well, was that Saffron Tartan had indeed failed to stay and was all but stone cold underneath him. Even coming into the last Winter was wondering if his horse had the physical strength left to surmount it. And after ,it there was the hill to be faced. Somehow he sat there, and suffered and nursed and drove Saffron Tartan up it towards the post.

Dick pulled Pas Seul together and sent him in pursuit. But the race had been run at a slashing pace and those mistakes had taken their toll. Pas Seul, too, was desperately tired. Even so, he rallied and began to cut down Saffron Tartan's lead. By now Saffron Tartan was throwing out every possible sign of distress. Yard by yard Pas Seul closed the gap. But, driven, urged and coaxed by Winter, all at the same time and in a manner only riders of genius possess, Saffron Tartan just held on. A stride past the winning post he was, in Winter's own words 'down to a walk' – but he had won or, perhaps it is more correct to say that Winter had won on him. Pas Seul had got to a length and a half of him and Mandarin, having lost his place and come again, finished fastest of all to be a further three lengths away, third.

His fellow jockeys gave Winter a spontaneous ovation when he returned to the weighing room. Dave Dick, having been in some position to judge, said that after this race he knew Winter was the best he'd ever seen. 'There'll never be another like him,' he added. By completing the Champion Hurdle – Gold Cup double, Winter became only the fifth rider to do so, the others being Tim Cullinan, Gerry Wilson, Aubrey Brabazon and Tim Molony – the last two, incidentally, on horses trained by Vincent O'Brien.

Saffron Tartan and Pas Seul were both horses on the verge of the highest class. Both may have been deprived of this accolade by the wind infirmity which necessitated hobdaying. In the case of Pas Seul there were, of course, those instances of 'his faculties deserting him', which probably cost him this race and his second Gold Cup. At all events he went on to win the Farnborough Chase at Stratford over two miles, a distance considered too short for him. In this race he was ridden by Winter, since Dick was not available. It was the first and only time that Winter rode Pas Seul, and when he dismounted he paid him the uncommon tribute of saying he was the best he had ever sat on. Taking into account the many fine horses Winter rode in his career, the Nationals, Champion Hurdles and Gold Cups that he won, this judgment, after one race, is testimony indeed to Pas Seul's claim to greatness.

Substantial recompense for that lost Gold Cup was, in fact, in store for Pas Seul. In soft going and carrying 12 st on his back, he won the Whitbread Gold Cup at Sandown on April 22nd by four lengths from Nicolaus Silver, to whom he was giving 21 lb. The magnitude of this performance cannot be exaggerated. There was a field of twenty-three, amongst them Mandarin who, receiving 6 lb, could only finish sixth, Springbok, Knucklecracker, Taxidermist and Blessington Esquire. The range of weights went down to 9 st 8 lb. Furthermore, three fences out, he was stopped in his tracks by a falling horse. This time he was reunited with his old friend and partner Dave Dick, who rode him brilliantly, there were no mistakes or hesitancies, and he clinched his claim, despite his defeat in the Gold Cup, to be the best of his day. It was probably the finest performance of any steeplechaser since the war, and it makes one wonder to what heights this grand horse would have aspired had all gone well with him.

It is interesting, too, to note that Pas Seul, second in the Gold Cup, was set by the handicapper to give Nicolaus Silver, winner of the Grand National in the same year, no less than the 21 lb already mentioned. This, and the result, strikingly illustrate the decline of the Grand National and the rise of the Gold Cup. It was now a far cry from the days of Easter Hero and Golden Miller.

Pas Seul was then only eight, and before the Gold Cup the following year he ran up three successive victories under top weights. His former jumping errors seemed forgotten, and he won by margins of six lengths, twenty-five lengths and five lengths. It was good enough to establish him as a firm ante-post favourite. He looked, indeed, to have a tremendous chance of being the first winner of the race to regain the championship after a subsequent defeat, for the opposition that year did not appear particularly strong. Saffron Tartan had had tendon trouble and been retired. Fortria, from Tom Dreaper's powerful stable in Ireland, seemed the likeliest challenger. He had won the two previous runnings of the Champion Two-Mile Chase at the National Hunt Meeting, and was thought a certainty to win it again were he to run. He had, however, been hobdayed, and there was doubt about his stamina. Nevertheless, his owner very sportingly decided to go for the greater prize and have a cut at the Gold Cup. But there was against him, too, the fact that he had not actually won a race this season, though he had been gallant in defeat under big weights. Mandarin was there, too, but who, they said, could seriously fancy Mandarin? He had been soundly trounced by Pas Seul not once but twice the year before, he was eleven years old, he had broken a bone in his stifle, been fired and had had to be nursed back to confidence after that terrible fall at Chepstow. But all the same Mandarin had that year won each of his three starts, which included the Hennessy Gold Cup, carrying 11 st 5 lb, second top weight to Olympia and no small burden for a small horse to shoulder in a high-class handicap. No one denied that Mandarin, small as he was, had the heart of a lion. Distance, too, did not seem to matter to him, and this year he was to have on his back none other than F. T. Winter. Earlier that season Winter had had to survive the longest losing run of his career – thirty-two rides without a winner – and immediately after breaking it he broke his collarbone as well. He was back, however, in all his brilliance by the time the National Hunt Meeting came round, and he had ridden Mandarin to victory in his last race before the Gold Cup.

Despite the presence of these two it did appear as if only his own failings or mistakes could get Pas Seul beaten. Then ill-luck struck again. A week before the race he developed a kidney complaint. It was thought to have cleared up, but any set-back, however apparently slight, in a horse's preparation for a championship, can never, in fact, be a trivial one. Although he opened in the betting at odds-on there were no takers, and he drifted out to 9–4, where he remained, still favourite. Fortria was well-backed at 3–1; Mandarin was third favourite at 9–2.

The weather nearly gave Pas Seul a chance of full recovery. It froze very hard the night before the race, and right up to the advertised time for racing to begin the stewards were in two minds whether to cancel or not. Finally the decision to go on was taken, but the start was put back twenty-five minutes.

Always a front runner, Mandarin was with the leaders from the start. But he was not giving Winter a particularly reassuring ride. After the water and up the hill the second time round Winter was hard at him, and getting little response. Here Pas Seul had gone on from the outsider Cocky Consort with Fortria hard on their heels. Then, suddenly, at the top of the hill, a wide gap opened on the rails in front of Winter. With that tactical sense and quickness of thought which had served him so well in so many races, Winter seized his opportunity. He gave Mandarin one with the whip and they were through the gap in an instant. With daylight in front of him and the slope of the hill beneath him, Mandarin took hold of his bit and began to race. In what seemed like a few strides he was up to Fortria's quarters.

Pas Seul jumped the third last still in front, but he compounded almost immediately and the whole race was transformed. At the bend Fortria had taken up the running. Winter, however, had the inside, and he was pressing the Irish horse. Fortria jumped the last still a shade in front, but now Mandarin had everything he wanted to give of his best – distance, rising ground and a challenge to his courage. He also had Winter on his back, and Winter was driving him as only he could. Half-way up the hill they had Fortria collared. Both horses ran dead straight and locked together. Then, suddenly, Fortria's suspect stamina and Mandarin's great heart and courage told their respective tales. Fortria faltered – and Mandarin forged ahead and won by a length. Cocky Consort was ten lengths behind Fortria in third place. A very weary Pas Seul, having been eased by his rider, came home fifth.

This was Winter's second successive Gold Cup. It was a wonderful performance by both horse and rider, and reminiscent of Tim Molony's feat on Knock Hard. It was also a fine training achievement to have brought Mandarin back after his injuries to win this great race. All the same, both Mandarin and Fortria may well have owed their positions to Pas Seul's kidney trouble. He did make a mistake, early on, at the fence past the stands, but it was not this that stopped him. 'All I know,' said a despondent Turnell, 'is that he ran three stones below his best.' It was a fair comment.

But worse was in store for the luckless Pas Seul. He fell in his next race at Stratford, and then, in the Whitbread, again under top weight, he broke down. He was fired and brought

Fortria (P. Taaffe) leads the eventual winner of the 1962 race, Madame K. Hennessy's Mandarin (F. Winter).

home to Guildenhurst, where he spent the next eighteen months. He was only nine when injury befell him, but by the time he had returned to the racecourse another who surpassed even him had appeared on the steeplechasing scene.

After their Gold Cup victory Fred Winter and Mandarin went for the 'Grand Steeple' in Paris in June. That race has been the subject of many accounts – all of them, and rightly, couched in terms of astonishment and awe. It has no bearing on this book, save insofar as it affected the Gold Cup situation in the following year. Suffice it to say that, after the third fence, Mandarin's rubber bit snapped in two. Winter and the little horse then proceeded to give performances which have passed into history, and which only superlatives can describe. In addition to the broken bit Mandarin's suspect tendon went at the third last fence. Despite all this, they defeated the cream of French steeplechasing and put themselves forever into that special hall of fame reserved for the truly great in skill and courage.

After this feat it was announced that Mandarin, full of years and distinction, would go into honourable retirement. This left the talent for the coming Gold Cup looking remarkably thin on the ground.

Pas Seul was out for the season; Fortria would have another year on his back and be aged eleven by the time the championship came round; Frenchman's Cove had never quite shown Gold Cup class, and anyway appeared to be losing his liking for the stress of battle on the racecourse. Where, then, were the other contenders?

There was one who was thought by many to be a rising star, but he was only five at the beginning of the season. Mill House was by the famous chasing sire King Hal out of a mare called Nas Na Riogh owned by the famous hotelier, Mrs Lawlor of Naas. Nas Na Riogh was a small mare, yet her most famous son stood fully 17 hands 2 inches. For all his build he moved like a bar of music and, at his best, the power and fluency of his jumping was such as to make even hardened observers gasp.

It was Dave Dick who was responsible for him coming to England. He rode him at Punchestown in a big novice hurdle in 1961. Although he fell, it was not before he had shown Dick that he was something quite out of the ordinary. Dick passed the word on, and eventually Syd Dale, the Epsom trainer, bought Mill House for a client, the wealthy advertising man, Mr Bill Gollings, who was looking for something extra special to carry his colours. The price was said to have been £7,500, a steep one indeed for those days.

The form Mill House showed in his novice races was inclined to the erratic. When he won, he won with brilliance. His stride, even then, was stupendous, and his jumping, when he got it right, pulverising. At that time the trouble was that he did not always, or nearly always, for that matter, get it right.

In his introduction to fences at Hurst Park he made a succession of mistakes which culminated in a crashing fall. This left his confidence badly shaken. Next time out, at Cheltenham, Tim Brookshaw had the ride. He found himself almost on the floor over the first two fences. After that he pulled the big horse out and rode him as if in a school. Gradually, during that race, Brookshaw brought Mill House's confidence back. Down the hill he really started to go, and he won, hard held, by two lengths. His great stride and speed over his fences, once he had got going, simply crushed the opposition. After the race, however, Brookshaw made a remark that was later to prove significant. 'It was not that we accelerated,' he said, 'the others came back.' The date was April 18th, and that was his last race of the 1961/62 season.

By the time the next season had come round Mill House had changed stables, for Mr Gollings had sent him to be trained by Fulke Walwyn at Lambourn. Mr Gollings' belief in his big horse was absolute. He was determined, novice though he was, that he would run in the coming Gold Cup and, what is more, he was certain he was going to win it. As long ago as the beginning of the preceding season Ralph Freeman, the London commission agent, had laid him 200–1 to £50 each way that Mill House would not win the Gold Cup in 1963, and Mr Gollings had taken the bet. He also had £50 each way with Ladbroke's at 100–1.

Mill House first came out at Sandown in the new season on November 10th. Ridden by G. W. Robinson, an ex-amateur from Ireland who had just been given the Walwyn retainer,

The 1963 field parading before the start.

he won easily and well-backed at 7–2. He was a short-priced favourite at Kempton twelve days later. King's Nephew beat him there, but jumping errors probably cost him the race. At Sandown again on December 15th, despite a mistake at the last, he won like a real champion. Then the weather closed in.

The King George VI at Kempton was the first big race to be abandoned through snow. It was by no means the last. From Christmas until early March the whole of England was in the grip of snow and ice. Day after day had to be sacrificed. Ninety-four days was the total that was ultimately added up, and it was not until Newbury on March 8th that racing could commence again.

During the long lay-off trainers had to keep their strings on the move as best they could. Other followers of the sport could only huddle over their firesides and talk. Mostly they talked about Mill House. He was now only a six-year-old, barely out of the novice class, and many who did not know of Mr Gollings' belief in his horse and his substantial wagers wondered if Walwyn would run him at all in the Gold Cup. But Walwyn had already won the championship with one handsome novice, Mont Tremblant, and, looking at the possible opposition, there seemed no reason why he should not repeat the achievement.

Mill House (*left*), winner by 12 lengths of the 1963 race, seen here running in the 1964 Hennessy Gold Cup.

Racing in Ireland was not quite as restricted as it was across the water, and Fortria was given an outing at Baldoyle. It was a two-mile chase – his best distance – and, although he was known to be in need of the race, he hardly distinguished himself by finishing sixth to the handicapper Brown Diamond. Frenchman's Cove was sent to Ireland to run in the Leopardstown Chase as his warming-up race, but he, too, did not add to his reputation by finishing well down the field.

Thus they all came to the big race with very little public form behind them. So resplendent did Mill House look on the day, however, dwarfing his rivals in size and far outstripping them in scope and class, and such was the stable confidence behind him, that he was quickly made and stayed favourite at 9–2. The ground was soft and it was thought that this might just be against him because of his size and stride, but this made no difference to the flood of public money for him.

The story of the race needs little telling. Mill House just galloped and jumped the rest of them into the ground. At the top of the hill the second time, Pat Taaffe tried to get Fortria on terms with him. It was a vain effort. Mill House simply strode away as he liked. He won without ever being off the bit, by the easiest of ten lengths. It could well have been twenty.

Then the superlatives began to fly about. He was hailed as the greatest steeplechasing prospect since Golden Miller. No horse, it was said, could live with such galloping allied to the spread, power and speed of his jumping. Almost everywhere he was proclaimed to be unbeatable. His exuberant owner collected £5,958 in stakes and about £25,000 in bets. He had, moreover, struck a similar bet with Mr Freeman that his horse would repeat his feat the following year.

It is easy to display the wisdom of hindsight, but it has to be said that amidst all the extravagant praise and publicity that flew about after the race one or two things were overlooked. 'It's not what he did but the way that he did it,' is a racing maxim which can and often does prove misleading. Mill House, in fact, beat a very sub-standard field in that Gold Cup. Fortria was past his best; he never really got the trip; he had been hobdayed, which may have taken the edge off his speed, and he hated the ground. Frenchman's Cove, the only other pretender to top class, was daily displaying a greater and greater dislike for the stern business of racing and, during the running, clouted each and every one of the open ditches good and hard, Mellor actually landing with his arms over his head at the second. The rest were either has-beens or handicappers. Moreover, Mill House had never yet been really tackled by a top-notcher and, free-runner that he was, he had never yet shown that he could accelerate.

Most important of all was another portent that was overlooked, save by a few percipient critics of whom Tom Nickalls, the leading writer on *Sporting Life*, was the chief.

On the first day of the meeting the Broadway Novices Chase was run over a distance just exceeding three miles. This was won every bit as impressively as Mill House had won the Gold Cup by another six-year-old. And he was announced as a certain runner in the Gold Cup the following year. He was trained by Tom Dreaper in Ireland. His name was Arkle.

11

Magnifico

'ARKLE', A VERY famous Irish trainer has said to the present writer, 'was extraordinarily lucky to find himself in the stable he did. They knew he needed time and were prepared to give it to him.'

Tom Dreaper never rushed his horses. His was a non-betting stable and his owners mostly rich men and women who understood horses and racing. Not terribly concerned about hurdling, the horses at Kilsallaghan were, therefore, for the most part built on steeplechasing lines. They were bought to run and race with the best, and trained by a master of his craft to do just that. This kind of horse needed time, and Tom Dreaper saw that he got it. His horses were never hurried. Patience, kindness, sympathy were the keywords, or some of them, to Dreaper's success. In Pat Taaffe, during all those years of unbroken association, he had as first jockey a man of courage and understanding that brought out the best in the great horses who thronged the yard. The same policies are, of course, now being pursued by his son, Jim, who has succeeded him.

Time, indeed, at first, was what Arkle needed above all things. He was by Archive, a useless racehorse himself who was nevertheless very well bred, being by Nearco out of Booklaw by Buchan out of Popingaol, and he had already sired Mariner's Log, second in the Gold Cup in 1954. His dam, Bright Cherry, was a mare with a chasing pedigree, and was no mean performer herself up to two-and-a-half miles.

It was Anne, Duchess of Westminster, his owner throughout his racing career, who spotted Arkle at Goff's Horse Show sales in Dublin in 1960. He was then a three-year-old, and she took Tom Dreaper to see him. He was not at that time a particularly prepossessing individual. 'Buy him if you like,' Tom Dreaper told the Duchess, 'but remember his dam never stayed an inch over two-and-a-half miles.'

Buy him she did, paying 1,150 guineas for him and bringing him over to Eaton Lodge in Cheshire. When he was four Tom Dreaper visited the Duchess to choose which of her horses he would train for her. Although not altogether impressed by Arkle's looks, for his hocks especially appeared then to be a weak feature in his conformation, Dreaper had an affection for the dam's breeding. He had ridden the grand-dam, Greenogue Princess, in point-to-points and knew well her toughness and courage. Greenogue Princess, too, was by My Prince – that marvellous sire of steeplechasers who was the parent of Prince Regent with whom Dreaper had won his first Gold Cup. Furthermore she had bred no less than twelve winners and Bright Cherry had won six steeplechases. By now the Duchess had named the gelding Arkle after a mountain on one of the Westminster estates in Scotland, and Tom Dreaper decided to have him.

When he came to Kilsallaghan Arkle was still gawky, unfurnished and a bad mover, especially behind. Generally, in the yard, he was not thought to be of much account. He had his first run in a bumper flat race at Mullingar just before he turned five.

Here he ran well enough to finish third, and at the Christmas Meeting at Leopardstown he was fourth in another bumper. As yet, however, he had not shown anything approaching brilliance. Then, unfancied and allowed to start at 20-1, he won a three-mile novice hurdle at Navan, far out-pointing the stable choice, Kerforo, which Pat Taaffe rode. This was the first time he displayed a flash of the phenomenon he was to become, for he simply went away from his field at the finish almost as if there was another gear available, had it been required. He had three more hurdle races that year, and won one of them.

After a summer's rest he came back to win a hurdle at Dundalk, which was followed by an easy victory in The President's Hurdle at Gowran Park, one of the principal races in Irish hurdling. He cut an artery in this race. Such, however, was his health and condition that, although Dreaper asked permission to bind it up before the dope test which is obligatory in Irish racing, it staunched itself before the bandage could be applied. But ever afterwards he was inclined to strike into himself when racing.

Now, at the age of five, he was just commencing to come to himself. The enormous depth through the heart, which is probably where the fantastic propulsion came from, was by this time beginning to be apparent. He was ready for his first steeplechase. There was never any suggestion of pushing him, but his very experienced trainer had at this time appreciated the potential that lay in him. His ultimate objective was the Gold Cup, though there was no question of subjecting him to this test so early in his career however well he came through these preparatory races.

Dreaper, however, knew that he was good enough to take on the smart English novices, and he was interested to see how he would fare against them and over English fences. On the same day that Fortria was sent to Cheltenham for the Mackeson Gold Cup, Arkle accompanied him to run in The Honeybourne Chase over two miles four furlongs.

Arkle's jumping was never as spectacular as that of his rival, Mill House. On the other hand, the sort of jumping powers Mill House displayed often court disaster and sometimes result in it, however strong and powerful the horse. Over his fences Arkle more resembled Golden Miller. Like Golden Miller, too, he never fell in a steeplechase. He was clean, economical and quick. Thus his great strength was conserved for the vital place where it was wanted – from the last fence to the line. In this, his first steeplechase, he did not blind the opposition with great leaps nor astound watchers with a free-running and devastating display of jumping. But he did something else. When Pat Taaffe let him go he showed he possessed the one essential attribute of a really great horse – the ability to accelerate. He won that race by no less than twenty lengths from opposition that was far from second class. He did it again in February at Leopardstown, and it has already been related how he won the Broadway Novices at Cheltenham a month later. He then took The Power Gold Cup, the most important novice race in Ireland, with contemptuous ease, and followed that by

winning the big novice at Punchestown as he liked. In all, that year, he had seven starts and, so far from being beaten, he was never extended.

He spent the summer, as he was always to do, on his owner's farm at Maynooth in County Kildare, and then went back to Kilsallaghan for his first tilt at the Championship. He had now built up from hip to hock, and this defect, if it was one, was to be further overcome as he came to full maturity during the year. There was still, however, the flaw from the hock down. He was, to use his trainer's phrase, 'a shade wide of his elbow' and was to remain so in his gallop to the end of his career.

The Dreapers had also discovered one curious fact about him. Each year, before the beginning of racing, he seemed to sense that a new season with its attendant excitements and clash of competition was about to start. He was possessed, of course, of exceptional intelligence. This, it appeared, enabled him to anticipate what was in store for him during the coming months and, with anticipation, came an unsettling eagerness to get on with it. He would sweat up in his box and out of it, and, for one normally so placid, begin to display unexpected signs of nerves and over-excitement. To cure this state they adopted a simple ruse that was found to work perfectly. He was put into a horsebox, driven to a racecourse and left there for an hour or so. Then he was taken home again. After the trip he immediately settled down and became his usually calm and placid self. Another peculiarity was that, like many humans, he did not welcome the attentions of the dentist and, towards the end of his career, he did not like being plaited up, so this practice was abandoned.

He began his campaign that season by winning a one mile six furlong flat race at Navan in the hands of T. P. Burns. He then went for the Carey's Cottage Chase over two miles four furlongs at Gowran Park. This was a race often chosen for top-class horses in Ireland to open their season's campaign. He won it with some ease. It was then announced that he and Mill House would meet on November 30th at Newbury in The Hennessy Gold Cup.

Mill House did not have a race before this encounter, in which he was set to give Arkle 5 lb. But what Mill House did have was a publicity build-up of quite astonishing proportions. He was said to be the steeplechaser of the century, unbeatable, a sort of amalgam of all the great horses that had won the Gold Cup rolled into one. No one near him would hear of defeat or anything approaching it.

The race was run in misty weather on ground that was soft and slippery. Mill House jumped into the lead at the first. He went on to give what appeared to be an unconquerable display of galloping and jumping in front of a high-class field. While the pride of Lambourn delighted his connections and the crowd with his great leaps and mighty stride, Arkle was nicely placed and doing just what he had to do and no more. Five from home he made a slight mistake, but it did nothing to check him, and, coming to the third last, Taaffe had moved him quietly up to Mill House. Here the leader threw another of his great leaps. Arkle appeared to take off with him. He slipped on landing, sprawled, and his race was gone. Mill House won by eight lengths from Happy Spring, who just beat Arkle for third place.

For the supporters of Mill House their triumph was complete, and they let it be known far and wide. From the stands that misty day it did indeed look as if the big horse had jumped his rival down. He had beaten him by eight and three-quarter lengths when giving

(OPPOSITE) Arkle and Paddy Woods on the lane to the gallops at Greenogue.

him 5 lb. Arkle could never make that up; he would never beat Mill House, wherever or whenever they met again, Mill House's jubilant supporters cried.

There were some, however, who were not so sure, though they kept their opinions rather more to themselves. Mill House, they thought, had once more failed to show that he could accelerate. In fact he looked tired enough ploughing home through the mud to his hollow victory over Happy Spring. Pat Taaffe, too, had his own opinion about the way the race had gone. At that time even he had not quite realised the quality of the racing machine he had under him, nor had he fully appreciated the colossal finishing speed he had in hand. Thinking it over, he came to the conclusion, as he told his trainer afterwards, that he had given Arkle a kick a stride too soon, with the result that his horse had stood off too far and slipped on landing. Thereafter he made up his mind that there was no need to push him into his fences, nor did he ever do so again in any of his races. A friend of his, standing by the fence, had examined the ground when the field had passed by. This examination convinced him that Arkle had struck a hole, and that it was this which had caused the slip. 'Don't worry, you'll win the Gold Cup', he told Taaffe afterwards.

But the whole of racing England, knowing nothing of any of these things, rejoiced. Mill House, having frightened off all the worthwhile opposition by his very presence, won a three-horse race for the King George VI Chase on Boxing Day just as he liked. On the same day, at Leopardstown, Arkle beat a better field, giving weight away all round. He was building up and strengthening fast now, and just over a month later he slammed another good field, again carrying 12 st, in the important Thyestes Chase at Gowran Park. He then went for the Leopardstown Chase on February 15th, and many of the English press came over to have a look at him.

Once more the ground was very heavy, and once more Arkle was set to give weight away all round. Flying Wild, a useful mare belonging to Raymond Guest, took him on at the second last and fell. He came home alone to win by an untroubled twelve lengths. It was not spectacular, nor breath-taking, nor any of the other adjectives which were currently being applied to Mill House. Most of the English representatives who returned to see their champion spreadeagle a moderate field at Sandown a few days later were content to write him off as a serious challenger.

So the day for the return match came round. The connections of Mill House were exuberantly confident. It seemed, oddly enough, as if the characteristics of the two nations were for once reversed. The taciturn English were loud and lavish in their pride and praise of Mill House, whereas the usually vociferous Irish were quiet and subdued, and content to await the outcome.

Taaffe and Robinson, the riders of the two horses, were firm friends. They had a bet between each other of a suit of clothes on the result of the race, and before it started they gave a television interview. In this Robinson exuded confidence. He would, he thought, gallop and jump Arkle into the ground. Taaffe quietly pointed to Arkle's remarkable powers of acceleration. They did not matter, Robinson felt, for Arkle would never get near enough to use them. Taaffe pointed to Arkle being much superior to Fortria, second to Mill House the year before, but the confidence behind the big horse remained unshaken.

These sentiments were virtually an echo of what everyone in racing England was feeling that day about Mill House.

Pas Seul was also in the field, but Pas Seul, though he had won a race at Kempton in January, was only a shadow of his former self. King's Nephew made up the fourth, and was the only other runner. Sad though it was to relegate Pas Seul to this lowly estate, the plain fact remained that neither of them mattered. The race was a match, and everyone knew it.

When they entered the ring the sense of occasion was immense, and the air was taut with rivalry. Just to heighten matters a sudden snow storm blew up and blotted out Cleeve Hill. As the storm eddied and flurried, Wing Commander Vaux came across to Tom Dreaper, and wondered if they would be able to run the race at all. 'The way I felt "down the middle" just then,' Tom Dreaper said afterwards, 'I wanted to tell him to let them go right away, storm, snow or anything else.'

The blizzard, in fact, went as quickly as it had come. The visibility was perfect as they paraded, and Mill House came back like a ballet dancer – 'as if he wouldn't crack eggs under him'. For a big horse he moved with astonishing grace and lightness. He looked and seemed unbeatable then. Arkle, by contrast, was less flashy. He provoked no murmur of admiration from the crowd as did Mill House, but he was hard and workmanlike, and ready to run for his life. Mill House was favourite at 13–8 on; Arkle 7–4 against.

Mill House jumped straight away into the lead, and delighted his supporters with the extravagant speed and power of his fencing. Arkle, pulling hard, was settled down with about four lengths between them. The champion met the open ditch in front of the stands all wrong, but the mistake hardly made him pause in his stride. He flung the next one behind him and then went for the water. The other two were out of it by now, and here the battle was really joined.

Robinson went on trying to fulfil his threat of losing Arkle. But all the time, like some menacing shadow, Taaffe tracked him. At the top of the hill he was still there, hard held behind the champion, and a real and living threat to his vaunted supremacy.

The two horses came down the hill at a terrific pace. Mill House had the inside, but he was gaining no ground. Arkle could close when he liked and signs of defeat were already in front of Robinson. His only chance was to gain in the air over the next. He hurled the big horse into it with the utmost bravery and brilliance. But it availed him nothing. His rival was still at his heels. He did the same at the next, with the same result. By now it was apparent that Taaffe was only biding his time.

As they came to the elbow Robinson went for his whip. There was a gasp of dismay from the crowd as they saw his arm go up. Then Arkle proved once and for all where the reality of greatness lay between the two. Taaffe asked him to go and in three strides he settled the issue. Without effort he surged into the full power of his finishing speed and left his rival beaten and struggling behind him. He was over the last clear and on the bit. Up the hill he simply strode away to win by an untroubled five lengths, a champion of champions.

Robinson lost his whip between the last two fences, but he was the first to say it made no difference. The two jockeys shook hands as they came back to the winners' enclosure. Afterwards there was talk of Mill House requiring a pacemaker and being provided with one the following year, but his immediate connections took the humiliation of their favourite with stoicism and grace. Mr Bill Gollings raised his bowler in symbolic salute as Arkle left the enclosure and Fulke Walwyn made no excuses. 'Mill House has come out of the race sound and well,' he told his friend Clive Graham afterwards, and added: 'I can still hardly

Arkle clears the last fence to win the 1964 Hennessy Gold Cup.

believe that any horse breathing could have done what Arkle did to him.' It was a fair and handsome comment in defeat, and served to underline the greatness of the joint achievement of Arkle and his trainer.

After that race the paths of Arkle and Mill House diverged. It was decided to give Mill House an opportunity of rehabilitating himself in the Whitbread, while Arkle went for the Irish Grand National.

By this time, looking at the results of his last three races - The Gold Cup, The Leopardstown Chase and Thyestes - it was apparent to the Irish stewards that they had no horse in their country within 21 lb of him. This made a virtual nonsense of the handicap, and they therefore instructed the handicapper that if he allotted a horse a weight of 14 lb or more below the top weight to the next horse in the handicap he was to prepare a second handicap, to be known as the 'B' handicap, in which the horse originally allotted top weight should be excluded. Both handicaps were to be published at the same time, but if the horse allotted the top weight were struck out or not declared then the 'B' handicap would apply.

This system was first put into operation in the Irish Grand National that year. As Arkle ran the 'A' handicap was used. It is perhaps interesting to note that, in the handicap as published, he was set to give another horse we shall hear of again, Fort Leney, no less than 30 lb. Fort Leney, also an occupant of the powerful Kilsallaghan stable, did not in fact run. In the race Arkle, carrying 12 st, beat the good mare Height of Fashion, receiving 30 lb, by one-and-a-quarter lengths, though he had to be given a slight shake up to do it. He was then retired to his summer quarters with six wins from seven starts, his only defeat being at the hands of Mill House in the Hennessy.

Mill House went to Sandown on April 25th. The going was holding, and the task he was set was a sterner one than that demanded of Arkle at Fairyhouse. Over a distance of three miles five furlongs, three furlongs more than the Irish race, he was asked to carry 12 st 7 lb, and give away a range of weights down to 9 st 7 lb. Starting favourite, he was in front at the last and looked all over a winner. Dormant, a useful handicapper who was later to gain something of a reputation as a giant-killer, was, however, closing on him. And Dormant was getting 42 lb from the big horse.

Mill House fought like a hero, but his lack of finishing speed, the crushing weight, the distance, the holding going and his own recent humiliation were all counting against him as they ran for the line. Half-way there Dormant had him collared. He went under by three lengths. His resolution in defeat regained him many admirers. He was cheered to the echo, and rightly so, as he came back to the enclosure. His was by far the best performance in the race; the honours were his if not the laurels but, in the last analysis, cheers are no substitute for defeat.

As one great star had emerged that year another left the stage. Winter retired from the saddle, the worthy recipient of the C.B.E. to mark his great services to the greatest of sports, and a guest of honour at a 'Fred Winter Tribute Luncheon' given by the Variety Club of Great Britain in the Savoy Hotel. In the following year he began a new career as a trainer, to which he brought those qualities of dedication, thoroughness, integrity and intelligence he had shown as a rider. The enormous and immediate success he achieved is written in the record books for all to see.

Arkle opened his campaign the following season with an easy victory – at 5–1 on – in The Carey's Cottage Chase at Gowran. This was just a sharpener for his repeat match against Mill House in The Hennessy on December 5th. Once more Mill House did not have an outing in public before the race.

This encounter was, perhaps, the real moment of truth between the two horses. The supporters of Mill House, though considerably more subdued, were far from being without hope. For now it was Arkle who had to defend his crown. What was more, he had to carry the full top-weight of 12 st 7 lb, and give Mill House 3 lb. There were some about who still thought he could not do it.

Arkle had, however, summered well. He had filled out; he was harder and more mature than he had been the previous season. Always easy to train and ready to eat anything, he had presented his handlers with no problems in getting him ready for this race. In the yard he was gentle and sweet in his disposition. Kind and appreciative to old and young, children and adults all came alike to him. During his preparation a visiting ex-M.F.H., aged over eighty, had ridden him and he had treated him with due respect as one gentleman to another.

But he was supremely intelligent, a trait not always noticeable in racehorses. Thus he always knew where he was, what he was about, and what was required of him. A lamb at home, he was beginning to be a lion on the racecourse. He was very well aware now of the fact that he was a champion and he intended to remain one. Earlier it had not required exceptional skill or strength to restrain him in his races. Now he was starting to take a really ferocious hold, as if to say to everyone that he knew the winner's berth was the proper place for him and that he intended getting there with as little delay as possible. What happened at Newbury on December 5th exemplified this. It dumbfounded the onlookers and con- founded those few sceptics who were left.

Arkle did to Mill House that afternoon what Mill House's supporters had once confidently predicted he would do to Arkle. He galloped and jumped him into the ground. As if to show that anything Mill House could do he could do better, straight from the first fence he took the big horse on, lying up with him instead of tracking him, matching him stride for stride. He even brushed aside the chief weapon in Mill House's armoury by taking off with him – and out-jumping him. Mill House took the punishment handed out to him as long as he could and then, under the onslaught, he cracked. Four from home he had had enough and dropped out. Finally he toiled into fourth place, thirty-two lengths behind Arkle, who beat Ferry Boat (receiving 35 lb) by ten lengths. The Rip was third.

In Arkle's next race his supporters in turn received a shock, for he was beaten, though on consideration the result hardly seemed to affect his chances in the coming Gold Cup. The race was another of the big sponsored races, the Massey-Ferguson Gold Cup at Cheltenham. Over two miles five furlongs, a distance surely too short for him to display his real powers, he went under by a head and a length to two useful horses, the mare Flying Wild and Buona Notte, who had won the first running of the Totalisator Novices Chase at the National Hunt Meeting the year before. Since Arkle carried 12 st 10 lb and gave the winner 32 lb and the second 26 lb, this could not be considered a serious blot on his record. Next time out he won the Leopardstown Chase, once more displaying all his old authority, and was then ready to defend his championship.

Mill House, for his part, turned the tables on Dormant at Newbury, beating him a head and giving him 32 lb, and then won the Gainsborough Chase at Sandown under 12 st 5 lb. It looked a good preparation for the Gold Cup, but everyone now knew that it was not good enough. The return match should only be a formality, and this is how it turned out. This year the full New Course was run over for the first time, and the Gold Cup was started from the chute in the same place as the Foxhunter's Chase.

Only two others took on the cracks – Caduval and Stoney Crossing. The latter deserves a further word. He was owned and ridden by Mr Bill Roycroft, a sporting Australian who, aged fifty-one, had never before jumped either fences or hurdles in public. He had, however, won on the flat, and had been a member of the Australian Olympic team at Tokyo. Mr Roycroft was indeed taking something on and, to add to the originality of his effort, he announced that his next objective would be the Foxhunters at Liverpool; after that he and his mount would revert to three-day-eventing at Badminton. It was an interesting pro- gramme for a Gold Cup horse!

(OPPOSITE) Anne, Duchess of Westminster leads in Arkle after he had won the 1965 Gold Cup.

At the time of the Gold Cup of that year Arkle, at the age of eight, had really come into the fulfilment of his splendid maturity. Before he had been a conqueror; now he was a king. And well he knew it. There was pride in his bearing and majesty in his mien as he paraded before the crowd in front of the stands. He had his crown, and he intended keeping it. On firm, hard, going he simply strolled away with his second Gold Cup, leaving the luckless Mill House toiling twenty lengths behind at the post. Mr Roycroft was repaid for his sporting effort to the tune of £1,089 for occupying third place, albeit a further thirty lengths behind Mill House.

Arkle was then sent for what may well have been his greatest test of all – The Whitbread.

The Whitbread Gold Cup, coming as it does at the very end of the season and being run over the extended distance of three miles five furlongs, has provided upsets in abundance during its short history. It has also proved the grave of reputations, and has dashed the hopes and aspirations of many good horses. Champions defeated under big weights in this race seem to take a long time to come back – if they do at all.

None of this counted for anything with Arkle. Carrying 12 st 7 lb, in the words of the form book he 'made all, drew clear approaching 2 out', beating Brasher as he liked by five lengths. Brasher carried 10 st, as did Overcourt; the rest of the field were on 9 st 7 lb. The figures speak for themselves.

Now, indeed, the champion bestrode the steeplechasing scene like a Colossus. There was no one remotely near him, for Mill House could scarcely be regarded as a rival let alone a contender any more. The English handicapper, at the beginning of the following season, was to put the big horse 16 lb below his conqueror, and many thought he could well have made the difference greater. It was obvious that, bar accident, Arkle could and would run up a string of victories in the Gold Cup – but what else was there for him?

His owner had definitely stated that he would never contest a Grand National, since the risk of interference and injury by loose horses was too great. 'The Duchess could ride him in the Newmarket Town Plate,' was Tom Dreaper's joking response when asked about future plans after his second Gold Cup victory. The Grand Steeplechase de Paris was mentioned as a definite possibility – and had he run, what a race that would have been! But for the present another Gold Cup was the immediate objective.

During the summer he was blistered for a joint jarred in the Whitbread, but it was nothing of consequence, and he was back to meet Mill House once more in a new sponsored race, The Gallagher Gold Cup, at Sandown on November 6th. As has been said, the difference in the weights was now 16 lb. He strolled away with the race, beating Rondetto (receiving 26 lb) by ten lengths, with Mill House toiling away again, a further four lengths away, third. In doing so, just by the way, as it were, he set up a new time record for Sandown.

In his next appearance he beat Freddie by fifteen lengths in the Hennessy. Although the distance of his victory in this race was of the magnitude that has been stated, nevertheless he had to get into top gear to achieve it. Brasher, too, had taken him on jumping down the back stretch, and had stuck to him for a few fences before he faded. Such was Arkle's reputation at the time that, even to have him tackled at all, made some critics wonder if the

(OPPOSITE) Mrs Linder with her sculpture of Arkle – Arkle looks on.

superb cutting edge of his speed was beginning to wear a little fine. It is sufficient comment on this to point once again to the distances, and to say that Freddie, a very useful and consistent horse, had been second in the National the year before under the steadier of 11 st 10 lb, and was now receiving 32 lb!

After an easy win at Ascot, Arkle went on to collect the King George VI at Kempton, beating Dormant by a distance. His next and only other race before the Gold Cup was the Leopardstown Chase. Before this race a vile period of apparently unending rain set in all over Ireland. It proved exceedingly difficult to give Arkle the work he required, and the race itself was postponed twice. Badly in need of the race, in heavy going, he was set to give the game little mare, Height of Fashion, 42 lb, and he had to run for his life to do it, only beating her by a neck. No one, however, really thought this in any way lessened his chances in the championship.

It was said that Mill House was to be subjected to another tilt at him in the coming race – and another inevitable hammering if the form book was any guide – but in fact he developed tendon trouble, and was out for the season.

There was, however, a big rangy chestnut in Tom Dreaper's yard called Flyingbolt, who was thought by many to be likely to make the champion look to his laurels. He had put up such spectacular performances in winning his last races that the 'A' and 'B' handicapping system in Ireland had to be scrapped, and was replaced by the extended handicap which is at present in use. But Flyingbolt was then only seven. It was decided not to pit him against the champion, and he contested the Champion Hurdle instead, finishing a creditable third.

The Gold Cup was considered to be a mere walk-over for Arkle, and this was how it turned out to be. It was not, however, an uneventful race, and Arkle provided his own sensation. Now in the fullness of his great strength and stride, his jumping was of a speed and power which matched or surpassed Mill House at his best. None of the other four horses in the race could, of course, live with him. He came to the eleventh fence, the last on the first circuit, moving with ease and grace; the race, even at that stage, handsomely won.

Perhaps it all seemed to him too easy. In any event, for whatever reason, he just did not look at the fence. Instead he concentrated his attention on the packed stands, many of whose occupants were already beginning to cheer their champion. As a result he took the fence by the roots and went straight through it. Scarcely believable though it may be, the mistake, which must without fail have floored any ordinary horse, did not even check him in his stride, nor did Taaffe move in the saddle. Without hesitation or pause they galloped remorselessly on, increasing their lead as they went. The final verdict was a thirty lengths win from Dormant. The other runners, if it matters, were Snaigow, Sartorius and Hunch – who fell three out and was killed. The race was run on St Patrick's Day. Arkle had a bunch of shamrock on his browband, and it was this, and St Patrick having backed him, it was said in the stable, that saved him from the consequences of his mistake!

He did not run again that season. Bad weather stopped him in his work, and it was very wisely decided not to submit him to another ordeal in the Whitbread on rain-soaked ground.

Dreaper's other crack, Flyingbolt, took the Irish Grand National, giving Height of Fashion 36 lb and beating her by two lengths. It is interesting to note that the Irish

(OPPOSITE) Pat Taaffe and Arkle clear the last fence to make it three in a row, 1966.

Anne, Duchess of Westminster with Arkle at Kempton Park stables following his injury in the King George VI Chase, 1966.

handicapper allotted Arkle 12 st 7 lb, and Flyingbolt 12 st 5 lb in the next handicap he made up that included them both. As he says, if Arkle was the best horse who won the Gold Cup, on the book, at least, Flyingbolt must be the best horse never to have won it.

Arkle's next appearance was his third Hennessy Gold Cup in November 1965. As always now he was, of course, top of the handicap, and he had 12 st 7 lb to carry. To everyone's astonishment and dismay he was caught by Stalbridge Colonist after the last, and beaten half-a-length. Stalbridge Colonist was getting 31 lb, but if Arkle was as good as he had been the other still should not have got near him.

The great British public had by this time taken Arkle to their hearts. Television had brought him to countless homes that until now had never thought of steeplechasing. His presence, dignity and wonderful achievements combined with the modesty and charm of his great rider had made him a universal favourite. To the many people who knew little of racing but who loved him, his defeat was unthinkable. There was an immediate and uninformed outcry that Arkle was being crippled by the great weights he had to carry.

The complaints had, of course, no substance at all though they did serve to show how a great horse can project himself and his image beyond the confines of the enclosed world of racing and racing people to capture the imagination of the whole public. The fact was that Arkle had been stopped in his work before that race. He had dragged his hind legs through a hurdle when schooling, and torn off a flap of skin in a manner reminiscent of the accident to Knock Hard. Ken Cundell told Mrs Dreaper afterwards that he knew they could never have beaten Arkle, even at the difference of the weights, had he been at his best.

He was indeed at his brilliant best in pulverising a field to whom he was giving the usual stones of weight away in the S.G.B. Chase at Ascot on December 14th. Then he was aimed at another win in the King George VI at Kempton.

Hard ground made the Kempton executive put the race back from Boxing Day to December 27th. Arkle was opposed by a pretty nondescript field which did, however, include Woodland Venture and Dormant.

The tragedy of the race is soon told. The ground may well have retained some slip in it after the frost; at all events, coming to the fourteenth, an open ditch, Arkle appeared not to take off properly. He hit the guard rail very hard, but galloped on, apparently unscathed and certainly, for the moment at any rate, unchecked. But at the second last Woodland Venture headed him. This did not look like the true Arkle. Woodland Venture fell here and the champion came to the last clear of Dormant. He jumped it all wrong and landed awkwardly. Up the straight he was in obvious difficulties, and labouring. Dormant came and caught him to win by a length. Clearly something was dreadfully amiss. Taaffe, coming back to scale, thought he had broken down.

In fact, as a listening world soon learnt, he had cracked a pedal bone in his off fore. As soon as he was well enough to be moved he was flown back to Ireland and installed in his own box at Kilsallaghan. At first there were hopes that he might respond to treatment sufficiently well to be able in time to race again. Eventually, however, the hopes dwindled. Despite the get-well cards that flowed in from all over the world to decorate his box, the prayers, the well-wishers who flocked in such abundance to the stables that the assistance of Securicor had to be called in to control them, it became clear that he was not responding to treatment sufficiently to ensure his reappearance on the racecourse. With infinite reluctance and regret it was announced that the greatest of them all would be retired forever, and would not race again.

Tom Dreaper was convinced that, at the time of his injury, Arkle was as good as ever he was and would have gone on to greater and greater things had he been spared. There can be little doubt that he was right. The mighty heart had shown no signs of flagging, the brilliant speed was still there. No horse then running could even think of living with him at anything approaching level weights. The Gold Cup for years to come looked entirely at his mercy.

He had won, in all, £75,206, in stakes, a huge sum for a steeplechaser even allowing for the tremendous increase in prize money resulting from sponsorship. But he had done far more than that. He had made himself into a world figure on a scale that no other steeplechase horse – and very few on the flat – has ever approached. He had brought back the crowds to the courses and, through the medium of television, made countless people who had scarcely heard of it before respond to the stir and struggle and excitement of steeplechasing. With his power, presence and dignity, he was a figure who inspired warmth and affection in the hearts of those who watched him perform. There was in him, too, something that made an especial appeal to the young, and with his enforced retirement a unique and irreplaceable figure went out of steeplechasing.

Arkle comes out of retirement to make a special appearance at the Horse of the Year Show. With him are Anne, Duchess of Westminster and Tom Dreaper.

12

Later Days

ALWAYS WHEN A great actor passes from the scene he leaves a sense of anti-climax behind him. With the disappearance of Arkle, this was indeed the case in the Gold Cup of 1967. To make matters worse for the Dreaper stable in particular and steeplechasing in general, the other rising star, Flyingbolt, suffered an operation for warts and was subsequently retired for the season. Thus none of the horses left to contest the championship were within 2 st of the reigning monarch who had had so sadly and suddenly to abandon his throne. Dreaper did have a third string in Fort Leney, owned by Colonel John Thomson, a Director of Barclays Bank, and bred by him. Fort Leney was by Fortina and out of Colonel Thomson's good mare Leney Princess. He was thus bred to chasing, and that he was more than useful he proved in winning the Troytown Chase at Navan and the Leopardstown Christmas Chase, by eight lengths in each case, and giving away big weights.

One wonders what either Arkle or Flyingbolt would have done to the rest of them including Fort Leney – had they been able to run, for it is interesting to note that after the Leopardstown Chase the Irish handicapper, Captain Louis Magee, had he been asked to do so, would have rated the three horses as follows: Arkle 12 st 7 lb; Flyingbolt 12 st 5 lb, and Fort Leney 10 st 12 lb.

Fort Leney went on to win the Leopardstown Chase under 12 st 4 lb by fifteen lengths, giving lumps of weight away all round and thus looking a very live Gold Cup prospect. But misfortune had not done with Tom Dreaper that season. In the Haydock Park National Trial Chase a horse called Thorn Gate fell at the second fence, fracturing Pat Taaffe's thigh. So, in the space of a few months, the Kilsallaghan stable had lost their two best horses and their first jockey. But the other contenders for the championship, on paper at least, with one notable exception, looked far from formidable.

The exception was Mill House. His tendon had been fired and the result was said to have been successful. He had had a rest for eleven months to recover from whatever ill effects the punishment he had received at the hands of Arkle had left behind. At the turn of the year he was only ten; the avowed intention of his connections was to regain his crown for him – and Arkle was out of the way.

Mill House had a couple of outings in the first half of the season, but his real warming-up race was the one which had often been chosen for him before – The Gainsborough Chase at

Sandown. He galloped and jumped in quite his old style to beat What A Myth by a length. Since they were level weights this did not look quite good enough, and by the time the National Hunt Meeting came round, Walwyn, too, had lost his first jockey, for Robinson had broken his ankle in a hurdle race. David Nicholson was booked to ride Mill House and Peter McLoughlin, a claiming jockey in Dreaper's yard, who had ridden Fort Leney throughout the season, kept the mount on the Irish horse.

Compared to the phenomenon that had gone before, the field may have looked second rate but, apart from the two who have been mentioned, as the season went on it showed that there were other useful horses about.

Stalbridge Colonist who, as we have seen, was one of the two horses who had had the distinction of beating Arkle in his prime (both, oddly enough, greys) was in it, as was Woodland Venture, who had been upsides with Arkle two out in Arkle's last ill-fated race; Dormant, who had beaten Mill House in the Whitbread and had passed the injured Arkle to beat him at Kempton; and the sometimes brilliant What A Myth, who was not far behind Mill House on current form.

Woodland Venture was to be ridden by Terry Biddlecombe, and Stalbridge Colonist by Stan Mellor. Biddlecombe had been champion jockey for the past two seasons. Tall, and of similar build to Pat Taaffe, Biddlecombe, like Taaffe, rode very short but, also like Taaffe, he could sit on a horse until he was virtually upside down. Mellor had been champion for three years at the beginning of the decade. He had survived appalling injuries to go on riding with his nerve and dash quite unimpaired. In his slight body there was an unquenchable will. Unorthodox in style, horses ran for him. He was later to ride more winners than any other steeplechase jockey in history and was – and is – one of the best ambassadors for the sport it has ever known.

The start of the race was delayed by Stalbridge Colonist, who spread a plate and had to be re-shod. It was an odd coincidence that the Derby that year had also been delayed by a similar occurrence to Charlottown. Some took it to be an omen in Stalbridge Colonist's favour for Charlottown, who had been last out of the Epsom ring, had been first home.

Mill House looked his magnificent and commanding self but backers fought shy of him, for there were reports of a muscle injury to his back. They made Fort Leney favourite at 11–4, despite the fact that he was said to need more give in the ground. What A Myth, a soft ground specialist, oddly enough was second favourite at 3–1, a point shorter than Mill House.

As it turned out none of these horses played any part in the finish. Fort Leney hit the second fence very hard and was never in the race after it; Mill House lobbed along in front at a steady pace until the last open ditch, which he simply took out for no apparent reason, and that was that; What A Myth's jumping, too, was far from perfect and, with the ground against him, he was at no time really in the battle.

Three fences out the race was between Stalbridge Colonist and Woodland Venture. On the top of the ground these two came for home at a great pace. Mellor had the grey a neck

(OPPOSITE, ABOVE) Woodland Venture (2) (Terry Biddlecombe up) taking the last fence in the 1967 race to win from Stalbridge Colonist (Stan Mellor up).
(BELOW) A smiling Terry Biddlecombe unsaddles Woodland Venture.

in front at the second last but, coming to the last, Woodland Venture was upsides of him. Both horses and jockeys were now flat out. Woodland Venture gained a little in the air over the last and landed a shade in front. But the grey came back at him under the swinging of Mellor's whip. They went up the hill locked together. Woodland Venture, the bigger horse, just held on to win by three parts of a length.

Woodland Venture's win was another triumph for a small and sporting breeder and for skilful training. Mr Harry Collins, a Somerset farmer, had bred the new champion himself. He was the first foal of his dam, Woodlander, whom Mr Collins had bought from Mr Sydney McGregor, breeder of April The Fifth, who won the Derby for the actor-trainer Tom Walls in 1932. Domaha had refused to cover Woodlander, so she was sent to Eastern Venture and the result was a Gold Cup winner. Woodland Venture had not been easy to train that season for he had had ringworm, then the fall in Arkle's race had badly shaken his confidence, and after that he had had trouble with his teeth. It was a first Gold Cup for Fred Rimell, who had also missed winning it as a jockey. Another point of interest in this race is that it was Mr Harry Dufosee who advised his friend Mr Collins to send the mare to Eastern Venture, and it was his advice also which led to the breeding of Stalbridge Colonist. In the uncertain business of breeding steeplechasers, to be responsible for the first and second in a Gold Cup is indeed an achievement.

The following season was interrupted by the plague of foot-and-mouth disease. Before this, however, it became certain that a new champion would have to be sought, since Woodland Venture went wrong and was immediately retired.

Fort Leney had suffered from intermittent heart trouble over the years. At one time a specialist had expressed the opinion that if he were to race again he must never be ridden hard or touched with the whip. It looked then as if he might have to be retired for when Taaffe rode him tenderly he simply pulled himself up and would not race at all. Nevertheless Taaffe knew that Fort Leney loved racing but to give of his best he needed to be shaken up. When this was done he set about his work and enjoyed himself. Further, as Taaffe said, there was no trace of a quitter in him and no braver horse ever looked through a bridle. He was, he said, a horse that not only needed to be ridden; he wanted to be ridden. He therefore asked to be excused riding him unless he was to be allowed to get at him. Next time out with another jockey on him who forgot his instructions and gave him a reminder he immediately acclereated, ran through his field and won as he liked. Furthermore, when he came back from Cheltenham that year his connections decided that the real reason for his indifferent display was not his heart but the fact that, when stabled near the racecourse, he had been upset by the noises all around him and had not slept. Certainly, in March 1968, he put up a smashing performance in winning the Leopardstown Chase under 12 st 7 lb, giving away 34 lb to the second, the highest weight carried against him being 10 st 3 lb.

Mill House was back for another try. Although he had just held on to win the Whitbread at the end of the last season, it really did look now as if his years and experiences were getting the better of him. In his favourite race, The Gainsborough Chase, he was beaten a length and a half at level weights by an up-and-coming young horse, The Laird. This put The Laird slap in the Gold Cup picture. He was owned by Mr H. J. Joel, trained by R. Turnell, and had been bred by Mr John Hislop. Mr Joel had already won the Two Thousand Guineas and The Derby that year with Royal Palace. It would be a unique achievement if

The 1968 field taking the second fence led by Fort Leney (6) (P. Taaffe up), Stalbridge Colonist (1) (T. Biddlecombe up) and The Laird (3) (J. King up).

he could also add the Gold Cup, the blue riband of steeplechasing, to these laurels.

Stalbridge Colonist had been third in the Gainsborough Chase, and was said not to have been suited by the slow pace at which it was run. He was, however, a very live candidate for the championship, for he had only just been beaten in the Hennessy, and had given What A Myth 3 lb and a two lengths beating in the Mildmay Memorial. But Stalbridge Colonist was beginning to become prone to jumping mistakes, and What A Myth, a certain runner once again, had never been cured of them. A very promising young horse called Sixty-Nine looked likely at one time to take them all on and beat them, but he, too, went wrong and had to be taken out.

Once again there was tremendous confidence behind Mill House, now re-united with his former partner G. W. Robinson. There was no doubt that the old warrior looked magnificent in the parade ring, but everything save his looks was against him. He was now eleven, and although older horses had won the Cup and would do so again it is not, by and large, a race for veterans. He had, as we know, suffered injury and semi-retirement, and there was, in addition, the suggestion in some minds that his increasing years had brought back the tendency to jumping errors which had marred his immaturity. Above all, there was the record which had stood throughout the history of the race that no horse who had won and failed had come back to win again. But despite all this the stable confidence told, and he was made favourite at the astonishingly short price of 2–1. The Laird, though his jumping, too, was far from above suspicion, and there was also against him the suggestion that he might not get the trip, was second favourite at 3–1. Stalbridge Colonist followed them at 7–2, and Fort Leney drifted in the betting before finally ending up at 11–2.

There was, in fact, some doubt about whether Fort Leney would run at all. Considerable precautions had been taken to prevent a repetition of last year's restlessness. He was brought over by air the day before and stabled at a farm away from the course. As a result he had a normal night's sleep, but even with that the final decision to run was not taken until the morning of the race, for the ground on the first two days had been desperately hard, and he needed at least some give in it to bring out his best. Luck was with him here, however, for there was rain during the night, and the morning was misty with occasional showers. The descision was then made to let him take his chance. This year, too, he had the inestimable assistance of Pat Taaffe's skill in the saddle. Though the failure of last year could in no way be ascribed to young McLoughlin, he would have been the first to admit that he had not, nor could he have had, the experience or tactical flair of the stable's first jockey. Taaffe's dash and judgment had been quite unaffected by the frightful fall that he had had at Haydock the year before. At this time he probably knew his way round Cheltenham better than anyone then riding. He had, after all, been placed in the Gold Cup as long ago as 1954, and not one of those who rode against him in that race were still in the saddle. He had won three championships, thus equalling the records of Rees and Brabazon. His tactical experience was unrivalled; and his professional abilities were only matched by his personal modesty. He was, too, told to ride as he liked.

Mill House, as usual, sailed into the lead. He was still there as they set out on the second circuit. But, as once before, on another and greater horse of Tom Dreaper's, Taaffe was close behind him and going easily, a picture of controlled menace waiting to pounce. At the open ditch past the water Mill House did exactly what he had done two fences further on the year before. He simply did not look at it, and took it out. This left Fort Leney in front, possibly a little earlier than Taaffe would have cared for. Almost immediately King on The Laird, and Biddlecombe on Stalbridge Colonist, moved up to threaten him.

Down the hill they stepped up the pace, and coming to the second last The Laird had headed Fort Leney. Here The Laird looked all over a winner. Peter Biegel the sporting artist, who was standing by the fence, told the Dreapers afterwards that, at that moment, he would have given any odds against their horse. Taaffe, too, knew that here was the place where the race would be won and lost. He drove Fort Leney with such power and strength into the fence that he landed all but level with The Laird. (Peter Biegel painted a superb picture of the scene, and it hangs in the Dreapers' dining room today.) Stalbridge Colonist made a mistake here, and his chance was gone. So The Laird and Fort Leney came alone and together to the last. The Laird landed first on the flat. But Taaffe put his horse into the fence as only he knew how, had him into his stride in an instant, and was first away from it. On up the hill he went, running straight as a gun barrel for the line. King sat down to ride The Laird right out. He, in his turn, was being threatened by Biddlecombe, who had got Stalbridge Colonist flying again after his mistake. The Laird beat off the grey, but, though he narrowed the gap with every stride, King could not close it. Fort Leney held on, and won by a neck.

Taaffe had suffered criticisms during this career for his apparent weakness in a finish. The result of this race must surely go a long way towards rebutting them. Although his style appeared to be unorthodox and untidy, horses nevertheless ran straight and true for him. Here he was able to hold off one of the strongest finishers in the business and keep his horse's head in front and unfaltering on the line. Shortly after this race, sitting at dinner next to one of the great jockeys of the day who had ridden much against Taaffe, Mrs Dreaper mentioned these criticisms. 'They say that, do they?' was the reply. 'Have any of them stopped to count the number of races he wins?' It was a fair and just comment from one who was in a better position to know than most of those who uttered the words of disparagement.

The result set up records. It gave Tom Dreaper his fifth Gold Cup, which meant that this quiet-spoken, wryly humorous master of his profession ('There wasn't much wrong with his heart today' was his comment in the unsaddling enclosure) had broken O'Brien's record for the number of winners trained. It was Taaffe's fourth win, and he thus excelled Brabazon and Rees.

Fort Leney, along with Mill House and Stalbridge Colonist, went on to contest The Whitbread, and once more that race provided an upset. Fort Leney did the best of them. Though virtually neglected in the betting he put up a sterling performance, only being beaten a neck by the useful handicapper Larbawn, to whom he was giving 19 lb. Mill House, now clearly a light of other days, got rid of Robinson at the thirteenth, and Stalbridge Colonist, too, unshipped his rider, at the sixth. This result does emphasise that it is normally only an exceptional Gold Cup winner who can go on to take this testing race.

The Gold Cup of 1969 was a sort of interregnum. The great stars, the crowd pullers, Arkle and Mill House, had now definitely gone forever from the scene. For Leney ran only

The Laird and Fort Leney jumping the second last, from the painting by Peter Biegel.

once that year; he had leg trouble, and was retired. Neither The Laird nor Stalbridge Colonist did much to enchance their reputations, though the little grey did beat The Laird with some ease in Mill House's former favourite race, the Gainsborough Chase. It seemed more and more likely that an altogether new name would be written on the list of champions. That is indeed what happened, but the name, when it emerged, proved to be one that most people, certainly at the beginning of the season, would have least expected.

What A Myth was now twelve years of age. Although he had been third in Woodland Venture's Gold Cup in 1967, he had never quite seemed to be really in the top-class. He stayed forever and he needed soft ground to give of his best, but he appeared to be short of speed, and his legs, too, had given him fairly constant trouble. He was high in the handicap and at the beginning of the season Ryan Price, who trained him for Lady Weir, advised her to have him hunted and put into semi-retirement. He was qualified with the Quorn and, although his name appeared in the entries for the Gold Cup, there was not then any great expectation of running him. He was a far from perfect hunter, being disinclined to treat the obstacles with the respect to which they were entitled, and he was quickly put to hunter-chasing. But it was a very wet year and the ground remained right for him. He ran away from his field in a hunter's chase at Market Rasen on March 1st, winning by twenty lengths. A week later he trotted up again in a similar race, this time at Newbury, the winning margin being eight lengths. It looked as if the old horse, enjoying himself in this company, had come back to his best. If the ground remained soft, since the opposition that year was far from strong, it was decided that he would be allowed to take his chance in the Championship.

The luck held. The meeting opened in such a deluge that it was even doubtful if racing could take place. On Gold Cup day the weather had cleared, but the ground was still desperately heavy – just what was wanted for What A Myth. Having been given his chance, he took it. The Laird and Stalbridge Colonist were out of it early. The Laird was brought down at the eighth, and Stalbridge Colonist fell at the tenth. Ridden with quiet confidence by Paul Kelleway, What A Myth made his way through the field, jumped the last well in front and, revelling in the conditions, stayed on up the hill to resist a late challenge from Biddlecombe on Domacorn by a length and a half.

What A Myth was not everybody's ride and Kelleway, who had ridden him in nearly all his races, had established with him that sort of special *rapport* which exists between some horses and jockeys. Kelleway had, earlier that season, refused an offer to be set up as a private trainer, and his courage in electing to remain in an uncertain and perilous profession was rewarded by his greatest triumph. Later, of course, he was to establish another splendid partnership with Bula in the Champion Hurdle.

After the race it was immediately announced that the winner would go into retirement. This he did, and next season was hunted a few times, but his liking for both the obstacles and the sport had not been increased by his accession to the Championship.

Without in any way detracting from his achievement it must be said that this was not one of the more distinguished races for the Gold Cup, and perhaps more interest was aroused by the race for the Cathcart Cup which immediately followed it.

This was won in the Arkle colours by a young horse of immense promise called Kinloch

(OPPOSITE) Paul Kelleway and What A Myth clear the last fence to win the 1969 race.

Brae. A six-year-old trained for the Duchess by her old friend from County Cork, the irrepressible Willie O'Grady, Kinloch Brae, though not so distinguished in appearance as her great champion, was a most taking mover and jumper, appearing almost to flow over his fences. The mud did not hinder or check him, and he won unheaded by twenty lengths. Here indeed was an exciting prospect for next year.

In fact, a whole new generation of high-class horses came to the fore throughout the following season. Spanish Steps, another six-year-old, had won the Totalisator Novices' Chase run over the full Gold Cup distance by fifteen lengths at that National Hunt meeting. This was in its way just as impressive a performance as that of Kinloch Brae in the Cathcart Cup. At the commencement of the new season, still only six, on the top of the ground with 11 st 8 lb to carry, he won the Hennessy Gold Cup, beating the vastly more experienced Larbawn by exactly the same distance as he had won the Totalisator Novices. He then went on to collect The Benson and Hedges Gold Cup and The Gainsborough, both at Sandown, in the latter giving The Laird 5 lb and a ten-length beating. Here, if ever, looked a live contender for the coming Gold Cup.

But he was not alone. Another talking horse had arrived, a six-year-old, a huge, ungainly ex-point-to-pointer called The Dikler. Possibly because of his size, possibly because he was one of the few really big horses by his famous sire, Vulgan, and perhaps because whatever he did either falling or winning, he appeared to do in the most spectacular way, he caught the imagination of the public. A tremendously hard puller and front runner, and, when he met them right, a great jumper, he was written up as a coming champion. The year before he had been running – and running out – in point-to-points. Despite the fact that this looked to be a vintage year and was his first season on the racecourse proper (both his early wins were in Novice Races, so he had only just graduated to handicap, let alone championship class) he was said to be aimed at the Gold Cup.

His story was certainly romantic enough for him to win a championship. Bought in Ireland as an unbroken three-year-old by Edward Bee, who died tragically and suddenly while the sale was being completed, he formed part of the residue of his estate which was beqeathed to his nieces Katherine Gregory and Peggy August in equal shares. Neither of them wanted him but when they came to try to sell him he was still leggy and unfurnished and no one would have him. Subsequently Mrs August acquired her sister's share and named him after a stream on her uncle's estate. He was still on the market however and since no one again wanted him Mrs August privately christened him Tuppence feeling that was all he was worth to her. Left with him she had him broken, hunted and point-to-pointed. Throughout these stages of his career he showed both his tremendous strength, his jumping ability when he was ridden with sympathy, and above all his independence. That there was something there worth going on with Mrs August sensed and, at the age of six standing 17 hands high she sent him to Fulke Walwyn to be trained. Walwyn, too, divined his quality, 'though we heard certain stories such as he was mad and dangerous,' met his challenge and the rest, as will be told, is history.

Titus Oates, sired by Arctic Slave, a prolific sire of winners in Ireland who yet never seemed to get horses quite of Gold Cup class, who won the Massey-Ferguson at Cheltenham and The King George VI at Kempton, was in the entries. On the book he had to be given a chance, as had Arcturus from the north. Also sired by Arctic Slave, Arcturus had won two races early in the season, and been third in the Mildmay Memorial. However, although useful, he appeared just to lack the necessary class, and to be more of a National horse. Gay Trip and Larbawn were also in the field.

As if all this wealth of talent was not enough, there were, besides Kinloch Brae, other live challengers from Ireland. One of these was French Tan. An eight-year-old by Trouville, French Tan had won his last three races impressively. The last of these was the Whitbread Trial Chase at Ascot, in which he numbered Flyingbolt, now trained in Scotland and attempting a comeback, and Stalbridge Colonist, among his victims. He was certainly more than useful, and was to have, too, the inestimable advantage of Pat Taaffe's assistance from the saddle. The second serious challenger from Ireland was L'Escargot. A seven-year-old by Escart III, L'Escargot had been bought for Mr Raymond Guest by Tom Cooper of The B.B.A. (Ireland). Although he wound quite considerably in front in his action, Mr Cooper liked him so much that he determined to secure him. Subsequent events were to prove how sound a judge he was. L'Escargot soon showed his trainer, Moore, that he was quite out of the ordinary. That season he won the ingenious and newly instituted novice chase competition thought up by the Haydock management and sponsored by W. D. and H. O. Wills. In it the qualifiers ran against each other in a number of differing regions, and the winners contested a final at Haydock in January. L'Escargot won this final from East Bound and Young Ash Leaf, and then went on to carry top weight into second place in the Leopardstown Chase, run on the Navan track owing to the re-building of the Leopardstown stands into a modern concourse. Herring Gull, a former winner of the Totalisator Novices and The Irish Grand National, was also a runner.

Despite the presence of these good horses, there was no doubt that the main Irish hopes were pinned on Kinloch Brae. He had won his last four races brilliantly, but the third of these had been a hurdle and his final race before the Championship was a two-mile four furlong conditions race at Thurles which hardly amounted to more than an exercise gallop. He had never yet, in his career, really had to jump on the stretch upsides with top-class horses. And there was at least one of the jockeys riding against him who was unlikely to overlook that fact.

Nevertheless, the race was regarded as virtually a match between Kinloch Brae and Spanish Steps. This revived all the old Anglo-Irish rivalry of the Arkle–Mill House days. Tremendous interest was aroused, a battle royal was anticipated, and a huge crowd thronged to see it. Added excitement was brought about by the definite presence in the field of the erratic and ungainly The Dikler, though some, less enthusiastic than his fan club, may have wondered what he was doing there at all.

L'Escargot very nearly did not run. Moore, his trainer, had doubts about his getting the trip, and wanted him to contest the Two Mile Champion Chase on the Tuesday. Mr Guest, however, was determined to have a go at the Cup. Although, as he freely confessed afterwards, he 'didn't think there was a horse in the world to beat Kinloch Brae', he wanted a runner in the Championship, and a runner he would have. L'Escargot was therefore declared for it but, with very little confidence behind him, was allowed to start at the long price of 33–1. Kinloch Brae was favourite at 15–8, with Spanish Steps close behind him at 9–4. The day was bright and sunny, and the going was good.

Titus Oates set a good gallop from the start. Arcturus went at the fifth, and The Dikler

L'Escargot (5) (T. Carberry up) and French Tan (P. Taaffe up) taking the last fence, 1970.
L'Escargot went on to win the race.

at the eleventh. Passing the stands, Hyde let Kinloch Brae stride along to join Titus Oates
in the lead. All down the far side he gave a delightful exhibition of galloping and jumping.
He was fencing with consummate ease, and obviously going so well within himself that, to
his supporters, defeat just then appeared unthinkable – especially since Spanish Steps was
in difficulties and had received a reminder from his rider at the fence before the water.

At the top of the hill Titus Oates cracked and dropped back. Here Kinloch Brae had a
clear lead, but Taaffe, the master tactician, was closing on him on French Tan, and Carberry
on L'Escargot was not far behind.

The third last fence on the Gold Cup course is set half-way down the hill, and there is a
slight fall of ground on the landing side. If a horse jumps it well he can and often does get

away from his field; if he takes a chance and meets it wrong he is almost doomed. No one knew this better than Taaffe. 'I remembered,' he said in a television interview afterwards, 'that Kinloch Brae had never been taken on in his earlier races. I thought I'd take him on here and see what happened.' He drove French Tan hard up behind the leader and, really racing now, they rose at it together. Whether it was cause and effect, or both, or neither, no one will ever know. What is indisputable is that down Kinloch Brae came leaving poor Hyde unhurt but disconsolate on the ground. Taaffe pushed on, making the best of his way home and chased by L'Escargot. Herring Gull, who was just beginning a late run that might have been dangerous, fell over the prostrate Kinloch Brae, and Titus Oates, a beaten horse at the time, came down at the same fence.

L'Escargot closed with French Tan at the last, and caught him. They ran on together up the hill. But L'Escargot, whose stamina was thought to be in doubt, in fact stayed on the better of the two to win by a length and a half. Strangely enough, both winner and runner-up had been hobdayed. Spanish Steps who, to the disappointment of everybody, was never really in the race at all, was a further ten lengths away, third.

Although the race was in many ways an anti-climax and the result was greeted in silence by the big crowd, L'Escargot was a worthy winner, for he had beaten a good field with the utmost authority and conviction. No one can say what would have happened if Kinloch Brae had stood up, but the third from home is some way out at Cheltenham, and much can happen between it and the winning post.

Mr Guest, at all events, had every reason to congratulate himself. It was on his insistence that his horse had run at all, and this insistence had now given him the blue riband of steeplechasing to add to his garlands on the flat. He had also every occasion to pay tribute to his luck, and indeed he did so. His first runner in the Derby, Larkspur, had won the race in 1962 when seven horses fell coming down the hill. He had won it again in 1968 with Sir Ivor. 'It is marvellous my luck has held so long,' he said. He was right and, as events were to prove, it was to hold even longer.

That Gold Cup proved to be Pat Taaffe's last. He retired at the turn of the year to farm and train, universally liked and respected, his record intact as the rider who had ridden most winners of this great race.

The preliminaries to the 1971 Gold Cup brought with them two terrible disappointments. The first was that Kinloch Brae developed leg trouble. This horse had already stamped his personality on the racing scene in a way that the reigning champion, L'Escargot, had quite failed to do. To many, he looked like becoming at least in some way a successor to Arkle. It was not, however, to be. His new trainer, Toby Balding, did everything possible for him, giving him time coupled with constant care and attention. He was not allowed to risk his suspect leg until the Jim Ford Challenge Cup at Wincanton on February 25th. In this race he displayed much of his old fluency and sparkle, but he was lame when he finished, and he did not reappear during the season. That left the Championship wide open and bereft of its most attractive contender. The other disappointment will be recounted in due course.

During the early part of the season The Dikler appeared to be about to justify at least some of the superlatives so freely used about him. But in his later races, though starting favourite, he failed. Much of the old unreliability seemed to have returned, and, what was worse, he did not run those races out like a true stayer.

There were, however, two live challengers from Ireland, Leap Frog, trained by Tom Dreaper and winner, as had been L'Escargot the year before, of the W. D. and H. O. Wills Premier Novices, and Glencaraig Lady, who had fallen at Cheltenham in 1970 at the last fence in The Totalisator Novices Chase with the race apparently at her mercy. She had won The National Hunt Centenary Chase at Punchestown in November, and The S.G.B. Chase at Ascot the following month.

L'Escargot himself had not had a very encouraging season. After his Gold Cup victory he was sent to America for the Meadowbrook Chase in June, which he won. Again in America, he was third in the Temple Gwaltheney Chase in October, and fourth in the Colonial Cup the following month. Back in Ireland, he ran in The Sweeps Hurdle at the Fairyhouse Christmas Meeting. He then unshipped his rider in a three-mile chase at Punchestown, and finished third under top weight in the Leopardstown Chase, run in very heavy going.

Spanish Steps, too, had a moderate season, but he did win the Stone's Ginger Wine Chase carrying 12 st 2 lb, and it was said that his connections were confident that he was going to redeem his failure of the year before.

Then the second terrible disappointment struck. Mrs Courage, wife of the trainer of Spanish Steps, in making the declarations to Wetherby's, submitted the name of another horse for the Gold Cup, by mistake, instead of Spanish Steps'. The mistake was not picked up, and Spanish Steps could not run. So the two most fancied horses of the year before were out of it and, to make matters worse, French Tan had also suffered injury and would not be in the line-up.

There was continuous rain for fifteen hours before the race. As a result, the stewards abandoned the chute start behind the stands and the horses came under orders instead at the three-and-a-quarter-mile start on the old course. This meant, oddly enough, that, in the waterlogged ground, the runners would have to jump twenty-three fences instead of the usual twenty-two.

L'Escargot, Leap Frog and Into View, a useful eight-year-old trained by Fred Winter who had, however, still to show he could stay three miles in this company, were favourites at 7–2.

The gallop, as might have been expected in that ground, was, to say the least of it, a steady one. Four out, it was Glencaraig Lady who was in the lead and, revelling in the conditions, apparently in full command. She was still there at the next – the fatal third last – and going well and easily when, for no apparent reason, she turned over and came down. This left L'Escargot in the lead from Leap Frog with The Dikler some way behind in third place.

Young Val O'Brien on Leap Frog tried to get on terms with L'Escargot, but it was a vain effort. The champion stayed on too well for him in the testing conditions and won by ten lengths, gaining what may have been another lucky victory. The Dikler hoisted himself into a tired third place fifteen lengths behind Leap Frog. It was not a very satisfactory race, but a horse can do no more than win, and this L'Escargot did and by a very substantial margin.

The 1972 Gold Cup made history in more ways than one. For a start Piper Heidsieck sponsored it, contributing £10,000 and a cup value £400. This made it the most valuable Gold Cup ever run, being worth £15,255 to the winner. It was the first time a sponsor had ever contributed to this race. The race was won by a mare, only the third time in history that this had happened. She did not win, however, without surviving an objection – the first

Glencaraig Lady (6) (F. Berry up) winner of the 1972 race leading The Dikler (3) (B. Brogan up) over a fence during the race.

time in forty-six years that one rider in the Championship has objected to another. Then, as if this was not enough, the rider of the third horse objected to the second!

The events which led up to these sensational happenings were ordinary enough. No new star appeared to dominate the scene, although Crisp, an Australian horse who had won the Two Mile Champion Chase the year before in brilliant style, was said by many to be one in the making. Crisp was no beauty and those with memories of India under The Raj wrote him down as a typical 'waler'. Although he could certainly go it was problematical whether he would act on every kind of going and some expressed doubts about his stamina.

For the second year in succession L'Escargot came to the Championship without a win to his credit. Indeed, he had had what looked on the book to be a thoroughly unsatisfactory season. He was fourth, eight lengths behind The Dikler in The King George VI at Kempton on Boxing Day, and second in a three-horse race at Leopardstown in February. He did not have a run between that race and the Gold Cup, missing the Leopardstown Chase owing to the desperately heavy going. His trainer announced that he was back at his best, he was said to be a horse who ran his best races in the spring – and his record seemed to show this – and his supporters felt sure that he would equal Cottage Rake's and Arkle's score of three Gold Cups.

Leap Frog's form looked better, for he had beaten The Dikler in The Massey-Ferguson, and had won handicaps at Naas and Fairyhouse, but he, too, missed the Leopardstown race owing to the state of the ground. He was now trained by young Jim Dreaper, who had taken over the Kilsallaghan stable on the retirement of his father at Christmas. Pat Taaffe, as has been said, had retired the year before but, although the old firm had been dissolved, the horses were still there as was the care which they received and the ability with which they were prepared and placed. Jim Dreaper, indeed, soon showed that he had inherited much of his father's skill with a series of brilliant successes gained almost as soon as he stepped into his shoes.

The Dikler, now partnered by Barry Brogan, who appeared to have mastered him, at last showed signs of running up to his reputation. He won at Kempton on Boxing Day, taking a classic steeplechase for the first time, but this gave no proof that he would stay the testing three miles at Cheltenham. And, again at Kempton, he failed a little later to give Crisp 6 lb over what was probably his best distance of two-and-a-half miles. He did seem a reformed character and Brogan rode him beautifully, but whether he was good enough was another matter.

Spanish Steps was in the field again, but he had hurt himself in the King George VI, and ran unconvincingly after it. The little mare, Glencaraig Lady, was there too, having a second try for the Championship, and a third attempt to overcome the jinx that pursued her at Cheltenham. This year she was to be ridden by young Frank Berry, a born horseman who, when apprenticed on the flat, had mastered the difficult Giolla Mear and won the Irish St Leger on him, making a temperamental and headstrong colt appear almost a child's ride.

It was a glorious National Hunt Meeting. The sun shone, the crowds poured in. Vouchers for the Members' Enclosure were abolished for the first time and during the three days every stand was packed. The climax, as usual, was the Gold Cup. It looked like proving an epic and exciting contest and this was what it turned out to be. Twenty-nine thousand people passed through the turnstiles to witness it, an increase of four thousand on the previous year.

Despite the sunny weather there was give in the ground, which favoured the chances of L'Escargot and also of Royal Toss, a game tough chaser from the West Country, who liked to feel his feet go in and stayed forever.

Possibly because of the immense stable confidence behind him, Crisp was made favourite at 3–1. L'Escargot and Leap Frog being next, at fours. It is perhaps worth noting that Gay Trip, winner of the 1970 Grand National and much fancied to win again this year, was neglected at 35–1. He was considered to be much above the average of recent National winners, and was set to carry 11 st 9 lb in it. Yet in this company his chances were known to be negligible. The enormous gap in class between the two races that then and now exists was thus doubly underlined.

They went a fair gallop in the heavy ground and it was, in fact, Gay Trip who made the running. Four from home Barry Brogan allowed The Dikler to jump to the front. He came down the hill with Glencaraig Lady and L'Escargot in close attendance. At the second last these three were almost in line with Crisp, who was clearly hating the ground, trying to get on terms. L'Escargot blundered here, and with the blunder went his chance of writing his name into the records.

It was The Dikler who landed first over the last. True glory was now perhaps at last within his grasp. His supporters rose to roar him home. But Berry had switched Glencaraig Lady to the inside. He had given her a copybook ride, and the little mare, hugging the rails, was catching The Dikler fast up the hill. Then a third threat loomed up. Young Nigel Wakley had made Royal Toss begin to fly. Going, it seemed, far faster than the two in front, he came storming at them. The Dikler, on the outside, was tiring rapidly. There appeared to Wakley to be room between the two. With his horse running on, he went for the gap.

Amidst a thunderous roar of cheering the three horses passed the post locked together. After a moment or two the numbers went up: 6, 9, 3. That was Glencaraig Lady, Royal Toss, and The Dikler. The distances were three-quarters of a length and a head. So, or so it seemed, at her third try at the National Hunt Meeting and her second in the Gold Cup, Glencaraig Lady, who this time had not put a foot wrong throughout, had laid her bogey, and had taken the coveted prize.

But had she? Unknown to almost everyone save those who stood by, Nigel Wakley said as he dismounted: 'I am going to object.' And object to the winner he did. The reason he gave was that the winner had 'taken his ground'. So, after a minute or two, the loudspeakers were announcing the first objection in the history of the race, and that a stewards' enquiry was about to take place. As if this was not enough the announcement was almost immediately followed by another to the effect that Brogan had objected to Royal Toss for boring in the last 150 yards.

The stewards were faced with a difficult problem. After lengthy deliberation and assisted by the camera, they came to the decision which was all but universally recognised as the right one. Glencaraig Lady may to some slight extent have left the fence and deviated from the direct line. The Dikler, as tiring horses will, may have drifted inwards. But the film showed no evidence of interference sufficient to alter the result. Twenty minutes of what must have been agonising suspense for the connections of the winner passed before the announcement was made that the placings would remain unaltered.

Glencaraig Lady is by Fortina out of the Turbulent mare Luckibash. She was bought as a three-year-old for eight hundred guineas. It was a tremendous triumph for her trainer, Francis Flood, a leading amateur rider in Ireland who had not long set up his string, for she had suffered set-backs and had not been entirely easy to train.

It had been a wonderful and exciting race for the richest prize ever offered for the Championship. Though not perhaps in the highest class of winners, the little mare had displayed those qualities of gameness, fortitude and jumping ability which make steeple-chasing the great sport that it is. With the coming of a sponsor, too, a new era of prosperity and fame was begun in this, the supreme prize in National Hunt racing.

13

Two Worthy Winners

PIPER HEIDSIECK WERE again the sponsors in 1973 and once more the Gold Cup gave every promise of being a classic contest. For a new star had arisen to challenge the reigning aristocracy of steeplechasing. This was Pendil, trained by F. Winter and ridden by his then stable jockey, the ex-amateur, Richard Pitman.

Winter had made swift transition from being leading rider to becoming leading trainer. Already by 1973 he had trained the winners of two Grand Nationals in Jay Trump and Anglo. The Gold Cup, however, had not been a lucky race for him and his last two runners Crisp and Into View had been down the field. From his very first appearance in the new season it looked as if Pendil was about to change all that.

A light-framed chestnut with two extraordinary protruberances or horns growing from his forehead Pendil had been introduced to racing as a hurdler. Immediately in that sphere he showed his quality by winning six races before breaking down in the Schweppes Hurdle of 1971 when looking likely to trouble the winner. Operated on successfully by the split tendon method he was back in training the following winter. Put to chasing he opened his account by spreadeagling a strong field of novices in the Bath Novices Chase at Cheltenham on December 10th. He then went on to win five chases off the reel, the last two being the Arkle Chase at Cheltenham and the Welsh Champion Chase at Chepstow. It was no wonder that he was being hailed as a successor to Arkle and that when he retired for his summer rest Winter and his jockey could look forward to the coming season with the liveliest of expectations.

Such indeed was the stable confidence behind Bula who had won the last two Champion Hurdles and Pendil the rising star that Ivor Herbert, Winter's biographer in *Winter's Tale*, has recorded Winter telling him: 'If I place Bula right and Pendil too I can – barring accidents – keep them unbeaten this season and possibly next. So what do I want to know about other people's horses?'

It certainly appeared that such super confidence was going to be justified when Pendil came out next season to win the Black and White Whisky Gold Cup at Ascot on November 18th and followed this with a victory in the Benson and Hedges Handicap Chase at Sandown in which he conceded no less than 27 lb to Red Candle, the runner-up. He then ended the first part of the season in triumph by slamming The Dikler in the King George VI Chase at Kempton by five lengths.

Although The Dikler had won the race the year before, with his great size and wayward steering he was never really suited to the sharp Kempton track which was tailor-made as it were for the handier type such as Pendil was. The Dikler camp, therefore, were in no way cast down by this defeat. But stable and public confidence in Pendil was increased by the fact that he had now shown that he stayed three miles in top-class company albeit the sharp three miles at Kempton, as has been said, bear little resemblance to Cheltenham with its stiff uphill finish.

Besides Pendil and The Dikler there were other contenders that year. Fulke Walwyn had in his stable Charlie Potheen, another unpredictable character who when he felt like it could be a very good horse indeed. Barry Brogan as stable jockey had his choice between these two and elected to ride The Dikler. Terry Biddlecombe, who had ridden him before, was engaged to ride Charlie Potheen, a task he undertook with mixed feelings. 'He was,' he says in his memoirs, 'a wild ride. He jumped left-handed, hung left-handed and was only run on left-handed tracks. On his day he was a smashing horse but quite horrific to ride.' L'Escargot and Spanish Steps were also in the field which was completed by Garoupe, Red Candle and Clever Scot.

Pendil finished his preparation by first of all making two top-class two-milers in Inkslinger and Tingle Creek look like hacks over 2 miles 160 yards at Newbury on February 10th. Then, a fortnight later, giving lumps of weight to the only two runners who took him on he romped away from them to win the Yellow Pages Pattern Handicap Chase at Kempton. As a result he became a roaring ante-post favourite for the Gold Cup, so much so that it appeared to many including perhaps his immediate connections that the race was only a formality. Prospective formalities in racing, however, have a way of proving otherwise.

The Dikler for his part went twice to Wincanton winning on both occasions, the second being a two-horse race against the novice, I'm Happy. Richard Pitman, a man never inclined to reticence, having watched the race, told the press that there was nothing there that impressed him. 'He'll regret those words,' was Walwyn's comment on hearing them. Time was to show how right he was.

Walwyn next sent The Dikler to Windsor for his winding-up race before the Gold Cup. No doubt he had his reasons but it does appear a strange venue to have chosen for it is a sharp figure-of-eight course unsuited, most would have thought, to The Dikler's big frame and great stride. In the event it proved to be so for on the run in The Dikler was all over the place taking Spanish Steps' ground and earning for himself in the stewards' room relegation to second place. It was not a very satisfactory Gold Cup trial and there was adverse comment on his prospects in the press. More bad news followed since Barry Brogan, who had ridden him so well, had for some time been fighting a battle against alcoholism which finally defeated him and he had to enter a nursing home in Ireland. A substitute rider for the big horse had therefore to be found. He was far from being anyone's ride and there was not much time to find one.

Terry Biddlecombe, on being consulted, recommended Ron Barry as the new jockey. Despite having been champion jockey the year before Barry, who had done most of his racing in the north, was virtually unknown to either Walwyn or Mrs August. 'Big Ron', as he was universally known, came from that nursery of great jumping jockeys, County Limerick. He had been apprenticed on the flat until, like many another, increasing weight turned his talents to steeplechasing. A strong, resolute horseman with gentle hands and an instinctive understanding of his mounts no better choice for The Dikler could have been made. But, since Walwyn knew little of him, he was at first dubious about the wisdom of engaging him. He was in no way reassured when he watched him on television show-jumping in the jockey's championship at Stoneleigh, a performance which he described to Terry Biddlecombe next day as a disaster.

When therefore Barry came to school The Dikler for his first and only time over fences Walwyn looked forward to their meeting with apprehension. He need not have worried. The Dikler, as was his wont, went like lightning over three schooling fences but Barry, at home with him at once, sat perfectly still and he and the big horse seemed to be instantly at one. 'Thank God; he's a better jockey than a show-jumper!' was Walwyn's comment.

It transpired afterwards that Barry's performance at Stoneleigh was not quite what it seemed for he had had a bet with Pat Buckley as to who could do the fastest time no matter how many jumping faults they incurred, which accounted for his sending the poles rattling and Walwyn's freely and strongly expressed dismay. But nobody knew then, since he kept it to himself, that another imponderable had come into the reckoning for Barry had broken a collarbone at Chepstow after his school on The Dikler and, although it was mending he still had a slight worry that the big horse, if he really took hold, might take off with him going down to the start.

Meanwhile although the Pendil camp still exuded confidence they had their own problems though these were not so many or so complex as those besetting The Dikler. No steeplechaser is ever perfect and Pendil was inclined to idle if allowed to go to the front too soon. In a championship race such as the Gold Cup and especially with front runners such as Charlie Potheen and Clever Scot in the field this was bound to present his rider with a difficulty in determining his tactics. Pitman and Winter discussed the coming race countless times, Winter being of the opinion that Pitman should be in the lead at the elbow and Pitman repeating his fear of what would happen were he to hit the front too soon. It appears that neither really considered the likelihood of defeat bar a fall and Pendil had never fallen yet. Moreover he had now won his last eleven races off the reel. There was no real reason on all known form why he should not make it up into the round dozen. This confidence was almost universally shared. No one, press or public, paused to consider that he had never won over a distance greater than the easy three miles at Kempton, while The Dikler had already won a handicap at Cheltenham over an extended three miles carrying 12 st and had twice been placed in the Gold Cup.

That National Hunt Meeting did not open auspiciously for Winter. Crisp, brought back from the Gold Cup distance to the Two Mile Champion Chase and starting at money on, could only manage to finish third to Inkslinger. Bula, confidently expected to make a hat-trick of Champion Hurdles and also starting at money on, finished fifth of eight to the rising star Comedy of Errors with, it should be noted, another name we shall hear of again, Captain Christy, in third place. However, it was confidently expected that Pendil in the Gold Cup would make up for all these disappointments and he was backed down to 4–6 on.

After all their discussions, Winter did not tie Pitman down with any strict instructions leaving the tactics to the jockey who knew the horse so well. He contented himself with saying, 'Enjoy yourself.' 'Thank you, I will,' was Pitman's reply.

The Dikler had been on edge all that morning. For the first and only time in his life he kicked his devoted lad 'Darkie' Deacon, who had done much to make him, on the thigh just as they finished saddling him. Deacon was in such pain that he could not lead his charge round the parade ring and had to hand over to one of the other lads and he said afterwards that he felt it an indication that the big horse was ready to run the race of his life. And to Barry's relief he went down to the start like a Christian causing him no trouble at all.

In the parade ring Walwyn had warned Barry of The Dikler's tendency to give himself a breather during the race and that he should not be deceived by this into thinking he was tiring. And he, too, cautioned against hitting the front too soon for The Dikler liked something to race against to bring out his bottomless staying power.

As expected Charlie Potheen set off at a headlong gallop jumping the second fence so fast and landing so far out that Biddlecombe, experienced as he was, said that it took his breath away. This ensured a strong gallop and Barry was able to place The Dikler where he wanted towards the rear of the field. Once there the big horse strode smoothly along under his hands. It was, 'almost like a good day's hunting,' he said afterwards. Walwyn's warning about the breather had been timely, too, for Barry found him faltering beneath him as they met the hill before the last open ditch and began to wonder what was happening until he recalled the trainer's words.

Pitman on Pendil was having his own problems for he had difficulty in settling him as he wanted, Clever Scot's fall early on, directly in front of him having upset him and momentarily knocked him out of his stride. He managed however to restrain him at the back of the field until, at the top of the hill, turning for home, he let him go. Devouring the ground eagerly Pendil closed with the leaders. By this time Charlie Potheen had shot his bolt and was dropping back.

At the third last Pendil threw a tremendous leap and went clear. He was still three lengths in front at the second last and appeared to have his race in hand. But Barry, riding a copy book race on The Dikler, had not yet moved on him. He had had to switch to the outside as Charlie Potheen hung towards the rails but the pause may even have helped him to conserve his run. At all events feeling the great power and thrust of the big, game horse beneath him he knew then he had every chance of closing the gap with the flyer in front. He sat down and sent The Dikler after him.

Over the last Pendil was two lengths clear and scarcely off the bridle. But by now Barry had The Dikler devouring the ground and he was catching the favourite with every stride. Left in front and facing the hill Pendil faltered. It was something he could not afford to do with that combination bearing down on him. Half-way to the line The Dikler came and caught him and went half a length up. Pendil fought back. Headed, he showed the class of the champion he might have been. Under Pitman's driving he came again and whittled down the lead. But it was too late. The Dikler had all the courage of his opponent and perhaps that extra ounce of staying power that makes the difference up that hill. He passed the post a short head in front in one of the most thrilling finishes ever seen in the Gold Cup. Mrs August's ugly duckling, her 'tuppenny' horse, had earned and well earned his niche in the hall of champions.

After the race there were the usual post-mortems. Talkative as ever, Pitman blamed himself freely for the defeat. He may have been out-generaled and out-ridden by Barry on

Pendil leading over the last fence from the winner of the 1973 race, The Dikler, with Charlie Potheen third.

the day but it must be remembered that the characteristics of his horse and the way the race was run presented problems that it would have taken no ordinary jockey to overcome. To their eternal credit he and his trainer were the very first to congratulate their conquerors. The whole race exemplified all that is best in steeplechasing and perhaps the fairest comment when the tumult and the shouting had died was that of the anonymous scribe in *Chasers and Hurdlers* that The Dikler had won because he was fractionally the better stayer. After this victory which stamped him as a true champion The Dikler was retired for the season. His jockey, Ron Barry, ended a memorable year by becoming champion jockey once again.

Before the 1974 renewal of the race came round another milestone in its history had been passed for this was its jubilee year and Piper Heidsieck celebrated the occasion by giving a dinner at the Berkeley Hotel. To this dinner were invited every owner, trainer and rider of past winners together with other racing luminaries as guests of the Marquis D'Aulan, the managing director. In his after-dinner speech Major-General Sir Randle Feilden, the chairman of Cheltenham, compared the prestige of the Gold Cup in jumping to that of the King George VI and Queen Elizabeth Stakes and the Prix de L'Arc de Triomphe on the flat and went on to say that over the years it had proved itself the true championship of steeplechasing. There could be no doubt now that from its humble beginnings and through war, trouble and tribulation the Gold Cup had survived to become the supreme accolade of the steeplechasing year.

The handicap, too, endorsed this view for it is worth pointing out that in the 1974 renewal of the Hennessy Cognac Gold Cup the handicapper set Charlie Potheen, a horse placed third in the Gold Cup, to give no less than a stone to Red Rum the then twice victorious hero of the Grand National thus underlining the relative importance in the hierarchy of steeple-chasing of the two races and the class of horses contesting them.

Whether The Dikler could repeat his victory of the previous year was a matter of speculation. History has shown how hard it is to win more than one Gold Cup. Many still held that he had been a lucky winner and that when they met again Pendil would avenge his defeat. Pendil himself gave credence to this view when he slammed The Dikler in the Massey-Ferguson Gold Cup at Cheltenham. At level weights – 12 st 7 lb – he had The Dikler twenty-one-and-a-half lengths behind him with a useful horse, Helmsman, receiving no less than 32 lb from them both, separating them. Pendil, however, had then had the benefit of a race under his belt which The Dikler had not but he repeated his triumph in the King George VI at Kempton on Boxing Day with The Dikler again third, this time as much as thirty-two lengths adrift. It had also to be remembered that Pendil was a year younger than his rival who would be eleven when the race was next run, an age when the edge might just be gone or be beginning to go from his greatness.

The claims of another, still younger, competitor, were at this time at least, largely overlooked.

Like The Dikler and Charlie Potheen, Captain Christy was something of an unpredictable character but on his best behaviour he unquestionably could claim right of entry to championship class. The season before he had proved himself one of the elect over hurdles by winning the Scottish Champion Hurdle at Ayr in record time, the Irish Sweeps Hurdle and, as has been said, had finished third to Comedy of Errors in the Champion Hurdle.

Pat Taaffe, Arkle's jockey, had Captain Christy in his charge. The horse had been introduced to jumping by his owner, Major Pidcock, who trained and rode him himself. During the summer of 1972, however, he met Taaffe and asked him if he would take over his training. When he arrived at Taaffe's stable Captain Christy brought with him the reputation of being something of a handful. Taaffe had had experience of horses by Mon Capitaine and knew that many of them were self-willed, that they made up their own minds what they wanted to do and by and large did it. He was, however – and is – a horseman as well as a jockey and, riding Captain Christy himself as soon as he got him, he found him little trouble. He was keen and sharp but, like many such horses, did not take a lot of work and did most of it himself. Soon he had him ready to run at Tralee. Ridden by his owner he gave a very disappointing performance. That night when he got home, Taaffe received a telephone call from Major Pidcock to say he did not think he got on with the horse and if Taaffe could find a buyer at the same price as he had given for him – £10,000 – he was to let him go. Fortunately Taaffe knew that Mr and Mrs Samuels, recently come from New Zealand who had a couple of horses with him, were looking for a high-class chaser to carry their colours. He mentioned Captain Christy to them and the deal was made.

R. 'Bobby' Coonan rode him in his first hurdle race at Naas for Mrs Samuel, in whose colours he ran throughout his career, but when he was due to come out again Coonan was claimed by Paddy Sleator for whom he had a retainer. Taaffe went to Sleator and discussed with him the question of Coonan's replacement.

H.R. 'Bobby' Beasley had won the Cheltenham Gold Cup for Lord Fingall on Roddy Owen in 1959 and was one of the best and most stylish jockeys to come out of Ireland in the post-war years. But Beasley had, like Brogan, succumbed to alcoholism and had gone out of racing. Introduced to Alcoholics Anonymous by Nicky Rackard, a member of the great County Wexford hurling family who had won his own struggle with the bottle, who was a

Twenty-five winning jockeys attended the Piper Heidsieck fiftieth anniversary dinner in 1974, they are:
standing left to right – Davy Jones, Willie Robinson, Bill Rees, Michael Scudamore, Jimmy Power, Tommy Cusack, Dave Dick, Aubrey Brabazon, Martin Molony, Tim Molony, Tony Grantham, Stan Hayhurst, Fred Winter, Pat Taaffe, Dickie Black
sitting left to right – 'Frenchie' Nicholson, Danny Morgan, Evan Williams, Ted Leader, 'Tim' Hamey, George Owen, Roger Burford
front row – Terry Biddlecombe, Ron Barry, Paul Kelleway

neighbour of Beasley's and who trained a small string with success, and helped too by Dr Austin Darragh, Beasley fought his battle against drink and won it. 'Nicky Rackard,' Beasley has recorded, 'has saved five men from dying of drink. I reckon that's something to be proud of.' And it was Nicky Rackard who encouraged Beasley to get back into racing. Lord Fingall, one of the best ambassadors for the sport of steeplechasing Ireland has ever had, hearing of his return, offered him the ride on his good horse No Other in the Leopardstown Chase of 1971. So Beasley got his second start. In his heyday Beasley had ridden for Sleator with success. Now, having watched his comeback, he recommended him to Taaffe. 'He's as good a jockey as you'll get,' were his words.

By this time Taaffe had realised that Captain Christy was not everybody's ride. Mostly he was in too much of a hurry and it was this which caused his jumping errors. He was temperamental; he wanted to be in front except when he took another notion and would settle and jump fluently from behind. Taaffe remembered Beasley's former brilliance, for they had ridden at the same time. He engaged him and found a man to match the horse.

Beasley was up when Captain Christy came out again in the Rossmore Hurdle at Naas. They won by five lengths and went on to win their next two races the last of which was the Scalp Hurdle which was virtually the Irish Champion Hurdle at the time. Even at that early stage Captain Christy seemed to be able to gallop his opposition off their legs though there

Amongst those at the anniversary dinner were Mrs Wyndham, widow of Major H. Wyndham, Red Splash's owner. Mrs Wyndham is seen with Fred Winter.

Two of the great names of the past at the dinner, Danny Morgan (*left*) and Tim Molony.

was still a question mark over his jumping. Indeed after the Scottish Champion Hurdle one of the other jockeys told Taaffe that his horse had left so many of the hurdles flattened behind him there was nothing left for the other horses to jump!

Before the end of his hurdling career Taaffe himself schooled him over fences and from the first felt that he had all the attributes of a champion – a tremendous relentless gallop, staying power and, when things went right, brilliant, fast jumping. Even when things went wrong such was his power and strength he could often hit a fence really hard and yet have that invaluable 'spare leg' which kept him on his feet. Just the same even that spare leg could not save him from the chances he took in his two steeplechases in England before the Gold Cup. Against Bula in the Black and White Chase at Ascot he fell at the second last and, deceived by the drop, did the same thing in the Wills Premier Chase final at Haydock. In England, as a result of these falls, his chances in the championship were largely written off. He was looked upon as a novice, which indeed of course he was at that time, and held to be outclassed by the more experienced horses.

Despite the fact that he had never proved he could stay the extended three miles of the Gold Cup Pendil was backed for this year's race as if defeat was out of the question. He started at odds of 13–8 on, The Dikler was at 5–1, a handsome price many thought for a horse who had beaten the favourite fair and square the year before. Captain Christy was at 7–1. The remainder of the field was made up by Inkslinger, The Queen Mother's Game Spirit whom Terry Biddlecombe had chosen to ride in preference to Charlie Potheen and the rank outsider and chancy jumper High Ken.

By the time the Gold Cup had come round Captain Christy had had two more races and two more wins under his belt. To get his confidence back Taaffe had run him in a two and a half mile novice chase at Punchestown early in February which he had had the speed to win by ten lengths. On the last day of that month he contested a conditions race at Thurles which he won by the same distance from an undistinguished field. Even then he succeeded in giving his connections a fright for, when well clear at the last, he ploughed through it and only that 'spare leg' and Beasley's horsemanship held him up.

His chances in the championship were still largely discounted by the pundits and the general opinion may perhaps be summed up by a remark made by one good Irish judge. 'They're mad to run him in it with the novice chases at their mercy,' he said. Though he did add the rider: 'And having said that now the bugger will probably go and win it!'

There were, in fact, several good reasons influencing Taaffe's decision to take on the cracks. First there was both his own and Beasley's opinion of the horse as something quite exceptional; he also reasoned that Captain Christy jumped better in good company and on the stretch than 'messing about with novices'; he felt that he had had Bula beaten at Ascot when he fell and Bula was fancied as a first-class chasing prospect. Further he knew he would stay every yard of the distance and that if he stood up he would test the stamina of anything that tried to match strides with him. And there was, too, the point that his owners liked to see their horses run in top-class events.

Taaffe and Beasley did decide, however, that with a tearaway like Charlie Potheen in the field it would be best to let Captain Christy settle – if he would – for they knew he had the speed to go on with his field whenever it was wanted.

It was for once at Cheltenham a mild almost summer day and the ground was on the good side of soft conditions which were all in Captain Christy's favour. Charlie Potheen as usual set off in front and took them along. To say that the race was not without incident would be a massive understatement. At half-way Inkslinger fell and all but brought Captain Christy down. It might have been expected to unsettle him but in fact it appeared to make him concentrate on his work. He went on measuring his fences just as and where Beasley wanted him, happily settled towards the rear of the field.

At the top of the hill, turning for home where the race is accustomed to sort itself out, things began to happen. As he had done the year before Pendil, feeling the fall of the ground beneath him, took hold and closed rapidly on the leaders. Approaching the third last Charlie Potheen weakened and High Ken, whose jumping had been far from perfect throughout, took over on his outside. Pendil, striding out, heading for home, was tracking him. As he passed Game Spirit Terry Biddlecombe called to Pitman: 'Don't get too near that bastard; he'll go arse over head.' But by this time The Dikler had ranged alongside Pendil with Beasley on Captain Christy, having noticed High Ken's erratic jumping and pulled out from behind him, in close attendance.

Down indeed High Ken came slap in front of Pendil. There was no escape for Pitman. The favourite turned a somersault over the fallen horse and was out of the race.

This fall left The Dikler in front but Captain Christy was closing him fast. At the last they were together. Up in the stands all those with an interest in Captain Christy were holding their breaths. He had jumped perfectly so far but now he was under pressure and upsides with one of the strongest jumpers in training. He hit that last fence hard and The Dikler went clear. Generations of Beasleys had met this situation and this sort of crisis before. Beasley sat tight and that spare leg saved Captain Christy once again and when it was most needed. Knowing what he had under him Beasley gathered his mount together and sent him on. The Captain's courage and the relentless gallop he could call upon apparently at will did the rest. He came to and caught The Dikler as if the older horse were standing still and went on to win by the handsome margin of five lengths. There were four years in age between the two horses; the edge had surely gone from The Dikler's speed, but this is not to detract from a great performance by a virtual novice running in only his seventh steeplechase. For that victory, too, much credit must be given to his rider who rode him superbly and who, by winning the Gold Cup for the second time after an interval of fifteen years, had made probably the greatest comeback steeplechasing has ever known.

Writing his memoirs of his days with Arkle published before this race Pat Taaffe recorded: 'If I have one dream it is that one day I shall school and train an Arkle of my own.' It looked, then, as if that dream might just be coming true.

It looked even more like it when at Kempton on Boxing Day 1974 Captain Christy slammed Pendil in a truly run race over the latter's favourite course.

He was ridden throughout the season by his former first partner Bobby Coonan and his preparation for the Gold Cup went on without interruption though he showed his dislike of heavy going when beaten into fourth place in both the Thyestes and the Leopardstown Chases having to shoulder top weight of 12 st through the mud and giving 31 lb in each case to the winner. However he won his last chase before Cheltenham, The P.Z. Mower Chase at Thurles, proving his wellbeing and his readiness. But when Taaffe and the Samuels arrived at their hotel the day before the meeting and saw the torrential rains coming down they knew the writing was on the wall.

Captain Christy (Bobby Beasley up), winner of the 1974 Gold Cup.

Such was the downpour in fact that the first day's racing was abandoned altogether, on the second day it was in doubt until almost the last minute and when the course was declared fit for racing one fence and one hurdle were omitted. On Gold Cup day, Thursday March 13th, racing was again doubtful. The stewards having decided to go-ahead no less than two fences on the steeplechase course were omitted. The conditions, someone remarked, resembled something out of the trenches in the First World War, and in no way could they be construed as a realistic test of horse and man.

Despite his defeat by Captain Christy at Kempton, Pendil had been made favourite in the ante-post market. But three weeks before Cheltenham he broke down in the Yellow Pages Chase, also at Kempton, and was taken out of the race. It was yet another example of the cruel luck in the championship which had pursued him throughout his brilliant career. Fred Winter had, however, two other strings to his bow demonstrating yet again the strength of talent in his powerful stable. These were Bula and Soothsayer. Twice winner of the Champion Hurdle Bula had taken well to fences and was held by many to be likely to be the first champion hurdler to add the championship of chasing to his crown. Certainly he had credentials. He had won three of his last four steeplechases, the last one being the Fairlawne Chase at Windsor over three miles. Pitman, however, preferred to ride the American-bred

(OPPOSITE) Ten Up and his trainer, Jim Dreaper, at Greenogue.

Soothsayer leaving the mount on Bula to J. Francome who had ridden him throughout the season. Francome was then at the outset of a great career though at that time he was held to be ineffectual in a finish, a defect, if it ever existed, which has long since disappeared.

It did not look a particularly strong field. The Dikler was back again but surely now past his best and with his sights firmly set on the Grand National. High Ken was there again, too, but his chances could be discounted however poor the field.

There was nevertheless one strong contender from the powerful Dreaper stable in Ireland. Running in the familiar yellow and black colours of Arkle's owner, Anne, Duchess of Westminster. This was Ten Up, a big, strong hard-pulling Irish gelding by Raise You Ten. An eight-year-old, Ten Up had won his last two races the second of which was the Whitbread Trial Chase at Ascot over three miles. In this he had handed out a twenty-five-length beating to Soothsayer with Glanford Brigg, who was also in the Gold Cup field, three-quarters of a length away third. This was a good field for Crisp was in it as were Credo's Daughter, Bruslee (another Gold Cup contender), April Seventh and Canasta Lad. The going was soft as it had been in Ten Up's previous outings. Thus he had shown he could act in the mud and moreover he had not run a bad race yet. The omens were there for all who cared to see.

On the day it was probably the worst ground in which the Gold Cup has ever been run and resembled nothing so much as a quagmire. Captain Christy started favourite at 7-4 against, which on the book he was fully entitled to do but with the conditions what they were there was very little stable confidence behind him.

Although he made a mistake six from home Ten Up handled the mud better than anyone else and stayed on up the hill to beat a very tired Soothsayer by six lengths with Bula a further half a length away third. Captain Christy could not act in the ground at all and virtually never got into the race. He was toiling in the rear when pulled up approaching the fourteenth fence. 'You were quite right to pull him up,' Taaffe greeted Coonan as he came in. 'I didn't pull him up. He pulled himself up,' was the answer.

After the race the remainder of the meeting was abandoned.

Ten Up was trained by Jim Dreaper who had only recently taken over the reins at Greenogue and it was a great feat by this young man succeeding as he had so soon to such a responsible position. He was ridden by T. Carberry who went on to complete a riding feat which must surely be unprecedented for in the space of one month he won the Gold Cup, the Grand National, and The Irish Grand National, the latter on Brown Lad, a horse we shall hear of again, also from the Dreaper stable.

By winning the Gold Cup Ten Up gave Greenogue its sixth championship and the Duchess her fourth. She was a lucky owner but, given his potential, Ten Up was not a lucky horse. He was broken by Pat Taaffe who had him as a youngster. He was no trouble and Taaffe sensed something of championship class in him even then but when in his care he noticed that every few weeks his coat would become staring and he would go off his feed. He mentioned this to the Dreapers when he sent Ten Up to Greenogue. He was examined but nothing amiss could be found. Nevertheless it seems likely that these were early symptoms of the weakness that was to end his championship career.

(OPPOSITE) Anne, Duchess of Westminster, leads in Ten Up.

14

Ups and Downs

IT IS A TRUISM applicable to all sports as well as life that it is more difficult to stay on the top than to get there. Never was there a better example of this than the results of the Gold Cup for since its inception in 1924 only four horses have succeeded in winning the championship more than once and none had come back from defeat to win it again. But in 1976 Captain Christy looked all set to do so and write his name indelibly in the hall of fame. Between the Gold Cup and the King George VI on Boxing Day 1975 he had put up a series of sparkling performances in Ireland, England and America. Second under top weight in the Whitbread, beaten one and a half lengths by April Seventh to whom he was conceding 25 lb, second at Auteuil in the Grand Steeplechase de Paris, fourth in the Colonial Cup at Camden South Carolina and then a win in the Punchestown Chase in December with Davy Lad, Roman Bar and Ten Up all well beaten behind him. His performance in the King George VI, however, far surpassed all these and was perhaps the crowning achievement of his career.

Incapacitated with a broken arm sustained in a fall shortly before the race, Coonan was unable to take the ride. To the surprise of many Taaffe entrusted Captain Christy's chances to G. Newman then relatively inexperienced and still claiming the allowance. It appeared at first sight a rash thing to do but Newman was attached to Taaffe's stable, and Taaffe, none better, could judge a jockey's abilities: Newman had ridden the horse in his work and schooled him and knew him and Captain Christy more than most was a horse that needed knowing. Taaffe therefore gave him his great chance.

In the event both the horse and Newman surpassed even the stable's most sanguine expectations. Setting off in front at a headlong gallop he gave a superb exhibition of fast economical jumping. Taaffe had warned Newman that the year before he had hesitated at the bend past the stands as if wanting to get back to the stables and if he did it again to give him one down the shoulder. It was as well he had uttered this warning for that was what Captain Christy chose to do. Francome on Bula, thinking his rival was beginning to falter in his gallop, quickened to try to catch him. It was a hopeless task. Sent about his business again by Newman's slap down the shoulder Captain Christy resumed his remorseless gallop. He hit the sixteenth hard but it made no difference. Newman sat tight, and the field was spreadeagled behind him. Captain Christy passed the post to a storm of cheering thirty lengths in front of Bula having shattered the course record by more than four seconds.

The comments of the sporting press were ecstatic. Peter Willett, the breeding authority, writing in the *Sporting Chronicle* called it 'one of the great performances of steeplechasing history' and others were not far behind. Given good ground another Gold Cup seemed at his mercy. But it was not to be. A month later an injury to his off fore when being worked at home put him out for the season.

That injury to Captain Christy brought Ten Up very much back into the reckoning. But Ten Up had started to break blood vessels and as a result he had only three outings before Cheltenham. After his defeat by Captain Christy at Punchestown he finished second to Spanish Tan (receiving 27 lb) at Naas and then beat his solitary opponent, Ormond King, at Limerick Junction. Before this race he had received a coagulant, a fact which Jim Dreaper made known to the stewards who, however, took no action. But when he brought him to Cheltenham he was informed by the stewards of the meeting that if he administered this medication again and a coagulant was found on examination to be present it would be treated as a 'substance (other than a normal nutrient)' and render the horse liable to disqualification. Confronted with this Dreaper had little option but to withdraw Ten Up. This he did on the morning of the race earning as a result a fine of £125. This was the mandatory penalty for a late withdrawal. Whether it should have been remitted in the circumstances since at that time there were grey edges to say the least round the rules concerning coagulants is a matter of opinion.

The withdrawal of Ten Up robbed the race of much of its interest. Coupled with the absence of Captain Christy, with Pendil still sidelined through injury, and Soothsayer, too, also on the injured list, the entries then gave very much the appearance of a second eleven. It was true that The Dikler was there again but at thirteen he could scarcely be other than a light of former days and his objective in any event was now the National. The Dreaper stable displayed its strength by having two other representatives. One of them, Brown Lad, the winner of the previous year's Irish Grand National, looked on his best form as if he might be a threat to anything though he was thought to need a give in the ground. The other, Colebridge, had won the Irish Grand National in 1975 but he was twelve years old and had never quite perhaps even on his best form moved from being a high-class handicapper into championship class. None of the others were of much account with the exception of Bula who was immediately installed as favourite, at 6–4. Whether his qualifications justified that position is another matter. He had, as we have seen, been slammed by Captain Christy in The King George VI. Before that he had won at Haydock and been beaten at Ascot. After it he had had two bloodless victories, the second over a solitary opponent in the Fairlawne Chase at Windsor. Further he had given no evidence that he could stay the stiff three and a quarter miles at Cheltenham.

There was, in fact, a far more potent threat to all these fully exposed horses lurking in the entries in the shape of a seven-year-old gelding by Royal Buck called Royal Frolic who had come on by leaps and bounds since the beginning of the season. He was, however, still desperately inexperienced even by the time the Gold Cup came round. He had run once as a four-year-old and was then put by for a year. His chasing career had not started until December 1974 and the Gold Cup was, in fact, only the twelfth race of his career and his tenth steeplechase. But he had won four of his last races even if these, with the exception of the last, were in minor contests.

This last win was in the Greenall Whitley Breweries Chase at Haydock, a race for which his trainer, Fred Rimell, had specifically trained him. He had bought Royal Frolic for his octogenarian owner Sir Edward Hamner who particularly wanted a good win at Haydock, a course with which he had been intimately connected for nearly fifty years. Not only did Royal Frolic win it but he opened the eyes of all who watched him for he gave an exhibition of fast, unblemished jumping to leave Barona trailing ten lengths in arrears and with Glanford Brigg and Red Rum down the field behind them both.

Mrs Mercy Rimell had seen Bula run at Ascot and had not been impressed. She encouraged her husband to let Royal Frolic take his chance against the cracks; his owner agreed and Royal Frolic was in the line-up. He continued to improve and his trainer's confidence grew. Some days before the race he told a well-known bloodstock agent: 'Whoever beats me will win the Gold Cup.' It may have been this confidence which made Royal Frolic, though a virtual novice, start third favourite at 14–1.

The story of the race needs little telling. Despite the firm ground they went no great gallop on the first circuit. Royal Frolic was always lying handy and held fourth place just behind The Dikler as they climbed the hill for the second time. The Dikler made a thorough mess of the next fence and dropped out. At the third last Royal Frolic took over from Glanford Brigg and from there to the line it was a procession. Bula and Colebridge tried to get on terms but Bula, who had run lamentably throughout, hit the third last so hard as to put paid to what little chance he had. It was left to Brown Lad, who was hating the ground, and had had to be ridden by Carberry every inch of the way, to run on into second place after being virtually tailed off at the top of the hill. Even then he was five lengths behind the winner. Colebridge ran up to his best handicapping form to be third.

Royal Frolic gave Fred Rimell his second Gold Cup and Sir Edward Hamner £18,134.50 of which Piper Heidsieck contributed £12,000. Winter's wretched luck in the race continued with Bula's failure. He had now trained five of the last six favourites for it and none of them had won. 'I thought he was as well as I could get him,' he told *Sporting Life*, 'but somehow I felt on the journey here he wouldn't win. I've got a feeling about this race – like Gordon Richards about the Derby.'

There were new names in plenty for the 1977 race. Captain Christy, alas, had gone forever from the entries as had Bula who was aimed instead at the Two Mile Champion Chase in which he fell, sustaining injuries from which he later had to be put down. Royal Frolic, and Brown Lad, too, were absent through injury. Winter, however, had a new chasing star in the ascendant in Lord Howard de Walden's Lanzarote.

Lanzarote's entry on the chasing scene had been fortuitous. Previously his owner's interests had lain entirely on the flat where he was an owner and breeder of some magnitude. Lanzarote had not been of much account on the flat though he was bred well enough being by Milesian out of Slag by Mossborough. Contemplating him Lord Howard de Walden suddenly thought that it might be fun to have a jumper. Accordingly he had rung Winter to see if he had room for him and would take him. 'For you we'll build a box,' was Winter's reply and so Lanzarote had come to Uplands.

The sudden impulse and the choice of trainer had turned out well for Lanzarote had won the previous year's Champion Hurdle. Put to fences he had taken brilliantly to them and Winter thought it at least possible that he would succeed where Bula had failed and become

Fred Rimell, trainer of Royal Frolic, in the winner's enclosure, 1976.

not only his first winner of the Gold Cup but the first champion hurdler to take the chasing championship.

But, like Royal Frolic the year before, Lanzarote, brilliant though he was, was still only a novice. It was true he was an outstanding one winning his last three races before the Gold Cup in splendid style culminating in a twenty-five length victory over Never Rock in the Reynoldstown Novices Chase at Ascot on February 16th. Nevertheless, unlike Royal Frolic, he had never taken on experienced and top-class horses and it was asking a lot of him to do so in the championship for the first time especially since, with the proven Irish front runner Tied Cottage in the field, it was certain to be run at a strong gallop with its contenders jumping on the stretch throughout.

On the other hand, once more, it was not, on the face of it, an impressive field that year. Summerville, owned by that great supporter of racing both on the flat and over fences, the octogenarian, Jim Joel, was very good when he was good but he had a mind of his own and had taken to stopping or trying to run out. He had, too, recently been held up in his work with a suspect leg. April Seventh, the other runner from the Turnell stable, was also unreliable. Fort Devon, sent over from the States with this race in mind and with a victory in the Maryland Hunt Cup and numerous other races over timber behind him, had more serious claims to be considered. Originally a useless point-to-pointer in England he had come into his own as a jumper of timber and, returned, had won first time out at Wincanton under top weight. He might well have gone to the Gold Cup unbeaten had he not come up against Pendil, back once more in fighting trim, at Kempton and even then only gone under by a short head after a desperate struggle.

Pendil, even at twelve, having been nursed back to health under Winter's care, looked like being the one they all had to beat. Away from racing for almost two years he had made an amazing comeback winning his first three races off the reel and only failing by four lengths to give 33 lb to the winner of the Yellow Pages Pattern Chase at Kempton on February 26th. Then the bad luck which had dogged him throughout his career struck again. A fall on the road caused injuries which ended his racing career. Thus probably the best of the potentially great horses who have run in the Gold Cup without winning it passed into retirement and without him the race was once more wide open.

When chances could then be assessed the strongest challengers looked likely to come from Ireland. There were four of them – Tied Cottage, Bannow Rambler, Fort Fox and Davy Lad. There was not much to choose between the form of the first three. In the Thyestes Chase at Gowran Park Bannow Rambler in receipt of 7 lb and in bottomless going beat Fort Fox a short head. Just over a month later at Leopardstown in the Harold Clarke Handicap Chase (formerly the Leopardstown Chase) he beat Davy Lad a neck when giving him 11 lb. In this race Fort Fox fell and Tied Cottage was down the field.

Just out of the novice class but out of it longer than Lanzarote Bannow Rambler had caught the imagination of the Irish public. He had shown he could battle but his jumping was far from accomplished and most of his races had seen him make mistakes especially under pressure. It was true he had looked brilliant in beating the previous Gold Cup winner Ten Up and Davy Lad in the Punchestown Chase in December but time and again his jumping errors put him out of contention or on the floor. Fort Fox, too, had the maddening characteristic of throwing his races away by careless mistakes when well-placed.

Of the Irish runners it was Davy Lad who, on the book, appeared to have the least chance. Surveying the entries, however, his astute trainer, Mick O'Toole, realised that with the cracks of the previous seasons out of the way there was very little between any of the runners, that the jumping of both Bannow Rambler and Fort Fox was likely to let them down, and that his own horse was a courageous battler who would stay every yard of the distance. Moreover, though he was only seven he had two seasons' experience of jumping in handicap company behind him, he was improving all the time and he loved Cheltenham having won the Sun Alliance Novice Hurdle there as a five-year-old. He resolved to let him take his chance.

Davy Lad, his handler says, was an equable character who had been no trouble to break or train. He was, however, a much tougher horse on the racecourse than off it and when put to racing he showed that he had his idiosyncrasies and that he needed knowing. It was as well that in Dessie Hughes who rode him in all his races he found a stylist and a horseman who understood him and who had on the racecourse a strength and determination to match his own. For in all his races Davy Lad would somewhere or other, usually about half-way, persist in dropping himself out. 'He'd get out of any race at half-way; he'd look beaten and then come again,' his trainer recalls. Once the warning signals were out he required to be instantly and effectively got at to put him back into the race. Then, when he realised he was

Pendil, trained by Fred Winter, and seen here with John Francome up, was a firm favourite until a fall on the road ended his racing career.

mastered, he would run on and give of his best. This characteristic may have been one of the factors leading to his being under-rated in his most famous victory.

The weight of Irish money made Bannow Rambler favourite at 11–4; Lanzarote came next at 7–2 with Fort Devon third in the list at 4–1. Neglected in the betting Davy Lad was 12–1, Summerville stood at 15–1 and Tied Cottage at 20–1. Fort Fox, equipped with blinkers in the hope that they would concentrate his mind at his fences, was better than these three at 10–1. The ground was heavy.

Tied Cottage as expected set off in front at a great pace. Bannow Rambler and Lanzarote lay up close behind him but in this testing ground and against these experienced horses Lanzarote's jumping was not perfect. He made a mistake at the seventh fence, took the next in his stride and then, immediately after the ninth, disaster struck. Lanzarote appeared to jump the fence perfectly but a few yards beyond it, when clear of the fence, he slipped up and came down. Behind him Furlong on Bannow Rambler had no chance of taking avoiding action. Down he came too and so in the space of a couple of seconds the first and second favourites were out of it. Winter's jinx in the race was working overtime.

Tied Cottage continued to lead them at a merry gallop but at the last open ditch Summerville, on one of his going days, took over and headed him. Here Fort Devon fell putting the third of the well-backed horses out of the race and it was here, too, that Davy

Davy Lad clears the last fence from Tied Cottage and Summerville, 1977.

Lad decided to drop himself out. At the third last Summerville appeared to be safely heading for home and certain victory for only the tired Tied Cottage plugging on at the same speed was anywhere near him. But Hughes on Davy Lad, knowing what he had under him, was riding him hard and getting the response he was looking for. Down the hill, unnoticed by most, Davy Lad was eating up ground.

The race was not done with incident yet. Between the last two fences Summerville broke down. Davy Lad by now had caught Tied Cottage and passed him and was running on strongly. He was ahead of Summerville at the last which he jumped as well if not better than he had jumped anything in the race. He was a tired horse and he wandered slightly on the run in but the rest were stone cold behind him. Driven right out by Hughes he stayed on stoutly to win by six lengths. The toll of casualties exacted by the ground and the pace was such that only seven of the thirteen runners finished. O'Toole said afterwards that the horse owed his victory almost as much to his jockey as to himself for many riders would have given up so far behind was he at the top of the hill, but Hughes, like his mount, never surrendered.

This may have been a bad Gold Cup, it was certainly a tragic one. It is, however, worth stressing that Davy Lad was only seven and thus had not yet come to full maturity, and that he beat Tied Cottage fairly and squarely and Tied Cottage's record in the following years, showed him something above the average. The loss of Lanzarote, a greatly loved horse, robbed Davy Lad of much of the credit that was due to him.

Sadly Davy Lad never had a chance of proving his detractors wrong. He lost his form the following season mystifying his connections for he had always been an exceptionally sound horse with a splendid set of limbs. There seemed no point in trying for the championship again and eventually rheumatic trouble was diagnosed. His owners did not care to go on running him when it was clear he could not do himself justice and he was retired. Bannow Rambler, too, was plagued by back trouble and failed to win a race or recapture his old form. His fall on the flat over Lanzarote may have had something to do with this and indeed Lanzarote's own back may have had something to do with his slipping up for Pitman in his memoirs mentioned that he suffered from intermittent back trouble and it is not impossible that the mistake shortly before he came down on the flat may have jarred his back and caused the fatal fall.

As has been said Bannow Rambler, the previous year's favourite, had been nothing but disappointing throughout the season. He was well beaten by his old rivals Tied Cottage and Fort Fox in the Punchestown Chase in December, trailing into third place sixteen lengths behind the winner and again was sixteen lengths adrift to Kilkilwell at Leopardstown a month later. These were the nearest he could get to winning in six starts. Despite these failures his name appeared in the entries for the Gold Cup as, amongst the older and more experienced horses, did those of Fort Devon who, at the age of twelve had left his championship aspirations perhaps a little late, Fort Fox who flattered that his jumping might at last be relied on but was to prove that flattery a deception, Tied Cottage who was having a quiet season and Brown Lad who had missed all of the previous season through injury. Indeed Brown Lad, a courageous horse if ever there was one, was showing every sign of a return to his best form and that at the age of twelve he might well prove an exception to the general rule in that he was actually improving with advancing years. Best of all Royal Frolic was back on the racecourse again, his leg trouble apparently behind him, and appeared to be at least approaching his former championship form. Even so it looked as though he would have to prove himself something very special indeed if he were to establish a record by coming back to recapture his crown for there were several strong contenders for it amongst the younger up and coming brigade.

At first sight the most impressive of these was Bachelor's Hall who already in the first half of the season had set up one record for he had reeled off successive victories in the semi-classic Mackeson Gold Cup, Hennessy Gold Cup and King George VI Chases, a feat which had eluded even the mighty Arkle.

Bachelor's Hall then appeared to possess every attribute of a coming champion – staying power (the Hennessy Cognac is over the Gold Cup distance of three and a quarter miles), speed, jumping ability and, most importantly, the gift of instant acceleration. Ridden from behind by his then claiming jockey Martin O'Halloran, who got on so well with him and rode him in all his races, it was this turn of foot at the finish which made many hail him as the most exciting prospect to appear for several seasons.

Bachelor's Hall, fourth in the 1978 Gold Cup.

He was not alone amongst the newcomers to brighten the year for Fred Winter from the wealth of the talent available to him produced a young horse whose brilliance seemed likely to break his hoodoo in the race. On the advice of the ex-jockey Dave Dick he had bought Midnight Court for a hefty price (said to be £15,000) in Ireland and introduced him to racing the year before. At first he gave some trouble by getting his tongue over the bit but that was soon cured by fitting a special bit and he quickly showed his ability by winning two hurdles in convincing style. Put to chasing he had one win over two and a quarter miles at Ascot and was only once out of the frame in four starts. Looking more like a promising novice than a proven chaser at the beginning of the current season he proceeded to run up a series of wins and after Christmas convinced his handler that he could hold his own and probably more in experienced company. Although he had qualified for the Embassy Novice Final his speed and class decided Winter to aim him at the Gold Cup despite his youth – he was only seven – and the fact that it would be only his tenth steeplechase.

When Cheltenham came round it gave every promise of being an exciting championship but it was not to be. There was no Gold Cup at that National Hunt Meeting for the snow came down and the final day was abandoned. The race was reopened to be run on April 12th.

The abandonment altered the whole complexion of the race. Winter's luck was changing

Mrs Olive Jackson leads in Midnight Court after his win.

with a vengeance for from there on everything played into his hands. Tied Cottage went to Liverpool for the Grand National where he started second favourite but fell at the sixth fence. Fort Fox, Brown Lad and Bannow Rambler were all sent to Fairyhouse for the Irish Distillers Grand National run over three and a half miles. Here Brown Lad achieved the finest performance of his career in carrying 12 st 2 lb to a three-quarter-length victory over Sandpit to whom he was giving 26 lb. Fort Fox finished fourth to him. Bannow Rambler ran lamentably and was struck out of the re-opened Gold Cup as was Tied Cottage. Master H who had a victory over none other than Tied Cottage, Bachelor's Hall and Royal Frolic, admittedly when receiving weight, earlier in the season, appeared in the new entries but the considerable exertions of all these horses in the interval can have done their chances in the championship little good. Moreover Bachelor's Hall who had been on the strenuous go from November had almost certainly peaked too soon and the long postponement could only have further lessened his prospects. Best of all from Winter's point of view he was able to give Midnight Court another easy race in the interval in the Aynsley China Cup Chase at Chepstow in which with odds of 3–1 laid on him he trounced a moderate field by ten lengths over two and a half miles.

Despite the fact that he was by the Ascot Gold Cup winner Twilight Alley there was still the nagging doubt in the minds of many whether he could stay the three and a quarter miles at Cheltenham, and he did not start favourite this honour going to Fort Devon at 9–4. But here again Winter's luck held. With Tied Cottage out of the way there was no front runner in the field to take them along. The pace on the first circuit was one of the slowest if not the slowest seen in the race which enabled Francome to hold up Midnight Court and conserve his stamina. Moreover the ground was good to firm which was all against Brown Lad's chances.

Royal Frolic and Fort Devon were in the lead coming down the hill for the second time but behind them Francome could be seen sitting still, poised and ready to strike. Fort Fox had blundered away any chance he might have had by this time and Brown Lad, hating the ground, appeared hopelessly out of it.

At the last bend Fort Devon hung away from the rails and Francome was given the opening he wanted. He slipped Midnight Court through on the inside and set sail for home increasing his lead with every stride. He was about ten lengths clear at the last where Royal Frolic, in hopeless pursuit, toppled over to lose a certain second place. Midnight Court appeared to check as he met the hill. He may well have been tiring but there was no one near enough to find him out for Fort Devon, then in third place, was beaten and labouring. As it happened it was Brown Lad, recovering once more from an apparently hopeless position, who ran on under Carberry's driving to finish second with Master H a brave but struggling far away third. Bachelor's Hall whose blinding finishing speed had not surprisingly lost its edge was fourth and Fort Devon, fading to nothing at the finish, fifth.

This was not a satisfactory championship. Midnight Court may have been as good as his supporters said he was but he never had a chance to prove it in this class again. The wear and tear of modern steeplechasing found him out as it had done so many others. He suffered leg trouble and, despite some comeback attempts, never showed again form likely to win a championship. It is only fair to add, nevertheless, that when he was ultimately and finally retired in 1983 his rider Francome said of him that, 'on his day, he was one of the very best, a great jumper with a turn of foot and the ability of a class horse to act on any going'.

15

Alverton and Tied Cottage

BEFORE THE 1978 National Hunt Meeting was abandoned a big, strong steeplechaser named Alverton had gone through the mud like a hero to win the Arkle Chase and record his fourth win over fences in a row.

To those who looked forward to next year's Gold Cup this was an event of some significance though not perhaps fully realised at the time. But its former contestants were once more, as seemed almost inevitable during those years, succumbing to the wear and tear of steeplechasing at the top and falling by the wayside. Of its previous winners only The Dikler had survived fit and well to fight for his crown in successive years. Injury or illness had disrupted the careers of Captain Christy, Ten Up, Royal Frolic and Davy Lad. And now, as has been said, Midnight Court was also to be struck down and leave the racecourse, though not, as will be seen, forever.

Alverton's path to the top class had been a strenuous one nor did he enter it easily for he, too, had had his setbacks. Bought by Peter Easterby, his trainer, and sold by him to Mr Stanhope Joel whose interests lay mainly on the flat but who had had steeplechasers with Easterby before, Alverton, had, in fact, commenced his career on the flat and had won good races as a three-year-old before breaking down badly in a four-year-old hurdle at Newcastle. Fired and put by for over a year he came back to win again over hurdles and then to reel off five further victories on the flat before running second in the Ebor Handicap. His chasing debut came at Newcastle in January 1978 when he won the first of his four victories already referred to beating Sweet Joe, the winner of that year's Sun Alliance Chase.

By 1979 he was obviously ready for better things and a tilt at the cracks of whom, as it happened, there were then precious few left. Only Brown Lad survived of the placed horses in the 1978 Gold Cup for, as we have seen, Midnight Court was under treatment and Master H had broken a shoulder in the King George VI and had had to be put down. Brown Lad was now thirteen and even he, evergreen as he had shown himself to be, could scarcely be expected to improve at that age and no thirteen-year-old had ever won the Cup. Of the last five winners indeed four had been seven and one eight years old.

Alverton's 1979 campaign did not start auspiciously for he was brought down once and occupied second place twice in his first three starts though in the third of these he was giving away 3 lb to Diamond Edge soon to be written up as a future Gold Cup winner and who was

to have a distinguished career over fences. The initial stable plan had been to aim Alverton at the Grand National but when he won convincingly at Haydock early in March beating a useful field Easterby, in consultation with Mrs Brudenell Bruce, Stanhope Joel's daughter who then controlled the horse's destinies, decided to let him take his place in the championship.

As it happened Easterby had a second very live contender in the race. Night Nurse had won the last two Champion Hurdles. Put to fences he had taken to them well and looked as likely as any to break the hoodoo on hurdle champions reaching the top and become the first to win them both. He ran up a spectacular series of victories in novice events and a fortnight before the Gold Cup went down by two-and-a-half lengths to Silver Buck after a desperate struggle in the Embassy Premier Chase Final at Haydock. It could, however, be seen as significant that Jonjo O'Neill, the stable jockey, elected to ride Alverton. O'Neill a likeable and universally popular Irishman who had started his career on the flat was a shrewd judge of what and when to ride as he had demonstrated two years before when he had become champion for the first time with a record number of one hundred and forty-nine winners from five hundred and forty-five rides. This year he was well on course to become champion for the second time.

As well as Brown Lad, Royal Frolic and Tied Cottage were back in the field. Royal Frolic was only a shadow of his former self but Tied Cottage at eleven had retained all his zest for racing, he was at his best in the spring, he had never run a bad race at Cheltenham and, ridden by T. Carberry, probably the best and most experienced of the home-based Irish jockeys, he could be relied upon to give a good account of himself.

Within a few days of the opening of the Festival Meeting injury once more stepped in to disrupt plans, alter the betting and disappoint anticipation. Gay Spartan, the convincing winner of the King George VI Chase, the short priced ante-post favourite on every list, pulled up lame after a gallop on the Saturday before the race and had to be struck out. Then Diamond Edge, a Walwyn entry who was beginning to show real form, was found to be cast in his box the night before and he too had to be withdrawn. Immediately another runner from the Walwyn Stable, Gaffer, was installed as the early favourite. Whether he had done enough to deserve this exalted position is another matter. Only promoted from hurdling in January he had won two steeplechases before going under by two lengths to Gay Spartan in the Jim Ford Challenge Cup at Wincanton. It hardly looked like winning championship form though his vastly experienced trainer had publicly expressed the highest opinion of him. In the event Gaffer did not occupy the position for long being overtaken by both Alverton and, strangely, Brown Lad, who each started a point shorter than him at 5–1 against. To complete the story of Gaffer, when the tapes went up he never really got into the race at all, finished down the field, lame, and second last of those who completed.

It was a dreadful day, the going was heavy and just before the race the snow which had been threatening all the morning came down. Tied Cottage, as usual, set off to make all and, despite the state of the ground, the gallop he was able to go in it soon had many of his opponents in deep trouble. Brown Lad, always slow to warm up, this time never did so at

(OPPOSITE) Alverton (2) and Tied Cottage (21) jump the last but
Tied Cottage fell on landing and Alverton raced on alone to win by twenty-five lengths.

all. Night Nurse, quietly fancied to run a good race ran a diabolical one. Never jumping well he made a bad mistake at the thirteenth fence and was thereafter tailed off. Royal Frolic played no part at all and it was left to Alverton, who had always been in touch and who had jumped without the semblance of a mistake, to come through the mud to challenge Tied Cottage at the third last.

At the final bend the battle was joined. The two of them were then clear of their field not one of whom had a hope of catching them. They were level over the second last. Landing, O'Neill went for his whip with Carberry still sitting still.

Coming to the last Carberry had not yet moved while Alverton was being hand driven. Easterby has put it on record that as he approached the fence Tied Cottage changed his legs. Be that as it may he appeared to jump the fence perfectly possibly half a length ahead of his rival. Then, with the race, it seemed, in his grasp, he pitched on landing, slipped and came down. Alverton raced alone up the hill to win by twenty-five lengths. Royal Mail, a New Zealand import who would have been a distant third had Tied Cottage stood up, clambered into second place with Aldaniti, a horse who was to make history elsewhere later on, a further twenty lengths away third.

Whether Tied Cottage would have won had he stood up is, of course, a matter of speculation. In the first place the fences are there to be jumped, he did not stand up when it mattered most and Alverton, ridden with admirable courage and judgment by O'Neill, had him under pressure. Moreover Alverton had proved himself before and was proving himself then a redoubtable battler who responded to O'Neill's driving and, had the outcome of the fence been different, he might well have worn Tied Cottage down on the hill. It was a victory fairly won under testing conditions and nothing should be allowed to detract from it.

Alverton appeared to be thrown into the National handicap and was accordingly sent on there. At Becher's second time round he fell, broke his neck and was killed instantly. Apart from the tragedy of his death to his connections his loss was doubly unfortunate in that in build he looked to be the tough, strong sort who would stand up to the rigours of steeplechasing and make his reappearance in the Gold Cup for years to come.

That Alverton's type was sadly lacking from the modern scene was once more proved in the 1979/80 season when injury, accident and illness took their toll. Gay Spartan, Night Nurse, and Gaffer all went out as did Midnight Court who failed to sustain a comeback attempt.

On the other hand there were promising newcomers coming on to the stage. Jack of Trumps, trained in Ireland by Edward O'Grady, was being hailed there by many as a coming champion. At seven he was certainly of an age commensurate with most of the recent Gold Cup winners, furthermore he had greater experience than the majority of those of his age for he had been racing since he was a four-year-old when he won a point-to-point and then went on to win on the flat. He had been second in the Irish Cesarewitch and by the time he was five had five steeplechases under his belt. At six, the year before, he had been sent to take on the best running second in the King George VI at Kempton, beaten five lengths by Gay Spartan, indeed only a minor injury had prevented him from contesting that

(OPPOSITE) Alverton and Jonjo O'Neill being led into the winner's enclosure after winning the 1979 race.

year's Gold Cup. He was not particularly robust in appearance and it did pass through some minds to wonder whether these exertions might have their effect on his future.

Diamond Edge's name amongst the entries made the prospect of the race exciting, for at his best he was a fast, spectacular jumper though as often as not he was inclined to treat his fences with a disdain which led to his undoing. He, too, had started his career in point-to-points before being sent to Fulke Walwyn who brought him along in easy stages and he had, in fact, missed one whole season. In contrast to Jack of Trumps in appearance he was a tough, rugged gelding, built like a true steeplechaser, strong enough to sustain hard knocks and bred to stay three miles or more being by Honour Bound out of Six of Diamonds who was herself by Sayajirao the winner of the 1947 St Leger. He had a will of his own and took some riding but the stable jockey W. Smith got on with him admirably. Before the Gold Cup he had three successive victories under his belt, in the second of which, the Freshfields Holiday Chase at Sandown, a course on which he gave and was to give his best performances, he beat Tied Cottage by four lengths giving him 9 lb. He started a worthy favourite for the Gold Cup at 5–2 against.

It was clear nevertheless that Diamond Edge was not going to have it all his own way for despite defections this was a representative field. Jack of Trumps was there to threaten him as were last year's second Royal Mail, Master Smudge who he had beaten the year before at Sandown and, more interesting and exciting than these, Border Incident who had looked a prospective Gold Cup winner when beating a good field in the Embassy Final in 1977 but

Diamond Edge, trained by Fulke Walwyn with W. (Bill) Smith up, is seen here in the Compton Chase at Newbury.

Master Smudge, eventual winner of the 1980 race, jumps an early fence. He is third from the left and in the lead are Mac Vidi and Kas.

who had been plagued by injury ever since and had never arrived in the line up. Now, at last, at ten, he was taking his place in the championship.

Tied Cottage, at twelve and his third attempt, was largely neglected in the betting at 13–2. It was true that his form this season had been far from convincing but those who dismissed him overlooked several things. He loved Cheltenham and had never run a bad race there, he was at his best in the spring, and he was ridden by T. Carberry, who was one of the best tacticians in the business. Furthermore he revelled in the mud and the ground came right for him at the last moment when torrential rain the night before saturated the course. This deluge caused the late withdrawal of Silver Buck and Bachelor's Hall.

There was a new sponsor for when Piper Heidsieck dropped out the Tote came in making the race worth £35,997.50.

Although it is frequently said that it is virtually impossible to make a pillar to post win at Cheltenham, especially in the Gold Cup, knowing what he had under him, that his mount would stay every yard of the distance and that certain of his rivals had stamina limitations which this ground would mercilessly reveal, Carberry jumped Tied Cottage out of the gate and set out to make it all. He succeeded so well that it would be true to say no other runner got in a blow. Jack of Trumps was nearly down at the first but he was one of the few who looked as if he might deliver a challenge when brought down by Royal Mail falling in front of him five from home. Border Incident, too, was going easily enough when he got rid of his rider six out. Diamond Edge, who never really showed his best form at Cheltenham, was on one of his careless days and made early mistakes. Surviving those he was driven along to try to challenge, made more errors and was pulled up before the last. After the race he was found to be slightly lame.

Meanwhile Carberry in front was giving a masterly exhibition, worthy of Piggott at his best, of dictating the pace. So much was he in command that he was able to give Tied Cottage at least two breathers. He galloped on unfalteringly up the hill to win by no less than eight lengths from Master Smudge. Mac Vidi, a fifteen-year-old, who started at 66-1, profited by the mistakes and falls of his more illustrious companions to run on strongly through the mud to finish third. Tied Cottage was the third twelve-year-old to win the race the others being Silver Fame and What A Myth. It was a thoroughly deserved victory, a reward of courage, consistency and superb jockeyship. Alas he did not keep it. A routine test revealed traces of a contaminated substance - theobromide - in his urine.

The Disciplinary Committee of the Jockey Club had no option when they sat to consider the case but to disqualify Tied Cottage but they completely exonerated his trainer and all connected with him being satisfied that all reasonable precautions had been taken and waiving all fines. To lose the championship under such circumstances was the cruelest of hard luck especially since the stable was such a sporting one and his owner Mr A.S. Robinson was gallantly resisting the onset of a fatal disease which was to lead to his early death. The verdict was accepted without demur and the record amended to show Master Smudge the winner, Mac Vidi second and Approaching, who had been a very distant fourth to the true winner, third.

Tied Cottage (T. Carberry up) racing up the hill to win. A routine dope test, however, proved positive and he was later disqualified.

16

The Men from the North

THE LAST THREE years of the championship to be covered by this history all belong to the North. Little Owl, the 1981 winner was bred in Ireland by G. Ferris in County Armagh but he was sold at the Doncaster sales for 2,200 guineas to P.W. Easterby who trains at Habton Grange in Yorkshire from which he had already, as has been seen, sent out one Gold Cup winner in Alverton two years before. Easterby passed Little Owl on as an unbroken three-year-old, to Mrs 'Bobbie' Grundy in whose colours he ran until, on Mrs Grundy's death, she left him to her nephews Robert and Jim Wilson all of whom came from a well-known North of England family. By Cantab out of the Black Tarquin mare, Spangle, Little Owl was chasing bred and, a big, strong gelding, he looked like a true chaser far removed from the cast-offs from the flat that thronged steeplechasing and did it little good.

There was one, nevertheless, who was not impressed with his breeding however much he liked his looks. 'I promise you I would not have made another bid for him if I had not got him at that price because he was related to a whole lot of rubbish,' Easterby later told a reporter

At first Little Owl was something of a problem horse, difficult to break, unruly on the home gallops and 'working himself into a muck sweat over nothing' as his owner said. This unruliness persisted for some time as did the streak of the devil that was in him and it is the greatest credit not only to his skilful trainer but also to Olga Nicholson, the girl who looked after him, that he was tamed and came to hand. It was Olga Nicholson who always rode him in his work and Jim Wilson pays especial tribute to the skill, care and devotion she lavished on him not to mention the hours of patience she expended on him which made him into the lovely ride he became when he came into his hands.

On his very first appearance on the racecourse, Little Owl ridden by the stable jockey, Jonjo O'Neill, won the Harwood Novices Hurdle at Wetherby impressively by eight lengths. Thereafter, until he reached the peak of his career, he never looked back.

It was at the beginning of the 1981 season that Little Owl passed into the possession of Robert and Jim Wilson. He ran in the name and colours of Robert and was then and thereafter ridden in all his races by his brother. Jim Wilson was – and is – an outstanding amateur rider, probably the best now riding and certainly the best never to have headed the amateur's list. Unlike others he did not have the backing of a long purse or a powerful stable behind him. He had had to make his own way and the manner in which he rode Little Owl

showed how well he could seize his chances on a high-class horse once they were offered to him.

Before the Gold Cup Little Owl had had only seven races over fences but he had won all of them save the 1980 Sun Alliance Chase at the Festival Meeting when he had been hampered and brought down. He had also earned a considerable sum in prize money, his four victories in the 1980–81 season netting him £34,061. But he did not start favourite for the championship for this was probably the best Gold Cup field, horse for horse, seen out in the last ten years. The favourite's position was occupied by Silver Buck from the powerful Dickinson stable, also situated in the north. Silver Buck had won the King George VI Chase at Kempton for the second successive year. This race had been run at a terrific pace dictated by the tearaway Annalog's Daughter and Silver Buck had pulled up very tired raising doubts in some minds whether he would get the Gold Cup distance especially if the ground turned heavy. Moreover many believed that the dual champion hurdler Night Nurse, now turned successfully to chasing, might well have beaten him had he not blundered badly at the last giving his rider no chance of staying in the saddle.

Trained like Little Owl at Habston by Peter Easterby Night Nurse, although a champion hurdler, had the looks and physique of a champion chaser and on build alone appeared far more likely to be suited to the Cheltenham mud and uphill finish than Silver Buck. He had, however, been off the course for a year for he had broken down and had been fired on both his forelegs. Peter Easterby had done a wonderful job in bringing him back sound and strong enough to withstand the rigours of championship steeplechasing. He had, however, been far from foot perfect in that King George VI Chase and had blundered badly three out as well as at the last. But his courage, toughness and staying power were undeniable and he started joint second favourite with Little Owl at 6–1.

These three alone would have made the field both a competitive and a classic one but there were others to heighten the interest still further. Midnight Court, still only ten, was in the entries again but, despite a careful preparation, it had to be said that he looked unlikely to be the first previous winner to return successfully after a lay-off. Jack of Trumps was there, too, to represent Ireland together with an interesting newcomer Mrs Malcolmson's Royal Bond who had won four out of his last six outings including the Lambert and Butler Qualifier at Ascot back in October. Diamond Edge, also, was in the field though his jumping, especially in the highest class, was as unpredictable as ever. Old Tied Cottage, at thirteen the veteran of the field was present to make the pace a blistering one and another interesting entry was Spartan Missile winner of no less that twenty hunter chases.

As they so often do at Cheltenham the rains came the night before the race leading to speculation that Silver Buck might be withdrawn. He stood his ground however and excitement was intense as this very high-class field paraded in front of the stands.

As expected old Tied Cottage took them along at a cracking pace. Wilson who had never ridden in the race before quickly realised that, whatever the state of the ground, there would be no hanging about in the championship. The next year he was to warn his friend Oliver Sherwood that such was the pace at which the race was run he needed to be six lengths

(OPPOSITE, ABOVE) Night Nurse early in the 1981 race.
(BELOW) Little Owl (Mr A.J. Wilson up) goes to post.
(INSET) Robin (*left*) and Jim Wilson with the Gold Cup after Little Owl's victory in 1981.

nearer the leaders than he wanted to be. Immediately therefore he took close order on Little Owl lying fourth just behind Diamond Edge and Night Nurse. Tied Cottage's chances vanished when he fell at the sixth leaving the other three at the head of affairs. At the last open ditch Night Nurse, going strongly and, it seemed, well within himself, led from Little Owl with Diamond Edge, and Silver Buck all looking threatening behind him. Night Nurse now set sail for home with Little Owl and Silver Buck heading the others and chasing him down the hill. Both of them had him collared at the turn and the race looked between them as they came to the second last. Here Little Owl far outjumped Silver Buck who did not take it as well as he might have done. Landing a length in front and full of running Little Owl faced the last improving his lead and with victory in sight.

In his final preparatory race before the Gold Cup Little Owl had 'fiddled' the last and nearly been down. Wilson had blamed himself for letting him do it and he took no such chances here. Little Owl stood back, cleared it out of his stride and swept on.

Behind him interesting things were happening. Silver Buck had suddenly faltered giving his detractors grounds for their contention that he did not stay and Night Nurse, apparently well beaten three out, was now running on and to some effect. He passed Silver Buck after the last and, such was the strength of his renewed gallop that he actually began to gain on Little Owl in the climb to the post. Mr Wilson, however, still had something in hand. He kept Little Owl up to his task and won by a length and a half. Silver Buck was a further ten lengths away third and Spartan Missile, the hunter, ran the race of his life to finish fourth in a race that had lived up to the high expectations it had raised. Jim Wilson became only the third amateur in its history to ride the winner of the championship and amateurs occupied two of the first four places since Spartan Missile was ridden by his sporting owner Mr M.J. Thorne. As he was being led in Wilson raised his whip and pointed to the sky in silent tribute to his aunt Mrs Grundy who had left him the horse and given him the great chance which he had seized so well.

Little Owl was yet another seven-year-old to win the championship and by winning it he took his prize money for the season to the substantial figure of £78,318 a record for a steeplechaser in one season. Easterby's achievement in not only winning the Gold Cup twice in three years but in producing the first and second in this vintage year must be noticed. Not only that but Night Nurse had presented his trainer with a double problem for, despite his suspect legs he needed an immense amount of racing to get and keep fit having become utterly lazy on the home gallops. Yet he was produced sound, looking superb and ready to run for his life as indeed he did and very nearly broke the hoodoo on champion hurdlers making the Gold Cup double. Easterby also that year became only the fifth man to complete the 'Champion double' for Sea Pigeon, trained by him won the hurdle on the first day. To complete his great year Easterby ended the season as champion trainer.

Sad to say Little Owl did not escape the bad luck which appeared destined to dog seven-year-olds who won the championship. Easterby's yard suffered a visitation from the virus and Little Owl fell a victim to it. Apparently recovered the intention had been to run him in the King George VI as his seasonal reappearance. Heavy frost caused the abandonment of this race and so he was switched to the Colt Car Diamond Chase at Cheltenham on December 31st. Although looking on the burly side in the paddock he was made favourite at 9–4 with Royal Bond next in demand at 5–2. Little Owl led from the start but never appeared to be jumping with the zest expected of him. He fell at the eleventh fence, the race being won by Royal Bond who thus put himself firmly into the Gold Cup picture. Little Owl had fallen only once before in his steeplechases and the race did not augur well for his future. His next race was a three-horse affair at Kempton where he started at money on. Although he led from the start he never seemed happy in his work and when the bit slipped through his mouth he was pulled up leaving another Gold Cup possible, the owner-ridden Mr Oliver Sherwood's oddly named Venture to Cognac, to win at his ease. Little Owl failed in his next two outings and was withdrawn from the Gold Cup.

Other contenders were having their problems too. Venture To Cognac had been plagued by injury throughout his career. He had to be given a very light preparation and his victories before the Gold Cup were bloodless ones. Worse still Silver Buck whose record in the first half of the season had not, on the whole, been impressive, injured a hind foot in December and was off the course for the whole of January and February. In fact he did not run between November 25th when he won the Edward Hanmer Memorial Chase at Haydock and March 6th when he reappeared at Market Rasen to win the Cox Moore (Sweater's) Handicap Chase. He had thus presented his young trainer Michael Dickinson who had the year before taken over control of their powerful stable from his father, with a singularly difficult task in getting him ready to run in the Gold Cup at all let alone fit enough to fight out a finish. It

Venture to Cognac (Mr O. Sherwood up) winning the Geoffrey Gilbey Memorial Chase at Newbury.

is a measure of this young man's skill and dedication which he was to prove over and over again in the coming year, that Silver Buck was able to give away weight all round (no less than 35 lb to the second horse) and yet despite his long absence to win that Market Rasen race by a length and a half demonstrating his wellbeing for all who cared to see.

Dickinson also had Bregawn in the race but at that period Bregawn did not appear to have quite the ability, scope or quality of a Gold Cup winner and the chances of others were much preferred. Amongst them were Royal Bond the winner of the Harold Clarke Leopardstown Chase though he had to be driven right out to do it, Diamond Edge now the victor in two Whitbread Gold Cups and one Hennessy Gold Cup and Grittar, the reigning Grand National favourite. And, of course, Night Nurse. By now Night Nurse had become a tremendous favourite with press and public. During the season he enhanced his reputation for gameness and courage and gave the impression on each appearance that he was thoroughly enjoying both jumping and racing all of which served to widen his appeal and to prove himself one of the few horses whose name amongst the runners made people flock to see him run. Early in the season he slammed Captain John and Lesley Anne, two other Gold Cup possibles, in the Brabston Mandarin Handicap when giving them lumps of weight. He was then beaten twice by Bregawn when conceding him 19 lb and 21 lb respectively but he was so gallant in defeat and so impressive when slamming Midnight Court by twelve lengths in the Pennine Chase at Doncaster on February 27th that even though he was now eleven, he was fully entitled to start favourite for the Gold Cup which he did at 11–4.

There had been torrential rain the night before the race which was held to militate against Silver Buck's chances even raising in some minds the possibility that he might be taken out. Once more he stood his ground, however, and a record field of twenty-two faced the starter for a record Tote sponsored prize of £48,386.

As soon as the tapes went up Sherwood realised the truth of the advice given him by Jim Wilson. 'They all set off as if it was a two-mile race rather than three and a half.* And several of us were never going well,' he told an interviewer later. Venture To Cognac was taken off his feet by the championship pace so much so that at the start of the second circuit Sherwood feared he might have to pull him up. It is worth emphasising here that it is this pace from the start at which the race is almost invariably run that is one of the basic factors making it a true championship. It, together with the unforgiving ground and that steep climb to the finish, finds out hitherto undetected weaknesses, explains the number of fallers in an extended three miles over a park course and those with the letters p.u. after their names, conclusively proving the winner to be the best and soundest horse of the year on the day.

Night Nurse was another that year to suffer from the pace as was Royal Bond. Night Nurse, in fact, gave the impression like Venture To Cognac of being taken off his feet from the start. Driven hard from the first to lie up with the pace he ran a deplorable race and had no chance when pulled up two from home. Royal Bond, too, ran as if he had left his race behind him, as he may well have done since he had had a terribly hard race when winning the Harold Clarke Leopardstown Chase under top weight a month before, and he too, appeared to be struggling from the outset.

Meanwhile Silver Buck, ridden with admirable restraint by young Robert Earnshaw, was

* This is what he is quoted as saying. The distance is, of course, three and a quarter miles and was not altered that year!

about to prove all his doubters doubly wrong concerning his stamina and his ability to act in heavy going. Earnshaw kept him handy throughout, tracking the leaders, going easily within himself and ready to pounce.

After the fourth last old Tied Cottage was still in the lead but it was obvious from the stands that as they came down to the third last Silver Buck was galloping all over his field. The one question mark in everyone's mind was would he stay on up the hill when Earnshaw let him go? It was at the turn that Earnshaw unleashed him. He said afterwards that he thought it might have been too soon but his mount was pulling him so hard and was so full of running that he had no option. He jumped the last with a clear lead. Earnshaw kept him going up the hill; the winning margin was two lengths from his stable companion, Bregawn. At one point on the long climb Bregawn looked likely to threaten the leader but, brave though he was, he could not close the gap; nevertheless he, too, confounded those who doubted his class in this sort of race and proved conclusively that he could hold his own with the best.

So Silver Buck at the age of ten had at last worthily won his accolade and shown himself a true champion. With the Gold Cup prize money his total earnings amounted to £144,143 a record for a steeplechaser and he was voted deservedly the 'National Hunt Horse of the Year' by the racing journalists.

Michael Dickinson in his second year as a trainer had thus produced the first and second in the Gold Cup. Not only that but he had trained the riders too. When Tommy Carmody had left the stable at the end of the previous season most people had expected Dickinson to offer the retainer to another well-known name. Instead he had declared his intention of standing by the lads in his stable. Earnshaw and Bradley had well repaid his confidence and the triumph was a foretaste of even better things to come. Dickinson himself had, of course, all the qualifications as a trainer of jockeys as well as horses for he had ridden for some years as a distinguished amateur until a bad fall ended that phase of his career. It was he who had educated Silver Buck riding him in hurdles at the commencement of his career and he had, in fact, taught him and brought him on. He knew him out and out and had him exactly at his peak for that Cheltenham. 'He's a great ride until he hits the front,' he declared. 'Then he wants ten men on him!'

By the season's end Dickinson was champion trainer, his first prize money amounting to the record figure of £296,028, relegating no less than Fred Winter into a far away second place. In addition for the second year running he had sent out more winners than any other trainer, his striking rate of runners to winners being 44.9 per cent which was better, even, than Henry Cecil's on the flat. No wonder Timeform in their annual *Chasers and Hurdlers 1981/2* opened their account of him with the words 'Midas himself would have felt threatened by Michael Dickinson.'

An enthusiast, utterly dedicated, a perfectionist, loyal and able, always open as to his charges' chances with press and public, no better standard-bearer for the late twentieth century virtues of the jumping game could have been found than this young man. In himself and his approach he may have appeared to some of the older generation to be a far cry from the laughing cavaliers of the twenties and thirties but those days had long since gone forever. Moreover in many ways he was – and is – their modern successor for not only had he in his day ridden well enough to hold his own with any of them even in those vintage years of

Silver Buck (Robert Earnshaw up) leads over the last from his stable companion Bregawn (Graham Bradley up) to become first and second in the 1982 Gold Cup.

amateur riding but he declared his intention of continuing his career with jumpers and this he has done although it has recently been announced that he will take over the famous Whatcombe stables to train for Robert Sangster. Better still for the future of his stable and the sport it was, as Timeform was quick to point out, in its steeplechasers not its hurdlers that the strength of its powerful string lay. Sixty of the eighty-four winners were steeplechasers and his success rate in steeplechases was 56.1 per cent, a truly astounding figure. He was quick, too, to acknowledge the debt he owed to his father and mother, Tony and Monica, and that the fact that the stable at Poplar House ran like clockwork was the result of a ruling triumvirate at the top working amicably together and inspiring a magnificent team.

Although Dickinson had a wealth of talent to draw upon for the 1982–83 season it did not look at first as if he was going to have it all his own way and, after the manner of racehorses, especially good ones, they were providing their own problems. Things began well. Silver Buck won his opening race at Wincanton and then notched up his twenty-eighth victory in the Edward Hamner Chase at Haydock on November 24th slamming his field and returning to tumultuous cheering. Then Bregawn put himself into the limelight by beating his stable companion Captain John into second place in the Hennessy Gold Cup at Newbury the following Saturday. But trouble was waiting in the wings. 'You want 10–1 against any horse reaching Cheltenham at this stage, let alone against his winning the big race,' Dickinson said after Newbury and the words seemed prophetic when Bregawn pulled a muscle and Silver Buck injured a hock interrupting both their preparations for the King George VI on Boxing Day.

Nor at this period was the Dickinson stable without its challengers. Royal Bond had early on fallen by the wayside injuring a leg in training and being announced by his trainer as unlikely to run again that season. But Little Owl who had been hobdayed in June was said in a column of eulogy by Michael Phillips of *The Times* after a visit to him to be, 'big and well and hard with it' and 'now on the threshold of a comeback to the big time.'

These were brave words but the horse himself gave at least some promise of justifying them when after a bloodless victory in the Last Chance Chase at Nottingham early in December he went on to beat Bregawn by ten lengths at Haydock. This victory may not have been as impressive as it looked owing to Bregawn's pulled muscle but Dickinson, ever the realist, made no secret of his respect for Little Owl's comeback chances. 'Little Owl is the thorn in my side,' he said at the Derby lunch early in September.

But Little Owl was not the only threat to his supremacy. Winter had a promising newcomer in Brown Chamberlin who had scored a runaway victory in last year's Sun Alliance Chase at Cheltenham. Such indeed was his trainer's belief in him that, astounding for a novice with the wealth of talent about, early in the season he was quoted as second favourite for the coming Gold Cup. Winter had another challenger, too, in Sheik Ali Abu Khamsin's Fifty Dollars More. Night Nurse, though clearly going downhill, could not at this stage of the season be entirely disregarded nor could Bright Highway from Ireland, once hailed as a likely winner before injury interrupted his career, and who was also attempting a comeback.

The King George VI at Kempton was the moment of truth for several of those aspiring to the championship. Bregawn missed the race because of his pulled muscle and Dickinson warned that Silver Buck was not just as he would have liked him since he, too, had been stopped in his work.

Night Nurse led them for the first circuit and then faded quickly to be pulled up and dropped out of Gold Cup contention, a light, alas, of other days. Silver Buck and Little Owl were in front together at the third last. Just when it looked as though Little Owl might assert his class and quicken he, too, weakened with ominous suddenness and dropped out. At the last Wayward Lad, another Dickinson contender, and Fifty Dollars More had closed on Silver Buck. Wayward Lad, driven hard by John Francome who was having a chance ride for the Dickinson stable, held off Fifty Dollars More to win by two lengths with Silver Buck a further one and half lengths away third. Little Owl was a distant fourth twenty-five lengths behind him. It didn't really look Gold Cup form from him and when he was beaten nine lengths by Ashley House (another from Dickinson's yard) at Haydock in January and two and twenty lengths respectively by Observe and Royal Judgement a fortnight later at Sandown he was taken out of the championship; all those bright hopes of being the first to make the comeback into the winner's enclosure, dashed. But not, perhaps, for ever. He was later found to be suffering from a flap of skin in his throat and, operated for it, may well make a further and this time successful comeback.

So the real run up to the championship began with Dickinson holding an ever stronger and stronger hand. Bright Highway's comeback hopes had collapsed in Ireland and for the first time for many years Ireland would have no representative in the Gold Cup. Brown Chamberlin was prone to mistakes and had not really fulfilled his much boosted promise though it was decided to let him take his chance. Winter also ran Fifty Dollars More though he scarcely looked quite up to this class with the talent that was ranged against him.

For the first time in its history it did really appear as if the race lay between one trainer's selected – and there were no less than five of these to choose from! Silver Buck, the previous year's winner, had, of course to head the list though Dickinson warned right up to the off that he had not got him just as he would have wished. Then came Bregawn, last year's second, who had had his problems too in addition to which he had, on occasion, shown a reluctance to start, a trait which he may have inherited from his sire. Nevertheless it is worth quoting his summing-up from the previous year's *Chasers and Hurdlers*: 'He may lack the physique of some of the other leading chasers, but there is none outside his own stable we should back to beat him at level weights on his best form.' Wayward Lad, the King George victor who had not run since then and whose participation was in some doubt until he had undergone a searching gallop, Captain John, and, the least considered of them, Ashley House, who was in fact the only one of the quintet about whom Dickinson had had no training problems. No wonder, when asked, he said: 'The last month has been absolute hell.' But, like his one-time mentor, Vincent O'Brien, he left as little as possible to chance. On the Sunday morning he had a full time briefing in his office with his three home jockeys,

Sheikh Ali Abu Khamsin's Fifty Dollars More (R. Linley up), sixth in the 1983 Gold Cup, seen here winning the 1982 Red Rum Novices' Handicap Chase at Aintree.

Graham Bradley and Bregawn, winner of the 1983 race.

Richard Earnshaw, Graham Bradley and the stable amateur and assistant trainer, Dermot Browne who was to ride Ashley House. On the morning of the race he walked the course with these three and Jonjo O'Neill who had been engaged for Wayward Lad and David Goulding who had the ride on Captain John.

There was no question of hesitation at the start on Bregawn's part this time. He bolted from the gate and lay up behind the amateur-ridden 500–1 outsider Whiggey Geo who went into an early lead.

Whiggey Geo dropped out of contention at the fifth fence, sooner than Bradley either wanted or expected. Left in front he took the instant and courageous decision to stay there and to make it all – no easy task at Cheltenham in the Gold Cup. With his four stablemates in attendance he proceeded to gallop both them and the opposition such as it was into the ground. Brown Chamberlin made mistakes from the start and was pulled up at the end of the first circuit. Hitting the fifth and sixth fences from home really hard made not the slightest difference to Bregawn's relentless gallop. Bradley sat tight and his mount swept on unchecked. Fifty Dollars More found the pace in this class too much for him and fell at the last open ditch. Bregawn won unchallenged and the final tally read: Bregawn 1, Captain John 2, Wayward Lad 3, Silver Buck 4, Ashley House 5.

Dickinson had thus trained the first five runners home a feat never before accomplished and unlikely ever to be repeated. 'You'll never see that again in your lifetime,' John Francome said in the weighing room when he returned to it. In recognition of this unique training success the stewards permitted the first five horses to enter the space reserved for those placed in a race. The cheering was prolonged and went echoing up and over the surrounding hills.

Amongst those there to see this incredible finish was 'Frenchie' Nicholson who had

Michael Dickinson, trainer of the first five in the 1983 Gold Cup, at home with the successful horses and their lads. *Left to right*: Silver Buck (fourth), Ashley House (fifth), Wayward Lad (third), Captain John (second), Bregawn (first).

himself won the Gold Cup on Médoc in 1942 and with whom the young Michael Dickinson had been trained as a pupil.

Dickinson himself watched the race on the TV monitor in the weighing room. Burnt up with pressures and tension ('It's been almost unbearable. I've lost a stone since Christmas.') he sat in silence save for one involuntary exclamation which was typical of the man and his stable. 'Come on, my lot,' were the words which seemed almost jerked out of him as the field turned for home at the top of the hill. It was also absolutely in character that in the unsaddling enclosure he visited the last of his runners first lest he might appear to be devoting all his praise and attention to the winner.

'I was just shouting for the boys,' he said afterwards of his feelings as he watched the race. 'I can't relax. I'm fairly hard on myself and I'm very hard on them. I was very proud of them.'

The old timers would have lifted their hats to him, the tribute of the younger generation was paid in the cheers and congratulations, for in those words were embodied the true spirit of the sport of steeplechasing. It is a fitting note on which to close this history to date of the blue riband of the jumping game.

APPENDIX 1

Results of the Gold Cup

1924
Run March 12th

Major H. Wyndham's ch.g. Red Splash. 5 yrs. 11 st 5 lb.
(Copper Ore – La Manche) F. Rees 1
Major C. Dewhurst's b.g. Conjuror II. a. 12 st.
(Garb Or – dam by Juggler) Mr H. A. Brown 2
Major F. S. Murray's ch.g. Gerald L. a. 12 st.
(Captivation – Larenne) J. Morgan 3
Mr Bankier's Forewarned (J. Anthony) 4th. *Also ran*: Mr J. Bennett's Hawker (J. Hogan, jnr.); Mr W. Dixon's Old Tay Bridge (Mr H. Hartigan); Sir K. Fraser's Ardeen (A. Escott); Lord Westmorland's Royal Chancellor (E. Foster)
Trained F. E. Withington. Won h, n.
Starting prices – 3–1 Forewarned; 4–1 Hawker; 5–1 Red Splash, Gerald L; 7–1 Conjuror II.

1925
Run March 11th

Mr J. C. Bentley's ch.m. Ballinode. a. 12 st.
(Machakos – Celia) E. Leader 1
Mr W. H. McAlpine's b.h. Alcazar. a. 12 st.
(Yerres – Good and Gracious) F. Rees 2
Mr B. Lemon's ch.g. Patsey V. a. 12 st.
(Lord Garvagh – dam by Walmesgate) Owner 3
Major C. Dewhurst's Conjuror II. a. 12 st.
(Garb Or – dam by Juggler) Mr C. Dewhurst p.u.
Trained F. Morgan. Won 5*l*. Bad.
Starting prices – 8–13 Alcazar; 3–1 Ballinode; 10–1 others.

1926
Run March 9th

Mr F. Barbour's b.g. Koko. a. 12 st.
(Santoi – Persister) J. Hamey 1
Mrs W. H. Dixon's ch.g. Old Tay Bridge. a. 12 st.
(Bridge of Earn – Broken Reed) J. Hogan 2
Mr W. Filmer Sankey's br.g. Ruddyglow. a. 12 st.
(Ruddygore – Nell) Owner 3
Mr C. R. Horrell's Postinio (W. Speck) 4th. *Also ran*: Mr C. R. Barron's Mansin (E. Foster); Mr W. Newland Hillis' Trentino (Major Wilson); Col. J. H. Starkey's Vive (R. Burford), Mr H. Kershaw's Gerald L (A. Stubbs).
Trained Bickley. Won 4*l*, 5*l*.
Starting prices – 6–5 Ruddyglow; 3–1 Old Tay Bridge; 9–1 Gerald L; 10–1 Koko, Mansin; 100–8 Postinio, Vive; 20–1 Trentino.

1927
Run March 8th

Lord Stalbridge's ch.g. Thrown In. a. 12 st.
(Beau Bill – Va Largo) Hon. H. Grosvenor 1
Mr T. K. Laidlaw's br.g. Grakle. 5yrs. 11 st 5 lb.
(Jackdaw – Lady Crank) J. Moloney 2
Mr W. H. Midwood's b.g. Silvo. a. 12 st.
(Minter – Ever True) F. Rees 3
Mr H. Kershaw's Gerald L (L. Rees) 4th. *Also ran*: Mr C. H. Horrell's Postinio (W. Speck); Mr W. Hume's Grecian Wave (J. Meaney); Lady Helen McCalmont's Amberwave (Mr J. O'Brien); Mrs L. Wilson's Hackdene (J. Anthony).
Trained Anthony. Won 2*l*, ½*l*.

1927 continued
Starting prices – 13–8 Silvo; 4–1 Amberwave; 5–
1 Grakle; 8–1 Hackdene; 10–1 Thrown In;
100–8 others.

1928
Run March 13th

Mr F. W. Keen's b.g. Patron Saint. 5 yrs. 11 st
5 lb.
      (St. Girons – V.M.C.) F. Rees 1
Col J. H. Starkey's br.g. Vive. a. 12 st.
      (Minter – Ever True) L. Rees 2
F. Barbour's br.g. Koko. a. 12 st.
      (Santoi – Persister) P. Powell 3
Mr M. D. Blair's Aruntius (J. Hogan) 4th. *Also
ran*: Mr Deterding's Rathowen (W. Gurney);
Mr H. Kershaw's Meleaston (M. Rayson); Mrs
Partridge's Sprig (T. E. Leader).
Trained H. Harrison. Won 4*l*, 2*l*.
Starting prices – 4–5 Koko; 7–2 Patron Saint; 5–
1 Sprig; 8–1 Vive; 10–1 Rathowen; 20–1 others.

1929
Run March 12th

Mr J. H. Whitney's ch.g. Easter Hero. a. 12 st.
      (My Prince – Easter Week) F. Rees 1
Capt. R. F. H. Norman's ch.g. Lloydie. a. 12 st.
      (Vedanta – Lizzie Lane) R. McCarthy 2
Mr C. R. Taylor's br.g. Grakle. a. 12 st.
      (Jackdaw – Lady Crank) K. Piggott 3
Mr F. H. W. Cundell's Knight of the Wilderness
(W. Stott) 4th. *Also ran*: Mrs H. Mond's May
King (W. Gurney); Capt. F. E. Guest's Koko
(T. Morgan); Sir D. Llewellyn's Breconian (G.
Bowden); Mr E. A. Longworth's Kilbrain'(V.
Piggott); Mrs E. A. Ryan's Wild Edgar (C.
McCarthy); Mr S. Sanford's Bright's Boy (T.
Leader).
Trained Anthony. Won 20*l*, 2*l*.
Starting prices – 7–4 Easter Hero; 11–4 Grakle;
7–1 Koko; 8–1 Bright's Boy; 10–1 Knight of
the Wilderness; 100–9 Lloydie; 100–8 May
King; 100–6 others.

1930
Run March 11th

Mr J. H. Whitney's ch.g Easter Hero. a. 12 st.
      (My Prince – Easter Week) T. Cullinan 1

Mr C. R. Taylor's br. g. Grakle. a 12 st.
      (Jackdaw – Lady Crank) K. Piggott 2
Mr B. D. Davis's b.g. Gib. a. 12 st.
      (The Jabberwock – Bettyville) F. Rees 3
Col. Foljame's Donzelon (R. Lyall) fell.
Trained Anthony. Won 20*l*. Remounted. Bad.
Starting prices – 8–11 Easter Hero; 13–8 Gib;
10–1 Grakle; 50–1 Donzelon.
Tote – Win 3s 9d.

1931
No race

1932
Run March 2nd

Miss D. Paget's b.g. Golden Miller. 5 yrs. 11 st
5 lb.
      (Goldcourt – Miller's Pride) T. Leader 1
Lady Lindsay's br.g. Inverse. 6 yrs. 12 st.
      (St Giron's – Inversion) R. Lyall 2
Mr M. D. Blair's b.g. Aruntius. a. 12 st.
      (Call of the Wind – Wine Gall) D. McCann 3
Also ran: Mr B. D. Davis's Gib (Mr Thackray);
Mr Eric Platt's Kingsford (W. Stott); Mr C. R.
Taylor's Grakle (Mr J. Fawcus).
Trained Briscoe. Won 4*l*. Bad. 3 finished.
Starting prices – 10–11 Grakle; 3–1 Kingsford;
13–2 Golden Miller; 8–1 Inverse; 100–8 Gib;
20–1 Aruntius.
Tote – Win 15s Places 5s 9d, 6s 3d.

1933
Run March 8th

Miss D. Paget's b.g. Golden Miller. 6 yrs. 12 st.
      (Goldcourt – Miller's Pride) W. Stott 1
Mr J. H. Whitney's ch.g. Thomond II. a. 12 st.
      (Drinmore – dam by St Luke) W. Speck 2
Mr J. B. Snow's b.g. Delaneige. a. 12 st.
      (Santair – Kylestrame) J. Moloney 3
Mr M. Stephens' The Brown Talisman (J.
Goswell) 4th. *Also ran*: Mrs F. A. Clark's
Kellsboro Jack (D. Williams); Mr E. Tyrwhitt
Drake's Holmes (C. Beechner); Lady Lind-
say's Inverse (R. Lyall).
Trained Briscoe. Won 10*l* 5*l*.
Starting prices – 4–7 Golden Miller; 11–4
Thomond II; 100–8 Kellsboro Jack; 20–1
others.
Tote – Win 3s 3d. Places 2s 3d, 2s 3d, 3s.

1934
Run March 7th

Miss D. Paget's b.g. Golden Miller. a. 12 st.
    (Goldcourt – Miller's Pride) G. Wilson 1
Mrs Mundy's b.g. Avenger. 5 yrs. 11 st. 5 lb.
    (Black Gauntlet – Vendramina) R. Lyall 2
Mrs F. A. Clark's b.g. Kellsboro Jack. a. 12 st.
    (Jackdaw – Kellsboro Lass) D. Morgan 3
Mr J. H. Whitney's Royal Ransom (W. Speck)
4th. *Also ran*: Mr J. B. Snow's Delaneige (J.
Moloney); Lady Lindsay's Inverse (Sir P.
Grant Lawson); Mr E. Robson's El Haljar (W.
Parvin).
Trained Briscoe. Won 6*l*, 6*l*.
Starting prices – 6-5 Golden Miller; 11-2 El Haljar; 6-1 Delaneige, Avenger; 10-1 Kellsboro
Jack, Royal Ransom; 20-1 Inverse.
Tote – Win 4s 3d. Places 2s 6d, 3s , 3s 6d.

1935
Run March 15th

Miss D. Paget's b.g. Golden Miller. a. 12 st.
    (Goldcourt – Miller's Pride) G. Wilson 1
Mr J. H. Whitney's ch.g. Thomond II. a. 12 st.
    (Drinmore – dam by St Luke) W. Speck 2
Mrs F.A. Clark's b.g. Kellsboro Jack. a. 12 st.
    (Jackdaw – Kellsboro Lass) D. Morgan 3
Mrs Munday's Avenger (T. Rimell) 4th. *Also ran*:
Mr J. V. Rank's Southern Hero (J. Fawcus).
Trained Briscoe. Won ¾*l*, 5*l*.
Starting prices – 1-2 Golden Miller; 5-2
Thomond II; 100-7 Kellsboro Jack; 20-1 Avenger, Southern Hero.
Tote – Win 2s 6d. Places 2s 3d, 2s 3d.

1936
Run March 12th

Miss D. Paget's Golden Miller. a. 12 st.
    (Goldcourt – Miller's Pride) E. Williams 1
Mr H. Lloyd Thomas' bl.g. Royal Mail. a. 12 st.
    (My Prince – Flying May) Mr F. Walwyn 2
Mrs F. A. Clark's b.g. Kellsboro Jack. a. 12 st.
    (Jackdaw – Kellsboro Lass) D. Morgan 3
Mr G. Beeby's Brienz (J. Moloney) 4th. *Also ran*:
Mr M. D. Plain's Fouquet (G. Wilson); Mr
J. V. Rank's Southern Hero (J. Fawcus).
Trained O. Anthony. Won 12*l*, 2*l*.
Starting prices – 20-21 Golden Miller; 5-1 Royal
Mail, Brienz; 6-1 Southern Hero; 10-1 Kellsboro Jack; 25-1 Fouquet.
Tote – Win 3s 3d. Places 3s 6d, 3s 9d.

1937
Race abandoned

1938
Run March 10th

Lt.-Col. D. C. Part's b. or ch.g. Morse Code. a.
12 st.
    (Pilot – Heliograph) D. Morgan 1
Miss D. Paget's b.g. Golden Miller. a. 12 st.
    (Goldcourt – Miller's Pride) H. Nicholson 2
Mr H. A. Steele's br.g. Macaulay. a. 12 st.
    (Bolingbroke – Conette) D. Butchers 3
Mr J. V. Rank's Southern Hero (B. Hobbs) 4th.
Also ran: Sir F. Towle's Airgead Sios (T.
McNeil); Lord Latymer's Red Hillman (G.
Wilson).
Trained I. Anthony. Won 2*l*, 3*l*.
Starting prices – 7-4 Golden Miller; 3-1 Macaulay; 7-2 Airgead Sios; 13-2 Morse Code; 100-
7 Red Hillman; 100-6 Southern Hero.
Tote – Win 13s. 7d. Places 5s, 3s 7d.

1939
Run March 9th

Mrs A. Smith Bingham's b.g. Brendan's Cottage.
a. 12 st.
    (Cottage – Brendan's Glory) G. Owen 1
Lt.-Col. D. C. Part's b. or ch. g. Morse Code. a.
12 st.
    (Pilot – Heliograph) D. Morgan 2
Mr G. Whitelaw's b.g. Embarrassed. 6 yrs. 12 st.
    (Embargo – Lady Georgie) Capt. P. Herbert 3
Also ran: Sir D. Llewellyn's L'Estaque (Mr H.
Llewellyn); Mr G Whitelaw's Del et Bon (G.
Wilson).
Trained G. Beeby. Won 5*l*. Bad. Only placed
horses finished.
Staring prices – 4-7 Morse Code; 11-4 Bel et Bon;
8-1 Brendan's Cottage; 25-1 others.
Tote – Win 14s 6d. Places 3s 11d, 2s 8d.

1940
Run March 20th

Miss D. Paget's b.g. Roman Hackle. a. 12 st.
    (Yutoi – Waraya) E. Williams 1
Mrs C. Jones' b.g. Black Hawk. a. 12 st.
    (Eagle Hawk – Black Lamb) T. Rimell 2

1940 *continued*

Mrs C. Evans' bl.g. Royal Mail. a. 12 st.
    (My Prince – Flying Day) D. Morgan 3
Mrs A. E. Phillips's Rightun (Mr A Marsh) 4th
    Also ran: Capt G. Whitelaw's Bel et Bon (G.
    Wilson); Mr W. V. Goodbody's Up Sabre (W.
    Redmond); Col. Foljambe's Hobgoblin (J.
    Bissell).
Trained O. Anthony. Won 10*l*, 2*l*.
Starting prices – Evens Roman Hackle; 5–1 Bel et
    Bon; 6–1 Hobgoblin; 7–1 Up Sabre; 100–8
    Royal Mail; 100–6 Rightun; 20–1 Black Hawk.
Tote – Win 4s 9d. Places 3s. 6d, 7s 9d.

1941
Run March 20th

Mr D. Sherbrooke's ch.g. Poet Prince. a. 12 st.
    (Milton – Welsh Princess) R. Burford 1
Maj. L. Montagu's b.g. Savon. a. 12 st.
        (Schiavoni – Saffron) G. Archibald 2
Lady S. Phipps' b.g. Red Rower. a. 12 st.
    (Rameses II – Red Maru) D. Morgan 3
Sir E. Hanmer's Teme Willow (T. Rimell) 4th.
    Also ran: Lord Bicester's Red Prince (T.
    Carey); Mr A. Dann's Dominick's Cross (W.
    Hollick); Mr E. Johnson's Callaly (Mr J.
    Smith); Miss D. Paget's Roman Hackle (E.
    Williams); Mr J. V. Rank's Knight of Troy (R.
    Smyth); Mrs I. Strang's The Professor II (T.
    Isaac).
Trained I. Anthony. Won 3*l*, short head.
Starting prices – 5–2 Roman Hackle; 100–30
    Savon; 7–2 Poet Prince; 8–1 Teme Willow,
    Red Rower; 10–1 Professor II; 100–7 Red
    Prince; 20–1 Dominick's Cross; 25–1 Callaly;
    33–1 Knight of Troy.
Tote – Win 12s 3d. Places 3s 9d, 3s 3d, 4s 3d.

1942
Run March 21st

Lord Sefton's b.g. Médoc II. a. 12 st.
        (Van – Menthe Poivré) H. Nicholson 1
Lady S. Phipps' b.g. Red Rower. a. 12 st.
    (Rameses II – Red Maru) D. Morgan 2
Lord Bicester's b.g. Asterabad. a. 12 st.
        (Asterus – Carissima) T. Carey 3
Mr K. Cameron's Schubert (G. Wilson) 4th. *Also*
    ran: Mr E. Bailey's Golden Knight (Owner);
    Mr W. Tate's Sawfish (J. Dowdeswell); Major

J. Thomson's Dixie Kid (B. Marshall); Lt.-
Col. Sir E. Hanmer's Solarium (T. Rimell);
Miss D. Paget's Roman Hackle (R. Smyth);
Mr J. V. Rank's Broken Promise (M. Prender-
gast); Mrs D. P. Dick's Golden Luck (W. Hol-
lick); Mr D. Sherbrooke's Poet Prince (R. Bur-
ford).
Trained R. Hobbs. Won 8*l*, 4*l*.
Starting prices – 3–1 Red Rower; 9–2 Médoc II;
    5–1 Poet Prince; 8–1 Golden Knight; 10–1
    Roman Hackle, Broken Promise; 100–8
    Schubert; 100–6 Golden Luck; 20–1 Asterabad,
    Solarium; 50–1 others.
Tote – Win 12s. Places 4s 9d, 4s 3d, 16s 3d.

1943
No race

1944
No race

1945
Run March 17th

Lord Stalbridge's b.g. Red Rower. a. 12 st.
        (Rameses II – Red Maru) D. J. Jones 1
Mrs K. Cameron's b.g. Schubert. a. 12 st.
    (Lightning Artist – Wild Music) C. Beechener 2
Mr R. A. Holbeck's b.g. Paladin. a. 12 st.
        (Birthright – Saint Joan) G. Conlon 3
Mr D. Sherbrooke's Poet Prince (H. Nicholson)
    4th. *Also ran*: Mr W. Adlam's Nobletoi
    (Owner); Lord Bicester's Red Prince (T.
    Carey); Mrs Labouchere's India II (T.
    Farmer); Major H. Blount's Rightun (T. Ri-
    mell); Mr H. W. Smith's The Hack (J. Molo-
    ney); Miss K. Smith's Way Out (J. Taylor);
    Mr T. A. Spier's Farther West (P. Long);
    Major J. J. Astor's Ghaka (R. Smyth); Mr J. D.
    Norris' National Hope (R. Young); Mrs E. M.
    Halohan's Flying Saint (T. Isaac); Mr A. G.
    Chandler's Peaceful Walter (S. Magee); Mr
    C. E. Edward's Elsich (F. Wren).
Trained Owner. Won 3*l*, 1½*l*.
Starting prices – 11–4 Red Rower; 100–30 Pala-
    din; 11–2 Schubert, Poet Prince; 7–1 Red
    Prince, Flying Saint; 10–1 Chaka; 20–1 Righ-
    tun, The Hack; 33–1 Farther West; 50–1
    others.
Tote – Win 7s 9d. Places 3s 6d, 3s, 4s.

1946
Run March 14th

Mr J.V. Rank's b.g. Prince Regent. a. 12 st.
    (My Prince – Nemaea) T. Hyde 1
Mrs D. Nelson's b.g. Poor Flame. a. 12 st.
    (Flamenco – Poor Dale) T. Rimell 2
Lord Stalbridge's b.g. Red April. a. 12 st.
    (April The Fifth – Red Maru) G. Kelly 3
Miss E. Shortiss' African Collection (J. Fitzgerald) 4th. *Also ran:* Viscount R. de Rivaud's Jalgreya (F. Gurney); Mrs K. Edwards' Elsich (W. Balfe).
Trained Dreaper. Won 5*l*, 4*l*.
Starting prices – 4–7 Prince Regent; 9–2 Red April; 5–1 Poor Flame; 100–7 Jalgreya; 33–1 African Collection; 200–1 Elsich.
Tote – Win 3s. Places 3s, 3s 6d.

1947
Run April 12th

Lord Grimthorpe's ch.h. Fortina. 6 yrs. 12 st.
    (Formor – Bertina) Mr R. Black 1
Miss D. Paget's b.g. Happy Home. a. 12 st.
    (Cottage – Golden Emblem) D. L. Moore 2
Lord Bicester's br.g. Prince Blackthorn. a. 12 st.
    (Embargo – Alice Maythorn) R. Turnell 3
The Count de Rochefort's Fabiano (H. Bonneau) 4th. *Also ran:* Major J. J. Astor's Chaka (R. Smyth); Mr R. Coombe's Comique (J. Moloney); Mr A. W. Fletcher's Leap Man (B. Marshall); Mr H. Lensley's Bricett (M. C. Prendergast); Mrs D. Nelson's Nack (H Nicholson); Mrs C. D. Wilson's Rearmament (D. Ruttle); Mr W. F. Higham's Coloured Schoolboy (T. Rimell); Mr C. E. Edward's Elsich (R. Jenkins).
Trained H. Christie. Won 10*l*, 6*l*.
Starting prices – 3–1 Happy Home; 4–1 Coloured Schoolboy; 6–1 Fabiano; 8–1 Prince Blackthorn, Fortina, Bricett; 10–1 Chaka; 100–7 Rearmament; 20–1 Comique, Leap Man; 33–1 Nack; 100–1 Elsich.
Tote – Win 29s 6d. Places 7s 9d, 4s 6d, 5s 9d.

1948
Run March 4th

Mr F. L. Vickerman's b. or br.g. Cottage Rake. a. 12 st.
    (Cottage – Hartingo) A. Brabazon 1

Miss D. Paget's b.g. Happy Home. a. 12 st.
    (Cottage – Golden Emblem) M. Moloney 2
Mr W. F. Higham's br.g. Coloured Schoolboy. a. 12 st.
    (Grand Colours – Alpha Virginis) E. Vinall 3
The Conte de Chambourne's Salmiana II (R. Bates) 4th. *Also ran:* Mrs J. J. Astor's The Diver (D. Butchers); Lord Bicester's Freddy Fox (R. Black); Mr J. D. Clarke's Revelry (D. L. Moore); Mr J. Davey's Gallery (M. J. Prendergast); Mr T. Radmall's Klaxton (R. Smyth); Lord Stalbridge's Red April (G. Kelly); Major C. Stirling Stuart's Cool Customer (P. Murphy); Mr W. Noble's Barney's Link (J. Brogan).
Trained M. V. O'Brien. Won 1½*l*, 10*l*.
Starting prices – 7–2 Cool Customer; 11–2 Klaxton; 6–1 Happy Home; 13–2 Red April; 10–1 Cottage Rake, Salmiana II, Coloured Schoolboy; 100–9 Freddy Fox; 100–6 Revelry; 25–1 Gallery; 33–1 The Diver; 100–1 Barney's Link.
Tote – Win 17s 9d. Places 6s, 6s 9d, 7s 9d.

1949
Run April 11th

Mr F. L. Vickerman's b. or br.g. Cottage Rake. a. 12 st.
    (Cottage – Hartingo) A. Brabazon 1
Maj. R. Stirling Stuart's b.g. Cool Customer. a. 12 st.
    (Mr Toots – Never Worry) P. Murphy 2
Mr W. F. Highnam's br.g. Coloured Schoolboy. a. 12 st.
    (Grand Colours – Alpha Virginis) E. Vinall 3
Lord Bicester's Finnure (M. Moloney) 4th. *Also ran:* Mrs M. Harvey's Royal Mount (P J Doyle); Lord Stalbridge's Red April (A. Grantham).
Trained M. V. O'Brien. Won 2*l*, 6*l*.
Starting prices – 4–6 Cottage Rake; 11–2 Finnure; 13–2 Cool Customer; 8–1 Coloured Schoolboy; 100–8 Royal Mount; 20–1 Red April.
Tote – Win 3s 6d. Places 3s 9d, 8s 9d.

1950
Run March 9th

Mr F. L. Vickerman's b. or br.g. Cottage Rake. a. 12 st.
    (Cottage – Hartingo) A. Brazon 1

1950 *continued*

Lord Bicester's ch.g. Finnure. a. 12 st.

       (Cacador – Hazelly) M. Molony 2

The Marquis de Portago's ch.g. Garde Toi. a.
12 st.

       (Le Grand Cyprus – Grey Cloth) Owner 3

Mr J. P. Philipps' Nagara (R. Black) 4th. *Also
ran*: Mr C. H. Blunt's Clarendon (A. Mullins);
Lord Mildmay's Rideo (Owner).

Trained M. V. O'Brien. Won 10*l*, 8*l*.

Starting prices – 5–6 Cottage Rake; 5–4 Finnure;
28–1 Rideo; 100–1 others.

Tote – Win 3s 6d. Places 2s 3d, 2s 6d.

1951

Run April 25th

Lord Bicester's ch.g. Silver Fame. a. 12 st.

       (Werwolf – Silver Fairy) M. Molony 1

Mr J. V. Rank's b.g. Greenogue. a. 12 st.

(Knight of the Garter – Miss Muffsie) G. Kelly
2

Mr L. B. Chugg's b.g. Mighty Fine. a. 12 st.

       (pretorious – Miss Maureen) J. Bullock 3

Mr H. Lane's Lockerbie (A. P Thompson) 4th
Also ran: Mrs L. Brotherton's Freebooter (J.
Power); Her Majesty's Manicou (A. Gran-
tham).

Trained Beeby. Won short head, 2*l*.

Starting prices – 6–4 Silver Fame; 3–1 Lockerbie;
5–1 Freebooter; 15–2 Manicou; 10–1 Mighty
Fine; 12½–1 Greenogue.

Tote – Win 5s 6d. Places 3s 9d, 8s.

1952

Run March 6th

Miss D. Pagett's ch.g. Mont Tremblant. 6 yrs.
12 st.

       (Gris Perle – Paltoquette) D. V. Dick 1

Mr G. Hemsley's br.g. Shaef. a. 12 st.

       (Mansur – Rispana) F. Winter 2

Lady Orde's br.g. Galloway Braes. a. 12 st.

       (Norwest – Isola) R. Morrow 3

Mr J. P. Philipp's Nagara (P. Hieronimus) 4th.
Also ran: Mrs L. Brotherton's Cushenden (B.
Marshall); Mrs F. B. Watkin's Café Crème (R.
Black); Lord Bicester's Silver Fame (T. Mo-
loney); Mr J. V. Rank's Greenogue (G. Kelly);
Mr H. F. Craig Harvey's Lord Turbot
(Owner); Mrs L. Brotherton's Freebooter (J.
Power); Mrs M. H. Keogh's Knock Hard (Mr

A. S. O'Brien); Mr L. Carver's E.S.B. (M.
Scudamore); Mrs A. Warman's Injunction (J.
Dowdeswell).

Trained Walwyn. Won 10*l*, 4*l*.

Starting prices – 7–2 Freebooter; 5–1 Knock
Hard; 6–1 Silver Fame; 7–1 Shaef; 8–1 Mont
Tremblant, E.S.B.; 100–7 Cushenden; 100–6
Greenogue; 33–1 Injunction, Nagara; 66–1
others.

Tote – Win 14s. Places 6s 1d, 5s 11d, 30s 5d.

1953

Run March 5th

Mrs M. H. Keogh's ch.g. Knock Hard. a. 12 st.

       (Domaha – Knocksouna) T. Molony 1

Contessa di Saint Elia's br.g. Halloween. a. 12 st.

       (Court Nez – My Blue Heaven) F. Winter 2

Lady Orde's br.g. Galloway Braes. a. 12 st.

       (Norwest – Isola) R. Morrow 3

Miss D. Paget's Mont Tremblant (D. V. Dick)
4th. *Also ran*: Lord Bicester's Mariner's Log
(P. Taaffe); Mr. C Nicholson's Stormhead (G.
Slack); Mrs L. Brotherton's Cushenden (P.
Chisman); Mr H. Lane's Teal (A. P. Thompson); Miss D. Paget's Lanveoc Poulmic (R.
Emery); Mr L. Carver's E.S.B. (M. Scudamore); Mr G. Lawrence's Rose Park (T. Cusack); Mrs J. White's Statecraft (R. Francis).

Trained M. V. O'Brien. Won 5*l*, 2*l*.

Starting prices – 5–2 Halloween; 4–1 Mont Tremblant; 11–2 Knock Hard; 6–1 Teal; 100–9 Mariner's Log; 100–7 Rose Park; 100–6 Lanveoc
Poulmic, Statecraft; 20–1 E.S.B.; 33–1 others.

Tote – Win 10s 4d. Places 4s 1d, 3s 2d, 12s 6d.

1954

Run March 4th

Mr A. Strange's b.g. Four Ten. a. 12 st.

       (Blunderbuss – Undue Praise) T. Cusack 1

Lord Bicester's ch.g. Mariner's Log. a. 12 st.

       (Archive – She Gone) P. Taaffe 2

Contessa di Saint Elia's br.g. Halloween. a. 12 st.

       (Court Nez – My Blue Heaven) G. Slack 3

Miss D. Paget's Mont Tremblant (D. V. Dick)
4th. *Also ran*: Mrs M. H. Keogh's Knock Hard
(T. Molony); Mr G. Lawrence's Rose Park (A.
Freeman); Lady Orde's Galloway Braes (R.
Morrow); Mr C. Nicholson's Stormhead (P.

Farrell); Mr G. Hemsley's Shaef (J. Bullock).
Trained J. Roberts. Won 4*l*, 4*l*.
Starting prices - 6-4 Mont Tremblant; 9-4 Knock
  Hard; 6-1 Galloway Braes; 12½-1 Stormhead;
  100-6 Four Ten, Halloween; 20-1 others.
Tote - Win 26s 10d. Places 5s 6d, 17s 6d, 13s.

1955
Run March 10th

Mr P. J. Burt's b.g. Gay Donald. a. 12 st.
    (Gaylight - Pas de Quatre) A. Grantham 1
Contessa di Saint Elia's br.g. Halloween. a. 12 st.
    (Court Nez - My Blue Heaven) F. Winter 2
Mr A. Strange's b.g. Four Ten. a. 12 st.
    (Blunderbuss - Undue Praise) T. Cusack 3
Mr J. H. Griffin's Early Mist (B. Marshall) 4th.
  Also ran: Lady Orde's Galloway Braes (R.
  Morrow); Col. Lord Joicey's Bramble Tudor
  (R. Curran); Mrs D. M. Cooper's Crudwell
  (R. Francis); Sir P. Orde's Pointsman (T. Mo-
  lony); Mr G. Lawrence's Rose Park (A. Free-
  man).
Trained J. Ford. Won 10*l*, 8*l*.
Starting prices - 3-1 Four Ten; 7-2 Halloween;
  5-1 Early Mist; 6-1 Bramble Tudor; 10-1
  Galloway Braes; 12½-1 Pointsman; 25-1 Crud-
  well, Rose Park; 33-1 Gay Donald.
Tote - Win 109s 4d. Places 16s 11d, 3s 4d, 4s.

1956
Run March 8th

Mr J. Davey's ch.g. Limber Hill. a. 12 st.
    (Bassam - Mindoon) J. Power 1
Mr A. R. B. Owen's b.g. Vigor. a. 12 st.
    (Victrix - Château Neil Gow) R. Emery 2
Contessa di Saint Elia's b.g. Halloween. a. 12 st.
    (Court Nez - My Blue Heaven) F. Winter 3
Mrs A. C. Leggat's Cruachan (B. Wilkinson) 4th.
  Also ran: Sir P. Orde's Pointsman (R. Mor-
  row); Mrs John White's Lochroe (R. Francis);
  Wing Commander R. Stevenson's Wise Child
  (G. Milburn); Mr H. Freeman Jackson's Sam
  Brownthorn (T. Taaffe); Mr A. Strange's Four
  Ten (T. Cusack); Col. Lord Joicey's Bramble
  Tudor (R. Curran); Mr H. J. Joel's Glorious
  Twelfth (D. Ancil).
Trained Dutton. Won 4*l*, 1½*l*.
Starting prices - 11-8 Limber Hill; 9-2 Sam
  Brownthorn; 15-2 Pointsman; 8-1 Lochroe;
  100-8 Halloween, Cruachan; 100-6 Bramble

Tudor; 20-1 Four Ten; 25-1 Wise Child; 50-
1 others.
Tote - Win 4s 10d. Places 3s 6d, 20s 3d, 5s 11d.

1957
Run March 14th

Mr David Brown's b.g. Linwell. a. 12 st.
    (Rosewell - Rubia Linda) M. Scudamore 1
Mr G. H. Moore's br.m. Kerstin. a. 12 st.
    (Honor's Choice - Miss Kilcash) G. Milburn 2
Mr Guy G. Lawrence's ch.g. Rose Park. a. 12 st.
    (Pactolus - Primulas) G. Nicholls 3
Sir Percy Orde's Pointsman (R. Morrow) 4th.
  Also ran: Mrs John White's Lochroe (A. R.
  Freeman); Mr H. Freeman-Jackson's Sam
  Brownthorn (Mr J. R. Cox); Mr J. Morphet's
  Dovetail (Mr J. Morphet); Mrs Leonard
  Carver's E.S.B. (D. V. Dick); Wing-Comman-
  der R. E. Stevenson's Wise Child (F. Winter);
  Mr M. Kingley's Sir Ken (B. Marshall); Mr
  J. P. Burt's Gay Donald (A. Grantham); Mr
  S. T. Hill's Sea Captain (Mr R. McCreery); Mr
  H. Lane's Stroller (T. Taaffe).
Trained C. Mallon. Won 1*l*, 5*l*.
Starting prices - 6-1 Kerstin, Pointsman; 7-1
  E.S.B., Sir Ken; 8-1 Gay Donald; 10-1 Loch-
  roe, Sam Brownthorn; 100-9 Linwell; 100-8
  Rose Park, Stroller; 20-1 Wise Child; 50-1
  Dovetail; 100-1 Sea Captain.
Tote - Win 19s 7d. Places 6s, 4s 11d, 8s.

1958
Run March 13th

Mr G. H. Moore's br.m. Kerstin. a. 12 st.
    (Honor's Choice - Miss Kilcash) S. Hayhurst 1
Mrs P. Pleydell-Bouverie's br.g. Polar Flight. a.
  12 st.
        (Iceberg II - More Pure) G. Slack 2
Mr P. J. Burt's b.g. Gay Donald. a. 12 st.
    (Gay Light - Pas de Quatre) F. Winter 3
Mr M. M. le Masson's Jack V (P. Blancone) 4th.
  Also ran: Mr J. Davey's Limber Hill (T. Mo-
  lony); Mr Hugh Sumner's Hall Weir (W.
  Rees); Lady Barber's Game Field (J. Boddy);
  Mr David Brown's Linwell (M. Scudamore);
  Mme K. Hennessy's Mandarin (P. G. Mad-
  den).
Trained Major C. Bewicke. Won ½*l*. Bad.

1958 *continued*
Starting prices – 9–4 Mandarin; 100–30 Linwell; 11–2 Polar Flight; 13–2 Gay Donald; 7–1 Kerstin; 100–8 Hall Weir; 20–1 Limber Hill; 33–1 others.
Tote – Win 46s 6d. Places 8s 6d, 7s, 10s 4d.

1959
Run March 5th

Lord Fingall's b.g. Roddy Owen. a. 12 st.
    (Owenstown – Desla's Star) H. Beasley 1
Mr David Brown's br.g. Linwell. a. 12 st.
    (Rosewell – Rubia Linda) F. Winter 2
Mrs J. Mildmay-White's b.g. Lochroe. a. 12 st.
    (King Hal – Loch Cash) A. R. Freeman 3
Mr L. C. Denton's Hart Royal (D. V. Dick) 4th.
    Also ran: Lady Barber's Game Field (J. Boddy); Mr M. M. le Masson's Jack V (P. Biancone); Mrs P. Hasting's Taxidermist (Mr J. Lawrence); Mr G. H. Moore's Kerstin (S. Hayhurst); Mr J. Rogerson's Pas Seul (W. Rees); Mrs L. Carver's Flame Royal (M. Scudamore); Mr H. J. Joel's Caesar's Helm (G. Slack).
Trained D. J. Morgan. Won 3*l*, 10*l*.
Starting prices – 4–1 Taxidermist; 5–1 Kerstin, Roddy Owen; 11–2 Linwell; 100–9 Pas Seul, Lochroe; 100–8 Flame Royal; 100–7 Caesar's Helm; 100–6 Hart Royal; 33–1 Game Field; 50–1 Jack V.
Tote – Win 26s 2d. Places 11s, 9s 8d, 16s 4d.

1960
Run March 10th

Mr J. Rogerson's b.g. Pas Seul. a. 12 st.
    (Erin's Pride – Pas de Quatre) W. Rees 1
Mrs J. Mildmay-White's b.g. Lochroe. a. 12 st.
    (King Hal – Loch Cash) D. Mould 2
Mrs G. St John Nolan's b.g. Zonda. a. 12 st.
    (Dornot – Zanthene) G. Robinson 3
Lord Fingall's Roddy Owen (H. Beasley) 4th.
    Also ran: Mr M. H. Lait's The Bell (B. Lawrence); Mr A. Elliott's O'Malley Point (J. Fitzgerald); Mrs P. Pleydell-Bouverie's Polar Flight (D. V. Dick); Mr W. J. Roach's Knightsbrook (G. Slack); Mr W. C. Simpson's Mac Joy (A. R. Freeman); Mr W. Miller's Lotoray (M. Batchelor); Mr G. H. Moore's Kerstin (S. Hayhurst); Lady Sherborne's The Major (F. Winter).

Trained R. Turnell. Won 1*l*, 5*l*.
Starting prices – 7–2 Knightsbrook; 4–1 Kerstin; 5–1 Roddy Owen; Pas Seul; 8–1 Zonda, Mac Joy; 20–1 The Bell; 25–1 Lochroe, Polar Flight, The Major; 33–1 O'Malley Point; 50–1 Lotoray.
Tote – Win 21s 2d. Places 11s 2d, 34s 6d, 10s 10d.

1961
Run March 9th

Colonel G. R. Westmacott's br.g. Saffron Tartan. a. 12 st.
    (Tartan – Kellsboro Witch) F. Winter 1
Mr J. Rogerson's b. or br.g. Pas Seul. a. 12 st.
    (Erin's Pride – Pas de Quatre) D. V. Dick 2
Mme. K. Hennessy's b.g. Mandarin. a. 12 st.
    (Deux pour Cent – Manada) P.G. Madden 3
Mr S. Joel's Frenchman's Cove (S. Mellor) 4th.
    Also ran: Lord Donoughmore's Olympia (Mr M. Hely Hutchinson); Contessa di Sant Elia's King (W. Rees); Mr S. Nossell's Reprieved (P Taaffe); Lady Gunter's Devon Customer (J. Guest); Major L. S. Marler's Knucklecracker (D. Ancil).
Trained D. Butchers. Won 1½*l*, 3*l*.
Starting prices – 2–1 Saffron Tartan; 100–30 Pas Seul; 5–1 Olympia; 8–1 Frenchman's Cove, King; 100–7 Mandarin, Knucklecracker; 25–1 Sidbury Hill; 33–1 Reprieved; 100–1 others.
Tote – Win 15s. Places 7s 8d, 9s 4d, 12s 10d.

1962
Run March 15th

Mme K. Hennessy's b.g. Mandarin. a. 12 st.
    (Deux pour Cent – Manada) F. Winter 1
Mr G. Ansley's b.g. Fortria. a. 12 st.
    (Fortina – Senria) P. Taaffe 2
Mr W. Noddings' b.g. Cocky Consort. a. 12 st.
    (Happy Monarch – Sporty Ann) C. Stobbs 3
Mr J. Tilling's Duke of York (Mr D. Scott) 4th.
    Also ran: Mr J Rogerson's Pas Seul (D. V. Dick); Mr A. H. Wood's King's Nephew (M. Scudamore); H.M. Queen Elizabeth's The Rip (W. Rees); Mr F. Clay's John o' Groats (S. Mellor); Major L. S. Marler's Knucklecracker (D. Ancil).
Trained F. Walwyn. Won 1*l*, 10*l*.

Starting prices - 9-4 Pas Seul; 3-1 Fortria; 7-2 Mandarin; 7-1 Duke of York; 100-8 The Rip; 20-1 King's Nephew; 33-1 John o' Groats; 50-1 Cocky Consort, Knucklecracker.
Tote - Win 16s 8d. Places 6s 4d, 7s, 13s 2d.

1963
Run March 14th

Mr W. H. Gollings' b.g. Mill House. 6 yrs. 12 st.
(King Hal - Nas na Riogh) G. W. Robinson 1
Mr G. Ansley's b.g. Fortria. a. 12 st.
(Fortina - Senria) P. Taaffe 2
Mr J. Tilling's b.g. Duke of York. a. 12 st.
(Flush Royal - Queen of the Dandies) F. Winter 3
Mr A Dickinson's Longtail (J. Leech) 4th. *Also ran*: Mr S. Hewitt's Pride of Ivanhoe (Mr P. Hewitt); Mr B. Lubecki's Caduval (Mr L. Morgan); Mr S. Joel's Frenchman's Cove (S. Mellor); Lord Donoughmore's Olympia (L. McLoughlin); Mr A. Wood's King's Nephew (T. W. Biddlecombe); Mr B. Sunley's Nicolaus Silver (H. Beasley); Mrs A. Bancroft's Cannobie Lee (D. Nicholson); Mr S. L. Green's Rough Tweed (G. Scott).
Trained F. Walwyn. Won 12*l*, 4*l*.
Starting prices - 7-2 Mill House; 4-1 Fortria; 11-2 Frenchman's Cove; 7-1 Duke of York; 10-1 Caduval; 100-9 Rough Tweed; 100-8 Olympia, King's Nephew; 20-1 Longtail; 25-1 Pride of Ivanhoe; 33-1 Nicolaus Silver; 100-1 Cannobie Lee.
Tote - Win 15s 6d. Places 8s 4d, 9s 4d, 9s.

1964
Run March 7th

Anne, Duchess of Westminster's b.g. Arkle. a. 12 st.
(Archive - Bright Cherry) P. Taaffe 1
Mr W. H. Golling's b.g. Mill House. a. 12 st.
(King Hal - Nas na Riogh) G. W. Robinson 2
Mr J. Rogerson's b.g. Pas Seul. a. 12 st.
(Erin's Pride - Pas de Quatre) D. V. Dick 3
Mr A. H. Wood's King's Nephew (S. Mellor) 4th.
Trained T. W. Dreaper. Won 5*l*, 25*l*.
Starting prices - 13-8 Mill House; 7-4 Arkle; 20-1 King's Nephew; 50-1 Pas Seul.
Tote - Win 11s 10d.

1965
Run March 11th

Anne, Duchess of Westminster's b.g. Arkle. a. 12 st.
(Archive - Bright Cherry) P. Taaffe 1
Mr W. H. Gollings' b.g. Mill House. a. 12 st.
(King Hal - Nas na Riogh) G. W. Robinson 2
Mr W. Roycroft's br.g. Stoney Crossing. a. 12 st.
(North Riding Sunlit Stream) W. Roycroft 3
Mrs A. R. B. Owen's Caduval (O. McNally) 4th.
Trained T. W. Dreaper. Won 20*l*, 30*l*.
Starting prices - 30-100 Arkle, 100-30 Mill House; 33-1 Caduval; 100-1 Stoney Crossing.
Tote - Win 5s.

1966
Run March 17th

Anne, Duchess of Westminster's b.g. Arkle. a. 12 st.
(Archive - Bright Cherry) P. Taaffe 1
Mrs D. M. Wells-Kendrew's ch.g. Dormant. a. 12 st.
(Domaha - Miss Victoria) M. Scudamore 2
Lord Cadogan's b.g. Snaigow. a. 12 st.
(Vulgan - Nicotania) D. Nicholson 3
Lt.-Commander R. A. Lockhart-Smith's Sartorius (T. W. Biddlecombe) 4th. *Also ran*: Captain K. P. G. Harbord's Hunch (S. Mellor).
Trained T. W. Dreaper. Won 30*l*, 10*l*
Starting prices - 1-10 Arkle; 100-7 Snaigow; 20-1 Dormant; 33-1 Hunch; 50-1 Sartorius.
Tote - Win 4s 6d.

1967
Run March 16th

Mr H. H. Collins' b.g. Woodland Venture. a. 12 st.
(Eastern Venture - Woodlander) T. W. Biddlecombe 1
Mr R. J. R. Blindell's gr.g. Stalbridge Colonist. a. 12 st.
(Colonist II - Eesofud) S. Mellor 2
Lady Weir's ch.g. What A Myth. a. 12 st.
(Coup de Myth - What a Din) P. Kelleway 3
Mrs D. M. Wells-Kendrew's Dormant (J. King) 4th. *Also ran*: Mr C. Nicholson's Dicky May (P. McCarron); Colonel John Thomson's Fort Leney (P. McLoughlin); Mr C. P. T. Watkins'

1967 continued

Foinavon (J. Kempton); Mr W. H. Gollings' Mill House (D. Nicholson).

Trained T. F. Rimell. Won ¾*l*, 2*l*.

Starting prices – 11–4 Fort Leney; 3–1 What A Myth; 4–1 Mill House; 11–2 Stalbridge Colonist; 10–1 Dormant; 100–8 Woodland Venture; 25–1 Dicky May; 500–1 Foinavon.

Tote – Win 37s 8d. Places 8s, 7s 6d, 6s 8d.

1968
Run March 21st

Colonel John Thomson's b.g. Fort Leney. a. 12 st.
(Fortina – Leney Princess) P. Taaffe 1
Mr H. J. Joel's br.g. The Laird. a. 12 st.
(Border Chief – Pre Fleuri) J. King 2
Mr R. J. R. Blindell's gr.g. Stalbridge Colonist. a. 12 st.
(Colonist II – Eesofud) T. W. Biddlecombe 3
Mr W. A. Silvester's Bassnet (D. Nicholson) 4th.
Also ran: Mr W. H. Gollings' Mill House (G. W. Robinson).

Trained T. W. Dreaper. Won Nk, 1*l*.

Starting prices – 2–1 Mill House; 3–1 The Laird; 7–2 Stalbridge Colonist; 11–2 Fort Leney; 9–1 Bassnet.

Tote – Win 22s 6d.

1969
Run March 20th

Lady Weir's ch.g. What A Myth. a. 12 st.
(Coup de Myth – What a Din) P. Kelleway 1
Mr B. P. Jenks' br.g. Domacorn. a. 12 st.
(Domaha – Spring Corn) T. W. Biddlecombe 2
Mr P. Cussin's b.g. Playlord. a. 12 st.
(Lord of Verona – Playwell) R. Barry 3
Mrs D. Bowlby's Arab Gold (P. Buckley) 4th.
Also ran: Mr J. Lisle's King Cutler (B. Fletcher); Mr R. J. R. Blindell's Stalbridge Colonist (S. Mellor); Mr C. Nicholson's Dicky May (P. McCarron); Mr J. Roycroft's Furtive (Owner); Mrs P. Hackett's Castle Arbour (F. Dever); Mrs L. Prior's Kellsboro Wood (A. Turnell); Mr H. J. Joel's The Laird (J. King).

Trained Ryan Price. Won 1½*l*, 20*l*.

Starting prices – 7–2 Domacorn, The Laird; 4–1 Playlord; 9–2 Stalbridge Colonist; 8–1 What A Myth; 22–1 King Cutler, Dicky May; 25–1 Arab Gold; 50–1 Kellsboro' Wood; 100–1 others.

Tote – Win 22s. Places 6s 4d, 6s 10d, 6s 10d.

1970
Run March 19th

Mr R. R. Guest's ch.g. L'Escargot. a. 12 st.
(Escart III – What a Daisy) T. Carberry 1
Mr Kelso Stewart's br.g. French Tan. a. 12 st.
(Trouville – Kilted Angel) P. Taaffe 2
Mr E. R. Courage's Spanish Steps. a. 12 st.
(Flush Royal – Tiberetta) J. Cook 3
Mrs E. H. Vestey's Freddie Boy (R. Pitman) 4th.
Also ran: Mr H. J. Joel's The Laird (J. King); Mr A. Chambers' Gay Trip (K. White); Mr M. L. Marsh's Larbawn (M. Gifford); Mrs D. W. August's The Dikler (G. W. Robinson); Mr P. Cussins' Titus Oates (S. Mellor); Anne, Duchess of Westminster's Kinloch Brae (T. E. Hyde); Mrs N. Wilson's Herring Gull (J. Crowley); Lady Hay's Arcturus (P. Buckley).

Trained D. L. Moore. Won 1½*l*, 10*l*.

Starting prices – 15–8 Kinloch Brae; 9–4 Spanish Steps; 8–1 French Tan; 10–1 The Dikler, Titus Oates; 25–1 Larbawn, 33–1 L'Escargot, Herring Gull; 40–1 The Laird, Freddie Boy; 50–1 others.

Tote – Win 107s 6d. Places 18s, 7s 6d, 6s 6d.

1971
Run March 18th

Mr R. R. Guest's ch.g. L'Escargot. a. 12 st.
(Escart III – What a Daisy) T. Carberry 1
Mrs R. K. Mellon's b.g. Leap Frog. a. 12 st.
(Trouville – Maggie's Leap) V. O'Brien 2
Mrs D. W. August's b.g. The Dikler. a. 12 st.
(Vulgan – Coronation Day) Barry Brogan 3
Mrs P. P. Browne's Into View (P. Kelleway) 4th.
Also ran: Mr J. N. Davis' Fortina's Place (P. Jones); Mrs E. D. Dowley's Herring Gull (H. Beasley); Mr P. Doyle's Glencaraig Lady (R. Coonan); Mr H. Handel's Royal Toss (E. Harty).

Trained D. L. Moore. Won 10*l*, 15*l*.

Starting prices – 7–2 L'Escargot, Into View, Leap Frog; 7–1 Glencaraig Lady; 15–2 The Dikler; 10–1 Royal Toss; 33–1 others.

Tote – Win 60p. Places 23p, 17p, 18p.

1972
Run March 16th

Mr P. Doyle's ch.m. Glencaraig Lady. a. 12 st.
(Fortina – Luckibash) F. Berry 1
Mr H. Handel's br.g. Royal Toss. a. 12 st.
(Royal Challenger – Spinning Coin) N. Wakley 2

Mrs D. W. August's b.g. The Dikler. a. 12 st.
(Vulgan – Coronation Day) Barry Brogan 3
Mr Raymond R. Guest's L'Escargot (T. Carberry) 4th. *Also ran:* Sir Chester Manifold's Crisp (R. Pitman); Mr A. J. Kingsley's Bighorn (R. Cartwright); Mr J. J. O'Neill's Dim Wit (D. Mould); Mr A. J. Chambers' Gay Trip (T. W. Biddlecombe); Mrs Peter E. Burrell's Leap Frog (V. O'Brien); Mr E. R. Courage's Spanish Steps (W. Smith); Mr Philip Cussins' Titus Oates (R. Barry); Mr R. McDonald's Young Ash Leaf (T. Stack).
Trained F. Flood. Won $\frac{3}{4}l$, hd.
Starting prices – 3–1 Crisp; 4–1 Leap Frog, L'Escargot; 6–1 Glencaraig Lady; 10–1 Spanish Steps; 11–1 The Dikler; 22–1 Royal Toss; 33–1 Bighorn; 35–1 Gay Trip; 40–1 Titus Oates, Young Ash Leaf; 66–1 Dim Wit.
Tote – Win £1.05. Places 43p, 31p, 25p.

1973
Run March 15th

Mrs D. August's b.g. The Dikler. 10 yrs. 12 st.
(Vulgan – Coronation Day) R. Barry 1
Mrs C. Shallow's b.g. Pendil. 8 yrs. 12 st.
(Pendragon – Diliska) R. Pitman 2
Mrs B. Heath's br.g. Charlie Potheen. 10 yrs. 12 st.
(Spiritus – Irish Biddy) T. Biddlecombe 3
Mr R. Guest's L'Escargot (T. Carberry) 4th. *Also ran:* Mrs F. Williams' Garoupe (F. Berry); E. R. Courage's Spanish Steps (P. Blacker); Mrs C. O'Shea's Red Candle (J. Fox); M. Ritzenberg's Clever Scot (D. Mould).
Trained F. Walwyn. Won s.h, 6l.
Starting prices – 4–6 Pendil; 9–2 Charlie Potheen; 9–1 The Dikler; 10–1 Spanish Steps; 20–1 L'Escargot; 22–1 Clever Scot; 50–1 others.
Tote – Win 87p.

1974
Run March 14th

Mrs Jane M. A. Samuel's b.g. Captain Christy. 7 yrs. 12 st.
(Mon Capitaine – Christy's Bow) H. Beasley 1
Mrs C. August's b.g. The Dikler. 11 yrs. 12 st.
(Vulgan – Coronation Day) R. Barry 2
H.M. Queen Elizabeth's ch.g. Game Spirit. 9 yrs. 12 st.
(Game Rights – Castile) T. Biddlecombe 3

Mrs B. Heath's Charlie Potheen (W. Smith) 4th.
Also ran Mrs M. Sanger's Inkslinger (T. Carberry); Mr R. Hickman's High Ken (R. Davies); Mrs C. Shallow's Pendil (R. Pitman).
Trained P. Taaffe. Won 5l, 20l.
Starting prices – 8–13 Pendil; 5–1 The Dikler; 7–1 Captain Christy; 11–1 Inkslinger; 20–1 Game Spirit; 33–1 Charlie Potheen; 100–1 High Ken.
Tote – Win 75p.

1975
Run March 13th

Anne, Duchess of Westminster's b.g. Ten Up. 8 yrs. 12 st.
(Raise you Ten – Irish Harp) T. Carberry 1
Mrs M. Scott's b. or br.g. Soothsayer. 8 yrs. 12 st.
(Mystic 11 – Sagoma) R. Pitman 2
Capt. E. Heathcote's b.g. Bula. 10 yrs. 12 st.
(Rain Check – Pongo's Fancy) J. Francome 3
Mr P. Harpur's Glanford Brigg (S. Holland); 4th.
Also ran: Mr R. Hickman's High Ken (B. Brogan); Mrs D. Rees-Davies' Bruslee (A. Turnell); Mrs D. August's The Dikler (R. Barry); Mrs J. Samuel's Captain Christy (R. Coonan).
Trained J. Dreaper. Won 6l, $\frac{1}{2}l$.
Starting prices – 7–4 Captain Christy; 2–1 Ten Up; 5–1 Bula; 12–1 Bruslee; 20–1 The Dikler; 25–1 Glanford Brigg; 28–1 Soothsayer; 33–1 High Ken.
Tote – Win 25p.

1976
Run March 18th

Sir Edward Hanmer's b.g. Royal Frolic. 7 yrs. 12 st.
(Royal Buck – Forward Miss) J. Burke 1
Mrs P. Burrell's b.g. Brown Lad. 10 yrs. 12 st.
(Sayajirao – Calcos) T. Carberry 2
Mrs P. Burrell's b.g. Colebridge. 12 yrs. 12 st.
(Vulgan – Cherry Bud) F. Berry 3
Lord Chelsea's Money Market (R. Barry) 4th.
Also ran Mr P. Harpur's Glanford Brigg (M. Blackshaw); Capt. E. Edward Heathcote's Bula (J. Francome); Mr O. J. Carter's Otter Way (G. Thorner); Mrs D. August's The Dikler (A. Branford); Mrs D. O'Sullivan's Roman Bar (P. Kiely); Mr A. Watson's Flashy Boy. (D. T. Hughes); Lord Vestey's What-A-Buck (J. King).
Trained T. F. Rimell. Won 5l, 5l.

1976 *continued*

Starting prices - 6-4 Bula; 13-8 Brown Lad; 12-1 Colebridge; 14-1 Royal Frolic; 16-1 Flashy Boy, What-A-Buck; 33-1 The Dikler, Money Market; 50-1 others.

Tote - Win £1.02.

1977
Run March 17th

Mrs J. McGowan's b.g. Davy Lad. 7 yrs. 12 st.
(David Jack - Jim's Mother) D. T. Hughes 1
Mr A. Stanley Robinson's b.g. Tied Cottage. 9 yrs. 12 st.
(Honour Bound - Cottage Ray) T. Carberry 2
Mr H. Joel's b.g. Summerville. 11 yrs. 12 st.
(Bowsprit - Stella d'Oro) J. King 3
Mrs B. Meehan's April Seventh (S. C. Knight) 4th. *Also ran*: Mrs G. T. McKay's Fort Fox (F. Berry); Mr T. Metcalfe's Tamalin (J. J. O'Neill); Mr W. H. Davies' Master H. (Mr J. Weston); Mr J. Morley's Banlieu (B. R. Davies); Mrs K. White's Bannow Rambler (M. J. Furlong); Mr N. Whitcomb's Even Up (R. Champion); Mr C. S. Bird's Fort Devon (W. Smith); Mrs J. Greenhalgh's Zarib (R. R. Evans); Lord Howard de Walden's Lanzarote (J. Francome).

Trained M. A. O'Toole. Won 6*l*, 20*l*.

Starting prices - 11-4 Bannow Rambler; 7-2 Lanzarote; 5-1 Fort Devon; 10-1 Fort Fox; 11-1 Tamalin; 12-1 Zarib; 14-1 Davy Lad; 15-1 Summerville; 20-1 Tied Cottage; 50-1 Even Up; 60-1 others.

Tote - Win £1.09.

1978
Run April 12th

Mrs O. Jackson's b.g. Midnight Court. 7 yrs. 12 st.
(Twilight Alley - Strumpet) J. Francome 1
Mrs P. Burrell's b.g. Brown Lad. 12 yrs. 12 st.
(Sayajirao - Calcus) T. Carberry 2
Mr W. H. Davies' ch.g. Master H. 9 yrs. 12 st.
(Master Owen - Last Resort) R. Crank 3
Mr P. W. Harris' Bachelor's Hall (M. O'Halloran) 4th. *Also ran* Mr C. S. Bird's Fort Devon (W. Smith); Maj. W. Burdon's Cancello (D. Atkins); Mr K. Hogg's Forest King (J. J. O'Neill); Mr O. J. Carter's Otter Way (J.

King); Mrs G. T. McKey's Fort Fox (T. McGivern); Sir Edward Hanmer's Royal Frolic (J. Burke).

Trained F. Winter. Won 7*l*, 1*l*.

Starting prices - 2-1 Fort Devon; 5-2 Midnight Court; 7-1 Bachelor's Hall; 8-1 Davy Lad; 11-1 Royal Frolic; 18-1 Master H; 20-1 Fort Fox; 45-1 Cancello; 50-1 Otter Way; 80-1 Forest King.

Tote - Win 42p.

1979
Run March 15th

The Snailwell Stud Co Ltd's ch.g. Alverton. 9 yrs. 12 st.
(Midsummer Night - Alvertona) J. J. O'Neill 1
Mr S. Burgess' ch.g. Royal Mail. 9 yrs. 12 st.
(Bally Royal - Lency) P. Blacker 2
Mr S. Embiricus' ch.g. Aldaniti. 9 yrs. 12 st.
(Derek H - Renardeau) R. Champion 3
Mr Raymond Guest's Casamayor (B. R. Davies) 4th. *Also ran*: Mrs P. Burrell's Brown Lad (G. Dowd); Mr R. Watts' Gaffer (W. Smith); Admins. of late Mr P. Blackburn's Bit of Manny (R. R. Evans); Mr L. Smith's Mighty Honour (F. Berry); Sir Edward Hanmer's Royal Frolic (J. Burke); Mr M. Buckley's Strombolus (J. Francome); Mr O. J. Carter's Otter Way (D. Goulding); Mr A. S. Robinson's Tied Cottage (T. Carberry).

Trained M. H. Easterby. Won 25*l*, 20*l*.

Starting prices - 5-1 Alverton, Brown Lad; 6-1 Gaffer, Night Nurse; 7-1 Royal Mail; 10-1 Strombolus; 12-1 Tied Cottage; 20-1 Royal Frolic; 40-1 Aldaniti; 50-1 Bawnogues, Casamayor, Mighty Honour, Otter Way; 100-1 Bit of Manny.

Tote - Win 44p.

1980
Run March 13th

Mr A. Barrow's ch.g. Master Smudge. 8 yrs. 12 st.
(Master Stephen - Lily Pond) R. Hoare 1
Miss P. Neal's b.g. Mac Vidi. 15 yrs. 12 st.
(Vidi Vici - Jockette) P. Leach 2
Maj. D. Wigan's ch.g. Approaching. 9 yrs. 12 st.
(Golden Vision - Farm Hill) B. R. Davies 3
Mr G. Richmond-Watson's The Snipe (A. Webber) 4th. *Also ran*: Mr A. Warrender's Border Incident (J. Francome); Mr J. McManus' Jack

of Trumps (J. J. O'Neill); Mr S. Burgess' Royal Mail (P. Blacker); Westwood Garages Ltd's The Vintner (C. Grant); Mr Loughridge's Diamond Edge (W. Smith); Mr G. Daws' Kas (J. Burke); Mr P. Clarke's Kilcoleman (T. McGivern); Mr G. Rayes' Narribinni (R. Linley); Mr J. Heelan's Secret Progress (R. Barry); Mr A. Robinson's Tied Cottage (T. Carberry) disqualified; Mrs R. Eastwood's Chinrullah (F. Berry) disqualified.

Trained A. Barrow. Won 5*l*, 2½*l*.

Starting prices – 5-2 Diamond Edge; 5-1 Jack of Trumps; 6-1 Border Incident; 13-2 Tied Cottage; 9-1 Chinrullah; 11-1 Approaching; 14-1 Master Smudge; 33-1 Royal Mail; 50-1 Kilcoleman, Secret Progress; 66-1 Mac Vidi, Snipe; 100-1 others.

Tote – Win 43p.

Tied Cottage finished first, 8 lengths in front of Master Smudge, but was subsequently disqualified for failing a dope test. Chinrullah, who finished fifth, 8 lengths behind Approaching and 1½ lengths in front of The Snipe, was also disqualified. The Snipe was promoted to fourth place.

1981
Run March 19th

Mr R. J. Wilson's b.g. Little Owl 7 yrs. 12 st.
   (Cantab – Black Spangle) Mr A. J. Wilson 1
Mr R. Spencer b.g. Night Nurse 10 yrs. 12 st.
   (Falcon – Florence Nightingale) A. Brown 2
Mrs C. Feather's br.g. Silver Buck. 9 yrs. 12 st.
(Silver Cloud – Choice Archlesse) T. Carmody 3
Mr M. J. Thorne's Spartan Missile (Mr M. J. Thorne) 4th. *Also ran* Mr S. Loughridge's Diamond Edge (W. Smith); Mr J. McManus' Jack of Trumps (N. Madden); Lady Rootes' Royal Judgement (R. Rowe); Maj D. Wigan's Approaching (R. Champion); Mrs O. Jackson's Midnight Court (J. Francome); Mr A. Robinson's Tied Cottage (L. O'Donnell); Mrs R. Eastwood's Chinrullah (P. Scudamore); Mrs P. Fanning's Fair View (R. Barry); Mrs P. Fry's Raffi Nelson (S. Smith Eccles); Mrs G. V. Malcomson's Royal Bond (T. McGivern); Mr D. W. Samuel's So and So (Mr D. Gray).

Trained M. H. Easterby. Won 1½*l*, 10*l*.

Starting prices – 7-2 Silver Buck; 6-1 Little Owl, Night Nurse; 7-1 Jack of Trumps; 15-2 Tied Cottage; 10-1 Royal Bond; 14-1 Midnight

Court; 16-1 Diamond Edge; 33-1 Approaching, Chinrullah, Spartan Missile; 100-1 others.

Tote – Win 48p.

1982
Run March 18th

Mrs C. Feather's br.g. Silver Buck. 10 yrs. 12 st.
(Silver Cloud – Choice Archlesse) R. Earnshaw 1
Mr M. Kennelley's ch.g. Bregawn. 8 yrs. 12 st.
   (Saint Denys – Miss Society) G. Bradley 2
Miss C. Jawkey b.g. Sunset Cristo. 8 yrs. 12 st.
   (Derek H – Sunset Rambler) C. Grant 3
Mr S. Loughridge's Diamond Edge (W. Smith) 4th. *Also ran:* Mr M. Mouskos' Captain John (P. Scudamore); Mr F. Gilman's Grittar (Mr C. Saunders); Mr M. Sherwood's Venture to Cognac (Mr O. Sherwood); Mrs G. V. Malcolmson's Royal Bond (T. Carberry); Mr A. S. Robinson's Tied Cottage (G. Newman); Mr G. Steinborg's Two Swallows (A. Webber); Mr B. Gaule's Lesley Ann (C. Brown); Mr M. Shone's Sugarally (C. Tinkler); Mrs I. Hamilton's Peaty Sandy (T. G. Dun); Mr G. Sloan's Earthstopper (Mr G. Sloan); Mr A. Warrender's Border Incident (J. Francome); Mr H. Lutz's Drumroan (C. Dugast); Sir R. Wates' Henry Bishop (R. Rowe); Mr A. Barrow's Master Smudge (S. Smith Eccles); Mr R. Spencer's Night Nurse (J. J. O'Neill); Mrs Boucher's Snow Flyer (R. Champion); Mr D. Jackson's Straight Jocelyn (H. Davies); Mr David Lewis' Wansford Boy (R. Dickin).

Trained M. W. Dickinson. 2*l*, 12*l*.

Starting prices – 11-4 Night Nurse; 4-1 Royal Bond; 6-1 Venture to Cognac; 8-1 Silver Buck; 10-1 Lesley Ann; 11-1 Diamond Edge; 16-1 Grittar; 18-1 Bregawn; 25-1 Henry Bishop, Tied Cottage; 33-1 Border Incident; 40-1 Captain John, Peaty Sandy, Sugarally; 50-1 Sunset Cristo, Earthstopper, Two Swallows, Master Smudge; 100-1 Snow Flyer; 150-1 Drumroan; 300-1 Wansford Boy.

Tote – Win 95p.

1983
Run March 17th

Mr J. Kennelley's ch.g. Bregawn. 9 yrs. 12 st.
   (Saint Denys – Miss Society) G. Bradley 1
Mr F. Emani's ch.g. Captain John. 9 yrs. 12 st.

1983 *continued*

(Mon Captaine – Aprolon Light) D. Goulding 2
Mrs S. Trewlis' by.g. Wayward Lad. 8 yrs. 12 st.
(Royal Highway – Loughnamore) J. J. O'Neill 3
Mrs C. Feather's Silver Buck (R. Earnshaw) 4th.
Also ran: Mr R. Tory's Combs Ditch (C.
Brown); Sheikh Ali Abu Khamsin's Fifty Dol-
lars More (R. Linley); Mrs B. Samuel's Brown
Chamberlin (J. Francome); Mr J. McLough-
lin's Ashley House (Mr D. Browne); Miss Dal-
zell's Richdee (C. Hawkins); Carpenter's

Paints Ltd's Midnight Love (C. Grant); Mr
Sanderson's Whiggie Geo (Mr N. Tutty).
Trained M. Dickinson. Won 5*l*, 1½*l*.
Starting prices – 100–30 Bregawn; 9–2 Combs
Ditch; 5–1 Silver Buck; 6–1 Wayward Lad; 8–
1 Fifty Dollars More; 10–1 Brown Chamberlin;
11–1 Captain John; 12–1 Ashley House; 40–1
Richdee; 66–1 Midnight Love; 500–1 Whiggie
Geo.
Tote – Win £5.00.

APPENDIX 2

Table Showing Value of the Race
to the Winner

Year	Horse	Value	Year	Horse	Value
1924	Red Splash	£685	1954	Four Ten	£3,576
1925	Ballinode	£880	1955	Gay Donald	£3,775. 15s.
1926	Koko	£880	1956	Limber Hill	£3,750. 5s.
1927	Thrown In	£780	1957	Linwell	£3,996
1928	Patron Saint	£780	1958	Kerstin	£5,778
1929	Easter Hero	£776	1959	Roddy Owen	£5,363
1930	Easter Hero	£670	1960	Pas Seul	£5,414
1931	No race owing to frost		1961	Saffron Tartan	£6,043
1932	Golden Miller	£670	1962	Mandarin	£5,720
1933	Golden Miller	£670	1963	Mill House	£5,958
1934	Golden Miller	£670	1964	Arkle	£8,004
1935	Golden Miller	£670	1965	Arkle	£7,986. 10s.
1936	Golden Miller	£670	1966	Arkle	£7,674. 10s.
1937	No race owing to snow		1967	Woodland Venture	£7,999. 10s.
1938	Morse Code	£720	1968	Fort Leney	£7,713. 10s.
1939	Brendan's Cottage	£1,120	1969	What A Myth	£8,129. 10s.
1940	Roman Hackle	£495	1970	L'Escargot	£8,103
1941	Poet Prince	£495	1971	L'Escargot	£7,995.50
1942	Médoc II	£495	1972	Glencaraig Lady	£15,255.00
1943 } 1944 }	No race on account of the war		1973	The Dikler	£15,125
			1974	Captain Christy	£14,572.50
1945	Red Rower	£340	1975	Ten Up	£17,757.50
1946	Prince Regent	£1,130	1976	Royal Frolic	£18,134.50
1947	Fortina	£1,140	1977	Davy Lad	£21,990
1948	Cottage Rake	£1,911	1978	Midnight Court	£23,827.50
1949	Cottage Rake	£2,817. 10s.	1979	Alverton	£30,293.75
1950	Cottage Rake	£2,936. 10s.	1980	Master Smudge	£35,997.50
1951	Silver Fame	£2,783. 10s.	1981	Little Owl	£44,258.75
1952	Mont Tremblant	£3,232. 10s.	1982	Silver Buck	£48,386.25
1953	Knock Hard	£3,258	1983	Bregawn	£45,260